SCOTTISH COOKERY

Catherine Brown

Chambers

Published 1993 by W & R Chambers Ltd
43–45 Annandale Street, Edinburgh EH7 4AZ

First published by Richard Drew Publishing Ltd 1985

British Library Cataloguing in Publication Data

A catalogue record for this book is available from the British Library

ISBN 0 550 20006 1

Illustrations by Jane Glue

Designed by James W Murray

Printed by Cox & Wyman, Reading

CONTENTS

Oatcakes — Traditional Girdle Oatcakes with fine meal: Oven Oatcakes with coarse oatmeal.
Porridge, Brose — Oatmeal Brose: Pease Brose: Atholl Brose. Bannocks — Old-fashioned
Bannocks: Barley Bannocks: Modern Bannocks: Oatmeal Bannocks. Mealie Puddings and
Skirlie. Oatmeal and Barley Breads — Oatmeal Bread with molasses: Oatmeal Bread Rolls:
Sour Dough Oatmeal Bread: Cooked Potato Starter: Buttermilk Bread with oatmeal: Barley
Bread. Other uses of Oatmeal and Barley — Clootie Dumpling: Sweet Oaten Pudding with
raspberries: Buttered Oats: A Swiss/Scots Breakfast: Walnut and Oat Biscuits.

Atlantic, Wild Scottish and Farmed Salmon — Baked Salmon in butter: Grilled Salmon Steak
with parsley and lemon butter: Potted Salmon: Salmon Soup: Tay Salmon in Pastry with
Vermouth and Dill sauce. Smoked Salmon. Salmon Trout, Sea Trout, Brown Trout — Baked
Trout with herbs and lemon: Herring — Fresh Herring fried in oatmeal: Fresh Herrings as
dressed at Inveraray: Open Arms Herring with Drambuie butter: Grilled Herring with
mustard: Soused or Potted Herring: Sweet Spiced Herring. Atlantic Mackerel — Potted
Mackerel. Kipper — Potted Kipper: Grilled: Fried: Jugged: Baked: Uncooked. Salt Pickled
Herring — Tatties and Herring: Marinated Salt Herring: Salt Herring Salad with beetroot and
mushrooms. Haddock, cod and whiting — Haddock and Chips: Fresh Haddock in a light
creamy mustard sauce: Rizzared Haddock (Blawn Whiting): Grilled Fresh Haddock. Finnan
Haddock — Finnan Haddock with melted cheese and eggs: Baked Smoked Haddock with
cream and poached egg: Smoked Haddock Flan. Arbroath Smokie — Baked Arbroath Smokie
with baked potato: Arbroath Smokie poached in milk: Potted Arbroath Smokie with oatcakes.

Molluscs, Scallops — Scallops sautéed in butter with shallots: Steamed Scallops in a creamy
white sauce. Oysters — Served raw in their shells: Oysters with Whelks. Mussels — Mussel
Stew with crusty bread and butter: Mussels Grilled in their shells with wine. Horse Mussel —
Clabbie Dhubs with leeks and tomatoes. Periwinkle — Cooking and eating. Other Scottish
Molluscs. Crustaceans, Crab — Partan Pies: Partan Bree. Lobster — Grilled Lobster: Boiled
Lobster: Lobster Soup. Norway Lobster — Norway Lobster in cream sauce with sherry. Other
Scottish Crustaceans — Orkney Squid. Other Shellfish Recipes — Arisaig Seafood Pastry:
Shellfish Broth: Shellfish Sauce. Seaweeds, Caragheen — Caragheen Chocolate Pudding: For
thickening. Dulse and Tangle — Dulse Broth with lamb or mutton: Dulse Cakes. Sloke.

INTRODUCTION

It was a cold, wet, inhospitable day and the wild West Highland scenery looked unfriendly and menacing from where we sat inside the warm croft-house. As the light began to fade, Alistair lit the paraffin lamp and Maggie brought, from a cupboard in the corner, crisp oatcakes, butter, cheese, home-made jam and freshly made soft floury bannocks. These West Highlanders had lived on this croft all their lives and were into their seventies when a road was eventually built in 1972 linking the communities on this remote Applecross peninsula, which had depended on the sea as a means of communication for centuries.

The peat fire burned with a comforting steady glow, the wind and rain raged audibly without, while inside we warmed ourselves with whisky, and talked. Then Alistair took the lid off the pot sitting on the fire in the black iron range which dominated one wall, and the rich smell of broth suddenly pervaded the room. It had been cooking so slowly, and for so long, that only the faintest whiff of its existence had been noticeable till then. He removed the piece of mutton (from a Blackface sheep he had killed and salted himself) and sliced the meat off the bone in rough chunks. Then he threw a few handfuls of chopped leeks into the broth and we ate the meat first with a knife and fork and some oatcakes, while the broth finished cooking. It was thick with vegetables and barley and had the exquisite flavour only made possible with a piece of well-flavoured salt mutton from a mature sheep which had grazed long on the heather hills.

The memory remains vivid, as does the special warmth of their hospitality and their cheerfulness in the face of many hardships and extreme isolation. Also, one felt that these food traditions of great antiquity were a symbol of man's power to overcome in difficult conditions with scant resources, and yet produce superb food. It was like stepping backwards into the past, seeing the full force of available food resources and cooking methods dictating food traditions.

We made our farewells and left.

I did not realise, then, how much my curiosity had been aroused by this simple, satisfying meal or where that curiosity would take me. Driving back home along the winding single-track roads I made no unforgettable declaration of intent to write about Scottish food and hospitality. But I realise now that this was the inspiration, and the beginning of the pleasurable and fascinating affair which has resulted in this book.

Many other experiences in many other parts of Scotland, by the sea and in the mountains, in remote places and in cities, from childhood and brought to me through the writing of others often distant in time, have contrasted and blended together and shaped the content of my perception of Scottish cookery. The structure and theme of the book have been dictated by distinct primary Scottish raw materials and the chapters explore their place in the Scottish diet, past and present.

The fact that in Scotland today the emphasis of production is on barley and oats, not wheat; on sheep and cattle, not pigs and poultry; and on potatoes, not fruit and vegetables, has influenced my approach, while I have also taken into account the fact that this food production is not quite uniformly reflected in what is eaten, since Scots consume (per head) more beef, eggs and potatoes; but less lamb, pigmeat, poultry, fruit and vegetables, than the rest of Britain.

About 40% of the food eaten in Scotland comes either straight from farm or sea or via the food manufacturing industry. The importance to the Scottish food economy of trade with the rest of the UK and elsewhere is considerable. Scotland has been increasing its primary food production since the Second World War at a greater rate than domestic consumption, so while she is becoming more self-sufficient there is also more produce to trade with. As in the past, the rest of Britain and the world are influenced by primary Scottish food and food products of high quality.

Making the best use of them at home is something Scots need to think clearly about. Scottish food should be allowed to speak for itself — not in cooking styles which mask one flavour with another, or in fussy presentations which show no respect for the identity of the ingredient. Valuable possibilities must not be lost to indiscriminate gimmickery. Finding what conventions of form and detail can be dispensed with, while preserving the spirit of the whole through balance, best exploits the potential of Scottish food.

Gastronomic quality has no race or nationality and Scotland, like the rest of Britain has imported varied skills and cooking styles from many other cultures, which is what the last chapter describes. I have illustrated the Scottish facet in this now multi-national variety, through a mixture of styles high, low; formal, informal; traditional, modern. They reflect my own flexible approach to ingredients and the way we put them together, recognising their potential and letting them dictate, spending time wandering round food shops and markets, seeking out quality and freshness and then thinking of how to cook and combine.

The recipes in this book reflect my liking for cooking from scratch, which need not necessarily be more time-consuming than reaching for other alternatives. Things like one-pot-meals which, once quickly assembled, cook by themselves are an essential and constant part of my life, as is the need to get meals on the table in a hurry, without compromising on quality.

The 'short-order' aspect of feeding people is also important — having available a range of foods which will combine in a variety of ways to suit individual tastes, presented without unnecessary frills, but still making a good visual impact. Cooking large joints, which will sit happily in the refrigerator for several days, and can be instantly teamed up with interesting chutneys, preserved fruits or vegetables and served with good bread and butter are only one way of allowing you to cook today and stop worrying about what to have for the next three days. The time spent cooking is the same regardless of the size of the meat, etc. I'm not suggesting that we go back to the Victorian system, when they cooked such large joints on Sundays that it took them the rest of the week to consume. 'Hot on Sunday,' they said, 'Cold on Monday, Hashed on Tuesday, Minced on Wednesday, Curried on Thursday, Broth on Friday, and Cottage Pie on Saturday.' But there is a need to think ahead if not for the whole week at least for the next two or three days.

While I personally have made the selection, many people from all kinds of cooking philosophies have influenced the finished result. Some have had a more direct influence than others, but to them all I gratefully acknowledge their inspiration. To the personalities from the past who appear frequently throughout the text, I owe a special debt since they have captured the essence of their time and allowed us to see more clearly the origins of our Scottish traditions.

Catherine Brown, Glasgow 1989.

ACKNOWLEDGMENTS

Thanks to a multitude of people, this book has taken shape. It is the harvest of many people's creativity, imagination, knowledge and experience, and recognition of them all on a single page is impossible.

To all, I am sincerely grateful.

To each of the following I am particularly grateful for the time, aid, information and encouragement which they have given. In searching out the facts I fear that I have hurled many awkward questions which they have patiently answered:

Dr J.J. Connell, Director, Torry Research Station, Aberdeen; Martha Crawford, Secretary of the British Deer Farmers Association, Cluanie, Beauly, Inverness-shire; Keith Dunbar of Summer Isles Foods, Achiltibuie; Sheila Harley, Scotch Quality Beef and Lamb Association; Peter Hick, Director, Reawick (Shetland) Lamb Marketing Company: Professor George Houston, Department of Political Economy, University of Glasgow; James Keay, Torry Research Station, Aberdeen; D.S. MacDonald, Oatmeal Miller and Grain Merchant, Montgarrie Mills, Alford, Aberdeenshire; Elizabeth MacIntosh, Scottish Milk Marketing Board; Professor A.D. MacIntyre, Director, Marine Laboratory, Aberdeen; Donald MacLean, Chairman of the National Vegetable Society, Dornock Farm, Crieff, Perthshire; Dr Donald McQueen, Marketing Director, Scottish Milk Marketing Board; Dr David Mann, United Biscuits, Glasgow; Rosemary Marwick of Howgate Cheeses, Penicuik, Midlothian; I.G.A. Miller, Oatmeal and Pearl Barley Miller, Kelso Mills, Roxburghshire; George Motion, Assistant Secretary, The Red Deer Commission, Knowsley, Inverness; Hamish and Livingston Neil of S.L. Neil Glasgow; Carol Neilson of Barac Cheeses, Annan, Dumfriesshire; Douglas Ritchie of Strathaird Sea Foods; J. Russell, Manager of the Company of Scottish Cheese Makers; Archie Sinclair, Caithness Smoking Company, Latheronwheel; Stewart Sloan of Robert Sloan, Butchers; Susanna Stone of Highland Fine Cheeses, Tain, Wester Ross; Dr Charles E. Taylor, Director, Scottish Crop Research Institute; Invergowrie, Dundee; Richard Van Oss, Director, The Game Conservancy, Fordingbridge, Hampshire; Joseph Walker of Walkers Shortbread, Aberlour; Gillian Whytock of the Advisory and Development Service, Agronomy Department, The West of Scotland Agricultural College, Auchincruive, Ayrshire.

I am particularly grateful to the Chairman of the Taste of Scotland Scheme, Lt Col. H.C. Paterson, for his support and encouragement during the twelve years I have worked for the scheme as Food Consultant. Thanks also to John Leese, MBE, Food Information Office, Scotland, of the British Farm Produce Council, from whom I have also received much help and support, not least as a member of his Scottish Food Writers Circle when he has brought together food writers and producers to the great benefit of both. Though I have only been able to mention a random few, I wish to acknowledge the commitment of all members of the scheme who strive daily in the pursuit of excellence.

Many thanks also to — Paul Booth at Killiecrankie Hotel for his recipe for Smoked Fish Pie; Norma Hasham at Foveran Hotel for her Orkney Squid; Thelma MacBeth at the Wood'n Spoon, Kingussie for her Carrot Cake; Charles Price at Gleddoch House, Langbank for his Strawberry Shortbread; Claire Macdonald of Macdonald for Honey and Whisky Ice Cream; Arthur Neil and Chef Douglas at the Open Arms Hotel, Dirleton for Herrings with Drambuie Butter; Elizabeth Sandell at the Log Cabin Hotel, Kirkmichael for her Game dish; Paul Rogerson at Esk Valley Technical College for his Peach Highland Cream; Peter Slaney at Ettrickshaws Hotel, Selkirk for his Ice Cream; Janice Stewart at The Arisaig Hotel for her Seafood Pastry; and David Wilson at the Peat Inn, Fife for his Tay Salmon recipe.

There are some ideas for recipes from other sources, and while I have acknowledged them in the text, I would also like to thank their originators.

Sincere thanks to Antony Kamm for his editing expertise; he has been an ever constant source of patient, helpful advice and encouragement.

For the use of their kitchens, their stimulating company and their help, reading and correcting recipes, my thanks to Catherine Braithwaite (my mother) and Joan Campbell. My thanks also to Gwen Schenz of California for keeping me right on American variations and to Lorna Sinclair for similar help with the subtle differences between the Scots and the English.

To the many people who have helped in a practical way which has given me the time to spend on this book, adequate words of thanks escape me, and I can only say that without their help, it simply would not have been written.

Neither would it have been written without much help from Iain in many ways. Without Esther and Ailie it might have been written sooner, but I am grateful to them as honest, sometimes utterly deflating, critics of my cooking. I am grateful also that they are enthusiastic cooks themselves, despite the constant havoc in the kitchen.

WEIGHTS, MEASURES & ANGLO-AMERICAN TERMS

Quantities produced by the recipes

While I have given some indication for each recipe, it can only be an approximation since so much depends on serving size and on the position in the meal, not to mention individual appetites. A dish used as a starter will usually provide double the servings than if it is used as a main course. The yield for scones, biscuits, etc. will depend on unit size; again my quantities are only an approximation.

Converting from one system of measuring to another

Do not mix measures — stick to one system throughout a recipe.

Any conversion from one system to another can only be an approximation, not an exact equivalent. While not wishing to appear unduly careless, weighing out for everyday cooking does not need the same kind of measuring precision necessary for weighing out gold or silver. The odd half ounce here and there will not ruin the recipe.

In any case basic items like flour, sugar, butter and margarine vary in moisture content and also air content, which matters if you are measuring by volume, while results can also depend on whether the day is dry or wet, the kitchen hot or cold.

Converting from Imperial to Metric

Scales and measures are usually graduated in multiples of 25 g. If the conversion of 1 oz to 25 g is made (1 oz = 28.35 g), it is inevitable that there are illogical jumps, for example when you move from 3 to 4 oz, and instead of going up by 25 g I have mostly taken the jump to 125 g simply because then the metric measurements can be compared proportionately: i.e. $\frac{1}{4}$ lb = $\frac{1}{8}$ kilo; $\frac{1}{2}$ lb = $\frac{1}{4}$ kilo; 1 lb = $\frac{1}{2}$ kilo, etc.

For liquid measurements the same proportional system can apply with $\frac{1}{4}$ pt = $\frac{1}{8}$ L; $\frac{1}{2}$ pt = $\frac{1}{4}$ L; 1 pt = $\frac{1}{2}$ L, etc.

The main advantage of this method is that it makes measuring easier, quicker and more convenient, especially if you are using ingredients which are packaged in metric.

Where it matters, and each recipe has to be judged separately as to the effects of this method, then the quantities can be rounded up or down as appropriate, remembering that 500 g is actually about 2 oz more than 1 lb; and 1 litre is about $\frac{1}{4}$ pt less than 2 pts. When working in large quantities, special adjustments have to be made, since obviously the discrepancies multiply along with increasing quantities to the extent that when using, say, the metric equivalent to 1 gallon according to this system, it would be 4 litres, which would be about 1 pint short of a gallon. In the recipes I have adjusted accordingly.

Imperial to American cups

I have to confess that I like the way Americans weigh ingredients and when not testing recipes, would always prefer to use American cups, unless cooking in large quantities, when they become too time-consuming. American butter is packaged in 4 oz sticks, 4 to a box of 1 lb which makes for easy and quick measuring, especially since they are usually graduated on the wrapping paper.

The main point to remember when using the American system is that they have actually retained the old British measure for 1 pint at 16 fl oz (UK — 20 fl oz), which was originally the same as the solid measure and which the British abandoned in 1825. American cups are graduated in fractions of 16 fl oz. Sets of cups are available (I use a set made by CUISENA). There are five sizes in the set — $\frac{1}{8}$; $\frac{1}{4}$; $\frac{1}{3}$; $\frac{1}{2}$ and 1 cup.

I have used the following table as a basis for conversion though on occasions in the recipes I have had to adjust quantities to produce comparable results. Where the cup is described as scant then I have filled it to about $\frac{1}{4}''$ of the rim of the cup, while generous means that it was slightly heaped.

American names for commodities, where different from the British, are in brackets.

SOLID INGREDIENTS	IMPERIAL	METRIC	AMERICAN
Dry ingredients			
Beans, dry	8 oz	250 g	1 c
Barley flour	3 oz	75 g	1 c
Breadcrumbs dry	4 oz	125 g	1 c
fresh	2 oz	50 g	1 c
Cocoa Powder	4 oz	100 g	1 c (gen)
Cornflour (Cornstarch)	4 oz	100 g	1 c (gen)
Currants	5 oz	150 g	1 c
Flour — Plain	4 oz	125 g	1 c (gen)
(All-purpose flour)			
Self-raising			
(All purpose Self Rising)			
Wholemeal			
(Whole Wheat)			
Gelatine	$\frac{1}{4}$ oz	7 g	1 envelope
Glacé Cherries	4 oz	125 g	$\frac{3}{4}$ cup
(Candied)			
Ground almonds	3 oz	75 g	1 c
Nuts — broken or			
coarsely chopped	4 oz	125 g	1 c
Oatmeal, fine, med	4 oz	125 g	1 c (scant)
Coarse — Pinhead	4 oz	125 g	1 c (scant)
(Irish Oatmeal)			
Rolled Oats	3 oz	75 g	1 c
(Oatmeal)			
Pearl Barley	6 oz	175 g	1 c
Rice	6 oz	175 g	1 c
Suet (shredded)	4 oz	125 g	1 c (scant)
Sugar — caster, gran.	7 oz	200 g	1 c
	8 oz	250 g	$1\frac{1}{4}$ c
Brown	5 oz	150 g	1 c (scant)
Icing (Confectioner's)	4 oz	125 g	1 c (gen)
Sultanas and Raisins	6 oz	175 g	1 c
Yeast dry	2 level tsp	7 g	1 package (pkg)
fresh	$\frac{1}{2}$ oz	15 g	1 package or cake
Fruit, Cheese, Vegetables, etc.			
Butter and other fats	8 oz	250 g	1 c
	4 oz	125 g	1 stick
Cabbage, raw	3 oz	75 g	1 c
(scant) shredded			

Carrot, 1 med sliced	5 oz	150 g	1 c
Cheese, Cheddar, grated	4 oz	125 g	1 c
Cream, crowdie, cottage	8 oz	250 g	1 c
Herbs, fresh	2 oz	50 g	1 c
Mayonnaise	6 oz	175 g	1 c
Meat, raw or cooked, chopped, minced (Ground beef)	8 oz	250 g	1 c
Mincemeat	10 oz	275 g	1 c
Mushrooms, raw, sliced	2-3 oz	50-75 g	1 c
Onion, chopped	5 oz	125 g	1 c
Potatoes, cooked, mashed	8 oz	250 g	1 c
Treacle, black (Molasses) Golden Syrup (Light corn syrup)	12 oz	350 g	1 c

LIQUID	IMPERIAL	METRIC	AMERICAN
Water, milk, vinegar, cream, oil, etc.	8 fl oz	250 ml	1 c ($\frac{1}{2}$ pt US)
	$\frac{1}{4}$ pt (5 fl oz)	150 ml	$\frac{3}{4}$ c (scant)
	$\frac{1}{2}$ pt (10 fl oz)	300 ml	$1\frac{1}{4}$ c (scant)
	$\frac{3}{4}$ pt (15 fl oz)	450 ml	2 c (scant) (1 pt US)
	1 pt (20 fl oz)	600 ml	$2\frac{1}{2}$ c
	$1\frac{1}{4}$ pt (25 fl oz)	700 ml	3 c
	$1\frac{1}{2}$ pt (30 fl oz)	850 ml	$3\frac{3}{4}$ c
	$1\frac{3}{4}$ pt (35 fl oz)	1000 ml	$4\frac{1}{4}$ c
	2 pt (40 fl oz)	1150 ml	5 c

AMERICAN STANDARD MEASURING SPOONS

These are the same as the metric measuring spoons now widely available in Britain.

All spoon measures are taken as level

For Liquids:

1 teaspoon	= 5 ml
1 tablespoon	= 15 ml
2 tablespoons	= $\frac{1}{8}$ c = 1 fl oz = 25 ml (approx)
5 tablespoons	= $\frac{1}{3}$ c = $2\frac{1}{2}$ fl oz = 60 ml (approx)
8 tablespoons	= $\frac{1}{2}$ c = 4 fl oz = 100 ml (approx)
1 tablespoon	= 3 teaspoons

Anglo-American cooking vocabulary

British | American

Cooking Terms

British	American
Fry	Pan Broil (without fat)
	Pan Fry (with fat)
Grate	Shred
Grill	Broil
Gut	Clean
Knock Back	Punch down
Prove	Rise
Sieve	Sift

Commodities not already mentioned in conversion table

British	American
Anchovy essence	Anchovy paste
Bannock	Flat, round cakes
Bicarbonate of soda	Baking soda
Biscuits	Cookies or Crackers
Boiling fowl	Stewing fowl
Broad Beans	Lima Beans
Cake mixture	Cake batter
Caster sugar	Granulated sugar
Cornflour	Cornstarch
Desiccated coconut	Flaked coconut
Double cream	Whipping cream
Dripping	Meat dripping
Essence	Extract
Flaked Almonds	Slivered almonds
Haricot Beans	Navy beans
Hough	Shank of Beef
Icing	Frosting
Jam	Preserves
Jelly (sweet)	Gelatin dessert
Rasher	Slice
Roast Potatoes	Oven browned potatoes
Scone	Shortcake, biscuit
Single cream	Light cream
Soft brown sugar	Light brown sugar
Spring onion	Green onion
Stewing steak	Braising beef
Sultanas	Seedless white raisins

Cooking equipment

British	American
Ashet (Scottish)	Meat dish
Baking sheet or tray	Cookie sheet
Frying pan	Skillet
Greaseproof paper	Waxed paper
Stewpan or pan	Kettle
Large pot	Dutch Oven or deep cooking utensil with a tight fitting lid
Liquidiser	Electric blender
Roasting tin	Roasting pan with rack
Sandwich tins	Round-layer pans

CHAPTER ONE

OATS
& BARLEY

Oats

> . . . Oatmeal with milk, which they cook in different ways, is
> their constant food, three times a day, throughout the year,
> Sundays and holidays included. . . .
>
> J. Donaldson
> A General View of Agriculture of the Carse of Gowrie, 1794

Original and frequent use of oatmeal was a mark of Scottish nationality
to the extent that the English lexicographer Dr Johnson described the
Scots in his dictionary as 'oats eaters'. The English thought oats only fit
for horses and Dr Johnson did not spare the sarcasm in saying so —
'a grain which in England is generally given to horses, but in Scotland
supports the people'.

Yet the people seem to have survived on this frugal diet, and even
been quite healthy, if travellers' tales are to be believed. Thomas Pennant, one of the most eminent naturalists of the 18th century made a
tour of Scotland in 1789 and described the men as 'thin, but strong'. Travelling people like drovers who herded the cattle around the country
seem to have subsisted almost totally on oatmeal carried in 'great wal-
lets' hung round their 'broad and sturdy backs'. They mixed the oatmeal
with water and baked cakes on stones heated by the fire. Soldiers were
more sophisticated, carrying a 'flat plate' strapped to their saddle. Presumably foot soldiers made do with the heated hearth stones. The ascetic
Scottish student from a humble cottage home living a subsistence existence in his sparse garret on the bag of oatmeal which he brought from
home at the beginning and middle of the term is a legendary figure.
'Meal Monday', now simply a mid-term holiday, still exists, to the aston-
ishment of English and other academics who come to work in Scottish
universities.

It is not known where or when cultivated oats originated. Wild oats are said to have been cultivated before 1000 BC by cave-dwellers in Switzerland. The carbonised grains of both wild and cultivated oats, along with wheat and barley, were found at digs along the Forth and Clyde Canal and at Camphill in Glasgow and were dated to a hundred or so years BC. Specimens can be seen at the National Museum of Antiquities in Edinburgh. It is generally agreed among authorities, that although oats thrive best in cool climates, they originally came from some warmer country in the East, from south east Europe, central or western Asia or North Africa and were certainly cultivated on the European continent before they arrived in Britain. The fact is, that a cool climate is much more suitable for growing oats. When the growth is comparatively slow, the kernels get the best chance of filling out. In warm climates, where the growth is faster, the kernels are poorly filled and even oats grown in the south of England are not nearly so well filled as those in Scotland.

The flavour of oats depends on a number of factors. The variety is important but also the amount of moisture; the district where it is grown; the kind of season; the kind of soil; the manuring; the time of cutting the crop; and how the grain is threshed, dried and milled. Varieties of oats are continually changing and have a relatively short life compared with some of the varieties grown in the past. Around 1900 an old variety of oats known as Sandwich was favoured for its well flavoured oatmeal. This was due to a high oil and protein content compared with the oats which are grown today — the higher the oil content the better the flavour. Oats today contain 5-7% oil compared to only 1-2% in other cereals while oatmeal has an oil content of 6-10% compared to only 1% in other cereal flours. Oats not only have fat in the 'germ' but also in the 'endosperm' (the 'groat').

From a practical storing and cooking point of view the amount of moisture is important. Most samples of newly milled meal have 6-8% moisture and this is generally recognised as too high. At this level the meal lacks flavour and this is the reason why certain recipes say — 'Toast the oatmeal lightly in the oven before use.' It is simply to concentrate the nutty flavour. Similarly, oatcakes were always toasted before the fire to 'harden off'. Oatmeal used to be much 'harder dried' to only 3-5% moisture and the slower the process the better the flavour. If it is dried too quickly the flavour can be harsh and fiery. This applies also to oatmeal being dried off in the oven before use.

Since it does absorb moisture readily it is better to store oatmeal in an airtight container and press it well down. Oatmeal which is kept in open bags in shops for some time cannot be of the best quality. Scots used to keep their oatmeal in a 'girnal' (wooden chest) — the freshly milled oatmeal was tramped into it in the spring and lasted through the summer till harvest.

All the traditional oatmeal dishes such as porridge, oatcakes, brose and skirlie depend so much on the natural flavour of the meal, it is important to use freshly milled meal if possible. If stored for too long it absorbs moisture and may develop a bitter taste or 'nip'. This is caused by 'lipase' enzymes which break down the fat into a bitter unpleasant tasting fatty acid.

Today, the kernels or groats are ground and processed into a variety of products.

Oatmeal Grades

Pinhead — used for haggis, oatmeal loaves.

Rough — used for porridge or brose, sometimes rough oatcakes.

Medium/Rough — used by butchers for mealie puddings.

Medium
Fine — porridge, brose, skirlie, baking.

Super-fine — used in baking and in oatcakes along with a coarser grade.

To make **Pinhead** oatmeal the whole kernel is cut in half with any floury meal sifted out. **Medium Rough** is also known as **Coarse Medium.** Medium and fine grades are the most popular. There is also **Oat flour** which is distinct from Super-fine which still has a granule.

Other Oat Products

Rolled oats or **Oatflakes** were developed in America by the Quaker Oat Company in 1877 and are made by steaming and rolling pinhead oatmeal. While they have the obvious advantage of cooking more quickly than regular meal they have been specially heat treated with some loss of flavour and nutrients and this also applies to the other 'instant' oat porridges now on the market. **Jumbo Oatflakes** are made by steaming and rolling the whole groat.

Dietetic Value

It has taken an American professor, researching the problems of diabetics, to convince the world scientifically that oats are good for you. Professor James Anderson of the University of Kentucky College of Medicine has found a reason why we should eat more oats in future; namely, that oats contain a gummy fibre material (evident when porridge is made) which reduces blood cholesterol, blood sugar and fats. Oat bran is particularly rich in this 'water-soluble' fibre much more so than wheat bran, which contains the 'unsoluble' cellulose and very little of the gum. Oats also score on value for money since they contain more protein, more fat, more iron, more of the B vitamins, more calcium and also slightly more calories.

According to a National Food Survey in 1983 Scotland is by far the strongest area for oats products in Britain (1.15 oz per person per week compared with the North of England — 0.21 oz and Wales — 0.37 oz). It also shows the Scots as the lowest consumers of all other breakfast cereals (Market Research, 1983, No 23).

Barley

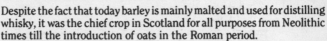

Despite the fact that today barley is mainly malted and used for distilling whisky, it was the chief crop in Scotland for all purposes from Neolithic times till the introduction of oats in the Roman period.

From this time onwards the oat crop developed but did not start to compete with barley till about the 17th century. By the 18th century, oatmeal was the predominant food crop and barley was used for distilling, making barley broth and bannocks. In the Highlands and Islands and among the lower classes in the Lowlands, barley continued to be used for making bread and is still used today in the Hebrides and in Orkney.

This distinct Northern variety of barley grown in upland areas of Scotland since ancient times is known as 'bigg' or 'big' (Hordeum Vulgare) and makes a dark greyish-brown bannock. Barley from 'bigg' is called 'bere' (pronounced 'bare'). There is no sweetening in the Beremeal bannock, which allows the natural flavour of the meal to predominate. It has a stronger, more definite flavour than oatmeal with a slightly astringent 'earthy tang' which combines well with creamy Orkney Farmhouse cheeses. Bere is ground on the island and made into Beremeal Bannocks by the local bakers. A few years ago Beremeal Bannocks were also available in Stornoway. Stoneground Orkney Beremeal is sold in the shops in Orkney and some specialist grain shops on the mainland sometimes have supplies. It is stone ground at the most northerly water-powered mill in Scotland, Boardhouse Mill, Birsay — the only remaining source of beremeal.

Pearl Barley, which is used for thickening Scotch Broth, is commonly available in all food shops. Barley flour is more of a specialist item but can be found in grain shops. Like oatmeal, they should both be bought in small quantities and stored in an airtight container. The flavour of this barley flour is not nearly so strong as that of the northern variety but nevertheless the distinctive earthy tang is still there.

Wheat

In fertile, lowland areas, wheat flourished, but the rest of the country grew mostly oats and barley. South-East Scotland, the Laigh of Moray, parts of Fife and Easter Ross were all developed by monastic farmers in the 11th and 12th centuries and wheat was grown in these parts, but mainly as a cash crop. Not much seems to have been eaten by the common people except at feasts and festivals. Higher up the social ladder, wheaten bread was initially something of a prestige food which made its social descent gradually till some time in the early 20th century when it had become a staple item for all people.

Oatcakes

Hear, Land o'Cakes, and brither Scots . . .

Robert Burns (1759-1796)

Burns meant, of course, land of **oatcakes** and not the sweet-flavoured cakes that have long been associated with the word. But why should the oat **cake** have come about, and why wasn't it just called oat bread or oat biscuit? It is a jigsaw puzzle of a problem, and to make the bits fit together the original meanings of loaf, bread, cake and biscuit are all relevant.

Bread, Loaf, Cake and Biscuit

'Loaf' is simple — it has always meant the undivided article. 'Bread' is more complicated since it originally meant only a 'piece or bit', later referred to as 'broken bread'. Finally it became known as the substance, 'bread'. The Lowland Scots and the Northern English have retained the original meaning of 'piece' when they say — 'Gie's-a-piece' meaning a piece of bread.

When bread, meaning the substance, was baked in a comparatively small flattened, round, oval or otherwise regularly-shaped form, this was known as a 'cake of bread'. It was usually baked hard on both sides by being turned in the process. We still talk of something being 'caked' hard or of making something into a hard round, flattish 'cake' like a cake of soap. In Wales, the North of England and Scotland (all oat-growing areas) this meaning survives in the oatcake.

'Biscuit' seems to have had a different meaning, though the end result is also a small, round, flattened, unleavened item which was eaten as 'bread'. The word, though, has the meaning 'baked twice' and seems to have been applied to something which was made for its keeping qualities. In England, at any rate, about the middle of the 16th century, it had these features — 'The bread was such as was provided to serue (sic) at need, or in Warrs, for it was BISCUIT, that is twice baked and without leaven or salt.' Sailors ate 'sea biscuit' which they sometimes called just 'bread'. And that makes our modern biscuits and oatcakes direct descendants of the oldest form of bread, the ground grain plus water, shaped thin and dried out, which also survives in things like Mexican **Tortilla**, Indian **Chapati**, American **Johnnycakes** and Chinese **Pancakes**.

Scots Oatcakes — shape and flavour

In their most basic and primitive form, Scots oatcakes are made with ground oatmeal, salt, a little dripping and water to mix. The Hebridean oatcake (Bonnach Imeach) is usually made with fairly fine oatmeal and is rolled out to between a quarter and half-an-inch thick, making it a fairly substantial cake. The Highlanders prefer a thinner, crisper variety usually rolled out to less than a quarter-of-an-inch thick and made with medium oatmeal. Lowlanders often add some wheaten flour, which makes the texture less brittle, but they may also use a coarser oatmeal (Pinhead) mixed with medium oatmeal, which makes an oatcake with a good bite to it. The taste in the North East is for a rough oatcake. The heavier Hebridean variety is really the exception to the general preference throughout the country for a crisp, crunchy cake, which means it must be rolled out as thinly as possible.

A quarter-of-an-inch is usually quoted in most cookery books; I find an eighth difficult to handle. They perhaps hit the right thickness in the Borders, if C. Lowther is to be believed when he says in his diary, Our Journal into Scotland, in 1629 — 'Three travellers in the Borders had oat bread cakes, baked a fifth of an inch thick on a griddle. . . .' At the other extreme there was the 'mill bannock' which was made twelve inches round and one inch thick, with a hole in the middle to simulate the mill wheel.

The usual shape is a round bannock (the size depends on the diameter of the girdle) cut with a cross into four. In pagan times, the Greeks and Romans cut crosses on their buns to represent the four seasons. Today we continue the custom, with a different symbolism, when we put crosses on hot cross buns.

A three-cornered piece of oatcake, scone or shortbread, the fourth part of a bannock, is known as a 'farl'. Old-fashioned 'farls' are not sold commercially today since they curl up at the edges and are difficult to package. So most commercial oatcakes are now sold in small round biscuit shapes though there are some shaped as small triangles. Michael Smith remembers seeing these old fashioned oatcakes 'like huge wash leathers' in bakers shops and refers to them in his book A Cook's Tour of Britain, 1984.

The fat which is used also affects the flavour of the oatcake. Bacon fat is preferred for flavour, though other drippings from beef and lamb roastings are also good. Dripping of one form or another is better from the point of view of making a shorter cake. Butter and oil are not traditional.

Oatcakes in the diet

For Breakfast . . . the cheese was set out as before, with plenty of butter and barley cakes, and fresh baked oaten cakes, which no doubt were made for us: they were kneaded with cream and were excellent.

Dorothy Wordsworth
Recollections of a Tour Made in Scotland, 1803

'Oatcakes are especially good with herrings, sardines, cheese, curds, buttermilk, broth, and kail; or spread with butter and marmalade to complete the breakfast.' Says F. Marian McNeill (The Scots Kitchen, 1929). Like porridge, oatcakes do not marry well with sweet things except perhaps with marmalade — but only when it is a bitter one. The delicate mealy flavour is perfect with an unsalted butter and some crowdie (traditional Scottish version of cottage cheese) mixed with a little cream, the soft cheese texture complementing the crunchy cake. In fact, all the traditional soft cheeses are good with oatcakes (see p. 244). Heather honey is often eaten with oatcakes. It doesn't have the sickly sweetness of blended honey but a particular bitter-sweet tang which goes well with the oatmeal flavour.

Records of meals show that oatcakes were commonly eaten at breakfast, dinner and supper as well as with tea at four o'clock in the afternoon. 'Oatcakes with milk' appears frequently in the diet charts of farm workers. In his Description of Scotland, in 1629, G. Buchanan says: 'They make a kind of bread, not unpleasant to the taste, of oats and barley, the only grain cultivated in these regions, and, from long practice, they have attained considerable skill in moulding the cakes. Of this they eat a little in the morning, and then contentedly go out a hunting, or engage in some other occupation, frequently remaining without any other food till evening.' Highland crofters who went up into the mountains with their flocks during the summer months and stayed in primitive 'sheelins' or 'bothays', made butter and cheese with cows' and sheep's milk which they ate with oatcake, according to Thomas Pennant writing in 1772.

Burns says that they 'are a delicate relish when eaten with warm ale'. Whether this means that amongst the very poorest classes they were regarded as a luxury is not clear, but amongst the inmates of the Poorhouse, oatcakes are never mentioned at any meal. Porridge and milk were their basic diet, more quickly and easily made than oatcakes, more filling and warming for hungry stomachs.

TRADITIONAL GIRDLE OATCAKES with fine meal

These attractive curled triangles have a crisp, 'short' bite to them. They can be cut into 4, 6 or 8 depending on when they are to be eaten. Larger ones are usually served at breakfast.

Mix and roll out enough for one girdleful at a time. Making up large quantities means that the mixture cools too much and is difficult to roll.

Quantity for one girdle

4 oz/125 g medium and fine oatmeal (about half and half or all medium oatmeal) (1 c)
1 tablespoon melted dripping*
Large pinch of salt
Boiling water to mix (about $\frac{1}{2}$ c)

Mixing and Shaping

Mix the meals and salt. Add the dripping, stir this through the meal. When well mixed, make a well and add enough boiling water to make the whole come together into a soft firm ball. The less water used, the crisper the oatcake. Knead into a round, dust with fine oatmeal and roll out on a board dusted with fine oatmeal to a circle about $\frac{1}{5}''$ ($\frac{1}{2}$ cm) thick. Keep bringing together round the edges to keep it from cracking. Cut with a cross into four, or into 6 or 8. Leave to dry for about $\frac{1}{2}$ hour before cooking — not necessary but helps to make them curl.

Heating the girdle (A large, heavy based frying pan will do instead)

Heat the girdle slowly to get an even heat. It should be moderately hot for oatcakes and the best way of testing is by holding your hand about 1″ ($2\frac{1}{2}$ cm) from the surface. It should feel hot, but not fiercely so. A steady slow heat is needed for drying out oatcakes.

Firing

Put the oatcakes on the girdle and leave till they have curled — they will curl upwards. If the cakes are too thick, they will not curl. Turn and leave for another five minutes till thoroughly dried out. This was originally done on a special toaster in front of the fire. Like toast, they should be put upright to cool since they continue to lose moisture till cold. Put in a toasting rack in front of the fire if you wish.

Note: Sometimes oatcakes were simply 'toasted very slowly at a distance from the fire, first on one side and then on the other on a toaster of open bars to let the moisture escape.' Meg Dods (1826).

Storing

Keep in an airtight tin or buried in oatmeal, which gives them a nice mealy taste. If they have been kept for more than a week it is a good idea to dry off slightly in the oven or in front of the fire to improve the flavour.

Serving

They can be served slightly warm but not so much that they make the butter run.

*Bacon fat is the most popular but lamb and beef dripping is also used. Oil and butter are not traditional but may be used.

OVEN OATCAKES with coarse oatmeal

This is a rougher textured oatcake which is the right vehicle for a smooth creamy cheese. Wheaten flour can be used instead of fine oatmeal and is almost invariably used in the commercial oatcakes to prevent them from breaking too easily. Barley flour adds its own distinctive flavour which tends to dominate the softer flavour of the oatmeal. Oatcakes made like this will not curl in the oven.

4 oz/125 g medium oatmeal (1 c)
4 oz/125 g coarse oatmeal (1 c)
4 oz/125 g fine oatmeal or barley meal (1 c)
2-3 tablespoons melted dripping
½ teaspoon salt
Boiling water to mix
Preheat the oven to 300F/150C/Gas 2

Put the meals into a bowl and add the dripping and salt. Mix thoroughly. Now add the water to make a stiffish dough. Roll out and cut into rounds or squares, using oatmeal to prevent sticking. Bake slowly without browning for 30-40 minutes.

Porridge

I took my porridge i'the morning an' often got naething again till night, because I couldna afford it.

W. Anderson
The Poor of Edinburgh. 1867

Goldilocks stole her porridge in the morning, soldiers marched on their morning porridge, and the Scottish peasant for many centuries started the day with a bowl of this sustaining food.

It is a morning ritual, porridge making — the handfuls of oatmeal running through your fingers into a large iron pot filled with boiling water, while the other hand stirs with the long tapered stick (spurtle); then the pot left at the side of the fire giving the familiar 'plop' every few minutes just to show it is still cooking.

It is true that it was also eaten for supper, and that leftovers were poured into the 'porridge drawer' in the Scotch dresser. The cold porridge set like a jelly and slices were cut off, known as 'caulders'. These were taken to the fields and eaten in the middle of the day, or slices were heated and eaten at night with eggs, fish or bacon.

Type of meal

Porridge is made with medium-ground oatmeal, sometimes with pinhead added, which gives it a rough texture. Fine oatmeal produces too smooth a porridge for Scottish tastes.

Many ways of cooking but only one way of eating

Wooden bowls (china or earthenware plates lose heat too quickly) were filled from the central pot, often placed in the centre of the table, and the porridge was eaten with a carved horn spoon. The spoon was dipped into the hot porridge, leaving enough room for the milk or cream on the spoon. The traditional carved horn spoon is quite large, round and deep, at least the size of a large tablespoon. The milk or cream bowl or cup was placed beside the larger one and the spoonful of hot porridge was then dipped into the cold milk/cream and eaten. This way the porridge remains hot till you have finished, whereas if you had put the milk in with the porridge it would have been cooled and the milk/cream heated. The essence of porridge eating is **hot** porridge and **cold** milk/cream.

There is nothing sacred about flavouring it only with salt. Robert Louis Stevenson made maps with the syrup on top of his porridge as a child and many people like it with honey. The point about sticking to a savoury taste is that the flavour of the oatmeal, otherwise overpowered by sweetness, is preserved. The sharp, bitter flavour of molasses is good with porridge and farm workers in the North East used to enjoy their porridge with some of the molasses which had been bought in drums to feed the horses.

To make porridge

4 Servings

Put 2 pts/1¼ L water (5 c) into a pot and bring to the boil. Sprinkle in 4 oz/125 g medium oatmeal (1 c) with one hand, while stirring with a spurtle (long wooden stick) to prevent lumps forming. Lower the heat, cover and leave to simmer for anything up to 30 minutes.

It does reduce and thicken so it is very much a case of how thick you like it. I prefer it cooked for a shorter rather than a longer time, about five minutes. Apart from saving time, it is less jelly-like in texture and the grains still have some bite to them (reduce water by half).

Season with a generous pinch of salt and serve in bowls with a smaller bowl of milk, cream or buttermilk. Natural yogurt, especially the Greek variety made from ewes' milk, is good with porridge and even better with a spoonful of molasses on top.

Brose

In these barracks the food is of the plainest and coarsest description: oatmeal forms its staple, with milk, when milk can be had, which is not always; and as the men have to cook by turns, with only half an hour or so given them in which to light a fire, and prepare the meal for a dozen or twenty associates, the cooking is invariably an exceedingly rough and simple affair. I have known mason-parties engaged in the central Highlands in building bridges, not unfrequently reduced by a tract of wet weather, that soaked their only fuel the turf and rendered it incombustible, to the extremity of eating their oatmeal raw, and merely moistened by a little water, scooped by the hand from a neighbouring brook.

Hugh Miller
My Schools and Schoolmasters. 1854

Brose is distinguished from porridge by its method of making. Single men living in bothies made brose in the morning: country people working in the fields or shepherds in the hills made brose. It was the quickest, cheapest way of producing food.

In rural areas day began at daybreak, about five o'clock, with perhaps a bowl of brose, then four or five hours later workers would return for breakfast. Dinner was in the middle of the day, supper at night.

Meal is put into a bowl — oatmeal, barley, pease meal, in whatever proportions available and boiling water, hot milk or the liquid from cooking vegetables or meat is poured over. Often a piece of butter is mixed in and perhaps some dried fruit. This was frequently a supper first course, the meat and vegetables eaten after with oatcakes. Today we eat Swiss Muesli for breakfast which is after all only a sophisticated version of Scottish Brose (see A Swiss/Scots Breakfast p. 40).

OATMEAL BROSE for breakfast

Put a handful of medium oatmeal or rolled oats into a bowl and pour over 1 cup of hot milk to cover the oatmeal, add a small piece of butter and stir while pouring. Season to taste with salt.

PEASE BROSE as eaten in the bothy

This is made in the same way as the oatmeal variety but instead the very fine peasemeal is used which gives it a richer flavour. Lots of currants and butter can be added as well as honey or sugar for sweetening.

ATHOLL BROSE

It was very common to mix whisky with honey in the past and equally common to mix liquid with oatmeal. Bringing the two together in this potent way is credited to a Duke of Atholl during a Highland rebellion in 1475, who is said to have foiled his enemies by filling the well which they normally drank from with this ambrosial mixture, which so intoxicated them that they were easily taken.

Some traditional recipes leave in the whole oatmeal while this one, reputed to have come from a Duke of Atholl, uses only the strained liquid from steeping the oatmeal in water.

6 oz/175 g medium oatmeal ($1\frac{1}{2}$ c)
4 tablespoons heather honey
$1\frac{1}{2}$ pt/$\frac{3}{4}$ L whisky ($3\frac{3}{4}$ c)
$\frac{3}{4}$ pt/450 ml water (2 c)

Put the oatmeal into a bowl and add the water. Leave for about an hour. Put into fine sieve and press all the liquid through. (Use the remaining oatmeal for putting into bread or making porridge — see p. 26). Add honey to the sieved liquid and mix well. Pour into a large bottle and fill up with the whisky. Shake well before use.

Uses

May be drunk as a liqueur; is often served at festive celebrations such as New Year, or may be mixed with stiffly whipped cream and served with shortbread as a sweet.

Bannocks

. . . bannocks and a shave of cheese
Will make a breakfast that a laird might please.

Allan Ramsay (1682-1758)
The Gentle Shepherd

A bannock is something large and round, thicker and softer than an oatcake, which was originally cooked on the girdle. In the past the type of meal used depended on what was available, with great variations throughout the year and from district to district. Despite this, there is constant reference to Barley Bannocks by travellers describing their meals.

Thomas Pennant, in 1772, talks about the 'fresh eggs, fresh barley bannocks, and tolerable porter, together with some smoked salmon' which they enjoyed in an Inn at 'Cree in La Roche' (presumably Crianlarich since he was travelling up Glen Falloch).

James Russel, writing in the 19th century, says that 'Oatcakes and bannocks of barley meal with an admixture of pease, were the ordinary table fare. Wheaten bread was scarcely known.'

Thomas Somerville, a minister in Jedburgh from 1741 to 1830, writes in his diary that — 'Though wheaten bread was partly used, yet cakes or "bannocks" of barley and peasemeal, and oatcakes formed the principle household bread in gentlemans' families; and in those of the middle class on ordinary occasions, no other bread was ever thought of.'

Early forms of bannocks were made without raising agents, which may sound unpalatable to modern tastes but the barley bannock which F. Marian McNeill describes in The Scots Kitchen as the 'old method' produces a good bannock.

OLD-FASHIONED BANNOCKS without raising agent

Something akin to an Indian Chapati since it doesn't rise. Its charm lies in the barley flavour, and in the contrasts of texture; the soft inside and harder but not quite crisp outside.

$\frac{1}{2}$ pt/300 ml milk ($1\frac{1}{4}$ c scant)
1 oz/25 g butter ($\frac{1}{4}$ stick)
4 oz/125 g barley flour (may be mixed with peasemeal) (1 c)
Salt to taste
Pre-heat the girdle till fairly hot. Flour lightly.

Making up the dough

Put the milk into a pan, add the butter and heat through to melt the butter; add the salt. Stir in the meal; it should come together into a softish paste a bit like the consistency for choux pastry. Turn out onto a floured board and knead lightly to a smooth ball, dusting well on top with barley flour. Press out to about 6" (15 cm) in diameter.

Firing

Place on girdle, press out evenly with your knuckles to about 10" × $\frac{1}{2}$" (25 × 1 cm) thick and cook on a moderate girdle till brown on one side, about 10-15 minutes. Turn, using two fish slices, or cut in half and turn in two pieces. (Bannock spathes were used in the past for this job, now only to be found in museums.) Cook on other side for 10-15 minutes. Place on cooling rack and eat warm.

BARLEY BANNOCKS wafer thin

Another early form was made with a much thinner mixture poured onto the girdle rather like the very large Breton pancakes (crêpes). Franco-Scottish connections may have had something to do with this, since there is a striking resemblance between the large Scottish girdles (a woman in Edinburgh had one five feet across which was used on a flat open hearth), and the large iron plates used in Brittany for making crêpes.

In his Travels in England and Scotland in 1799, Faujas de St Ford talks about 'barley cakes, folded over' — it is possible these are the cakes he was referring to.

They may be treated as for French crêpes, their flavour is stronger, but they are good filled with cream cheese, honey or preserves.

4 oz/125 g Beremeal or barley flour (1 c)
3 eggs
1 oz/25 g melted butter (¼ stick)
Water to mix

Heat the girdle till moderately hot or cook in frying pan or crêpe pan. Grease lightly.

Sift the flour into a bowl, make a well in the centre and add 3 eggs and the melted butter; mix with water till smooth. Beat well. Leave to rest. Pour onto heated girdle or crêpe pan in ladlefuls spreading out to the edges: this is best done by tilting the girdle to spread the mixture. Leave to cook 2-3 minutes, turn and cook on the other side for another 2-3 minutes. Place a filling in centre, fold in four and eat hot.

MODERN BARLEY BANNOCKS with raising agent

These are the round light bannocks which bakers in Orkney make usually about the size of an outstretched hand. (6"/15 cm approx.)

4 oz/125 g Beremeal or barley flour (1 c)
1 tablespoon plain flour
1 teaspoon baking soda
Pinch of salt
Buttermilk to mix

Heat the girdle till moderately hot and flour well.

Sift the dry ingredients together and mix with the buttermilk to a soft dough. Put onto the hot girdle, dust the top with flour and press down lightly with your fingers into a 6" (15 cm) round. Bake on both sides, turning once, about 5-10 minutes each side.

OATMEAL BANNOCKS

This sweet crumpet-style bannock comes from the North East where they call it a 'Sauty* Bannock'. They are thicker and heavier than the barley ones and should be eaten warm from the girdle.

12 oz/350 g fine oatmeal (3 c)
1 teaspoon salt
1 teaspoon bicarbonate of soda
1 tablespoon sugar
1 tablespoon syrup
1 pt/600 ml milk (2½ cups)
2 eggs

Pre-heat the girdle till fairly hot and grease lightly.

Dissolve the syrup in the milk and add to the oatmeal, salt, and sugar. Soak overnight. When ready to cook add the eggs and soda. Mix in more milk if necessary to make a thickish creamy mixture.

*From French 'sauter'.

Drop in spoonfuls onto a hot girdle — they should spread to 5-6″ (12-15 cm). Fire on both sides, pile on top of one another and wrap in a cloth to keep them soft. Serve hot, with butter and jam or crowdie.

Mealie Puddings and Skirlie

It fell about the Martinmas time
And a gay time it was then, O
That oor guidwife had puddens to mak'
And she boiled them in a pan, O.

Anon

In the days before the turnip was used as winter feed for animals, Martinmas, 11 November, was the time for killing the animals which people could not afford to keep during the winter. 'Mairt' was an incredibly busy time though several families would work together to get the job done. Every scrap of the beast was used — the meat mostly salted down and puddings made from the innards. Pudding is the original name for the innards of an animal, and Pudding Lane in London is so called, not because people ate puddings there, but because this was where the butchers used to wash out the innards of the animals (see Haggis pudding p. 150).

Mealie puddings, black and white, were made when beef cattle were killed. This is now mostly a butcher's job though some people still make their own. The oatmeal, onions, suet from the animal and salt and pepper were mixed in a large basin. Blood from the animal was added to make the 'bleedy' ones. The intestines were thoroughly washed, usually in a burn, and then stuffed loosely with the mixture. A writer in the 'North East Review' writes nostalgically of the puddings his mother used to make — 'Come time the skins were a' filled up, and tied, and jab-bit wi' a darner, and they were ready for the pot. They were biled an oor. It wis easy the langest oor I mind on. My teeth wid be watering till I slivert again, and when they lifted the lid o' the pot to see the water wisna biling in — oh! the guff that filled the kitchie. The tastings, or the preens as my mother ca'ed them, were first oot and nae wirds could tell ye fit they tastit like — as the poet his't — "warm-reeking', rich," ye dinna see the like the day.'

Skirlie is made with the same ingredients as mealie puddings but the mixture is fried in a pan. The noise of the frying or 'skirl' as in skirl of the pipes gave it its original name of 'skirl-in-the-pan'.

Skirlie has several uses. It can be served with roast meat and is particularly good with game. It can also be used as a stuffing for any kind of poultry or game or made into a steamed pudding using either a cloth or bowl.

Medium or coarse oatmeal is used. The type of fat varies, though fresh beef suet, meat or bacon dripping make the best flavoured Skirlie. Chopped onions are most commonly used, though an expatriate Scot told me recently of a Skirlie mixture she remembers using leeks, instead of onions.

To make Skirlie

Melt 2 oz/50 g fat in a frying pan. When hot, add 1 medium onion finely chopped and cook till soft and transparent but not coloured. (Some people add water at this point to soften the onion, but this seems to be a regional variation. A good idea if it is to be used for stuffing, since it helps to hold the mixture together.) Now add enough oatmeal to absorb the fat (about 4 oz/125 g/1 c), season well with salt and pepper and serve.

Oatmeal and Barley Breads

I was challenged by one of the leading health-conscious bakers of good bread in Glasgow recently to produce a loaf using oatmeal. Since it has no gluten strength he had never used it, but was aware of its potential in the market place as an additional healthy selling point. The following breads are the results of my experiments; with much help from Bernard Clayton's 'The Complete Book of Breads' (Simon and Shuster, 1973), and others.

Since oatmeal has no gluten it is essential always to use it along with flour with good gluten strength.

OATMEAL BREAD with molasses or treacle

makes 2 loaves

This striking loaf, richly brown on the inside, has a light speckled crust which happens when you line the tin with rolled oats.

6 oz/175 g rolled oats (2 c)
6 oz/175 g mollases or treacle ($\frac{1}{2}$ c)
$\frac{3}{4}$ pt/450 ml boiling water (2 c scant)
1 tablespoon salt
2 oz/50 g lard or margarine ($\frac{1}{2}$ stick)
1$\frac{1}{4}$ lb/625 g strong white flour (5 c)
1 oz/50 g fresh yeast ($\frac{1}{2}$ oz/15 g dried or 2 pkg)
2 eggs
2 tablespoons rolled oats to coat tins
2 × 1 lb/500 g loaf tins
Pre-heat the oven to 375F/190C/Gas 5
Put the oats, lard and salt into a bowl. Dissolve the molasses in the boiling water and pour over the oats. Activate the yeast if dried by mixing with a little warm water or mix the fresh yeast with a teaspoonful of sugar. Add the yeast to the oats and stir in half of the

flour. Beat well for three or four minutes — this can be done with the mixer. Beat in eggs and then work in the remaining flour gradually till the dough is soft and sticky but not too dry. Leave for 10 minutes to rest.

Kneading and Rising

Turn onto a board and knead till the dough is smooth and elastic. Cover and put to rise in a warm place for about $1\frac{1}{2}$ hours or until the dough has doubled in size.

Shaping

Grease tin well with lard or oil and coat the base and sides with rolled oats. Knead dough for a few minutes and then divide into two. Shape into loaves and put into tins. Cover with cling-film and put back in a warm place till they have risen to double their size again. Brush with milk and sprinkle with rolled oats. Bake for $\frac{3}{4}$ to 1 hour or until they make a hollow sound when tapped on the base. Cool thoroughly.

OATMEAL BREAD ROLLS

6-8 rolls

These moist, well-flavoured rolls are sprinkled on top with rolled oats before they are baked.

5 oz/150 g rolled oats ($1\frac{1}{2}$ c)
12 oz/325 g strong white flour (3 c)
$\frac{1}{2}$ oz/15 g fresh yeast, $\frac{1}{4}$ oz/7 g dried (1 pkg)
2 tablespoons sugar
1 tablespoon salt
2 oz/50 g softened butter ($\frac{1}{2}$ stick)
12 fl oz/50 ml warm water ($1\frac{1}{2}$ c)

Mixing the dough

Dissolve the dried yeast in a little of the water and leave in a warm place till it froths or blend the fresh yeast with a little sugar or sprinkle the packet yeast in with the flour.

Put half the flour, oats, sugar, yeast, salt, butter and water into a bowl and beat for at least 2 minutes either by hand or with the mixer. Then add the remaining flour gradually, mixing in by hand till the right soft sticky consistency is reached.

Kneading

Turn the dough onto a lightly floured board and knead till it becomes smooth and elastic and leaves the hand cleanly. Add more flour if it is too sticky.

Rising

Put in a bowl, cover and put in a warm place till it has risen to double in size.

Shaping and Proving

Knock back the dough and knead for a few minutes. Divide into 6 or 8 pieces. Leave to rest for a few minutes. Shape into rolls, place on baking tray, cover with lightly oiled cling-film and put in a warm

Baking

place till they have risen again to double in size.

Brush the tops with milk and sprinkle with rolled oats. Bake for about 30 minutes. Test by tapping the bottom of one — it should sound hollow.

SOUR DOUGH OATMEAL BREAD

Pioneer America perfected this idea of rising the dough, not by commercial yeast which was unavailable, but by a bubbling pot of aromatic starter, making use of the wild yeasts which are all around us. It seems that the Scots in remote areas had also discovered this phenomena — 'What some of them did was to twist an oak rod, four to eight inches long, boil it in wort (unfermented beer) and dry it well; then, when they steeped it in wort a second time, it fermented and made yeast'. <u>Domestic Life of Scotland in the Eighteenth Century</u>, Marjorie Plant 1952.

The dough is firstly a flour and liquid mixture which is allowed to ferment naturally in a warm place. Then more starchy substance is added for the yeast to feed on making a 'sponge' — now it is thoroughly fermenting and the yeast cells multiplying by the million. The life and movement in this dough is a constant source of wonder — the finished loaf with its unique flavour and aroma, a great delight.

How To Make a COOKED POTATO STARTER

4 tablespoons cornmeal (fine)
2 tablespoons sugar
1½ teaspoons salt
8 fl oz/250 ml milk (1 c)
Blend the cornmeal with milk and add sugar and salt. Put into a pan and bring to the boil, stirring constantly. Pour into a small bowl, cover and leave in a warm place for 2-4 days till it ferments and looks light and frothy.

Reserve the liquid from boiling 3 medium potatoes and make up to 2 pts/1.15 dl (5 c). Purée or sieve the potatoes and add to the liquid. Mix through 3 tablespoons sugar and 2 teaspoons salt. When cool, stir in the fermented cornmeal. Cover and leave in a warm place overnight, stirring down when it becomes bubbly. Next day put into a large jar, cover with some foil rather than a lid, since it continues to give off gas, and put into the refrigerator to age for about 3 days before using. Stir well each time before using. Replenish when the starter has been reduced to 1½-2 cups adding a new potato, potato water, sugar and salt mixture made as before.

¾ pt/450 ml boiling water (2 c)
8 oz/250 g medium oatmeal (2 c)
8 oz/250 g strong white flour (2 c)
3 tablespoons brown sugar
12 fl oz/50 ml Cooked Potato Starter (1½ c)

Day before baking

Pour boiling water over oatmeal and when lukewarm add flour, sugar and starter. Stir well, cover and leave overnight in a warm place.

The next day

Pre-heat oven to 350F/180C/Gas 4.
Prepare tins 4 × 1 lb/500 g loaf tins.

Add

12fl oz/350 ml warm water (1¼ c)
4 tablespoons dried milk powder
½ teaspoon ginger
5 teaspoons salt
4 oz/125 g butter (1 stick)
6 tablespoons syrup (maple)
2 tablespoons brown sugar

Mixing and Kneading

Stir well then start adding flour — 2 lb/1 kg (8 c). Add half to begin and mix for about two minutes, then add remaining flour gradually till the dough forms a soft mass. Turn out and knead till it is smooth and elastic and comes away easily from your hands.

Rising

Put dough back into the bowl, cover, and put in a warm place till it has risen to double its size.

Knocking Back and Shaping

Knock down the dough and turn out onto floured board. Divide into loaf sized pieces. Knead for a few minutes, shape and put into tins. Brush the tops with melted butter, cover with lightly oiled cling-film and leave in a warm place to rise to double their volume.

Baking

Bake for about 1 hour, test by removing from tins and knocking on base when it should sound hollow. Cool thoroughly.
Note: May also be rolled out into a rectangle and spread with a layer of maple syrup, about 2 tablespoons, cover with 1 tablespoon ground cinnamon and sprinkle a few currants on top. Roll up and put in loaf tin.

BUTTERMILK BREAD with oatmeal

This is a moist but not wet bread which has a sharp tangy flavour. It is ideal with cheese or a thick soup-stew and can be baked in a round and cut in pie-shaped wedges or baked in a pot or tin (see p. 211). It has the added advantage of being quick to make.
8 oz/250 g medium oatmeal (2 c)
1 pt/600 ml buttermilk (2½ c)

Night before baking

Put the oatmeal into a bowl and pour over the buttermilk. Stir well and cover.

Next day

10 oz/300 g strong white flour (2 c)
1 teaspoon bicarbonate of soda
1 teaspoon salt
Pre-heat the oven to 350F/180C/Gas 4.
Grease tin — 2 lb/500 g loaf tin or 7" (12 cm) round pot with lid which can be put in the oven or chicken brick.

Sift flour, soda and salt together and add to the oatmeal mixture. If it is too stiff, add some more buttermilk. Keep the mixture soft and elastic.

Either shape into a round, divide into four, and bake on a greased baking tray, or make into a loaf and bake in a tin or pot with a lid. Bake the round for 30-40 minutes. The covered loaf will take longer, about an hour. To test, remove from tin and knock on the base: it will make a hollow sound if ready. Remove and cool thoroughly.

BARLEY BREAD

The flavour of barley gives personality to this loaf, particularly if it is Orkney beremeal.

1 lb/500 g strong plain flour (4 c)
4 oz/125 g Beremeal or barley flour (1¼ c)
½ oz/15 g fresh yeast, ¼ oz/7 g dried (1 pkg or cake)
1 tablespoon salt
12 fl oz/350 ml water (1½ c)
2-3 tablespoons buttermilk
2 lb/1 kg loaf tin or 2 smaller ones 1 lb/½ kg — 4" (10 cm deep)
Pre-heat the oven to 450F/230C/Gas 8 for the first 15 minutes — reduce to 400F/205C/Gas 6 for the next 15 minutes to finish the loaf.

Remove from the tin and put on its side and bake for another 15-20 minutes at 350F/180C/Gas 4 when it should make a hollow sound when tapped on the bottom.

To make up the dough

Begin by sieving the flours and salt together and placing in a low oven for 5 minutes to warm through. This helps to get the yeast started: cold flour just takes longer, but make sure that neither it nor the bowl are above lukewarm. Pour some of the measured water over the yeast and leave in a warm place for ten minutes to activate. It should froth up (dried yeast needs a stir to dissolve and a pinch of sugar to get it started). Now make a well in the centre of the flour and pour in the yeast and water: mix with your hands to make a smooth elastic dough with plenty of stretch — only by working with your hands can you sense when the dough is the right texture. Give it a good kneading to develop the stretchy gluten — it should come away from your fingers easily. In other words if it is very sticky it may need more flour, or if too tight a dough, may need a little more water.

Rising

When ready, place in a floured bowl and cover with a wet tea-towel — this gives the necessary damp steamy atmosphere which it needs to rise. Place in a warm place and leave till it doubles in size.

Knocking Back and Shaping

Punch the dough down and knead for a few minutes to redistribute the yeast. Grease the tin with oil or fat. Shape the dough so that the folds are underneath, and put into the tin.

Baking and Cooling

Bake in the centre of the pre-heated oven testing for readiness. Cool on a rack till perfectly cold. Bread which has not been properly 'dried off' will go mouldy quicker.

Other Uses of Oatmeal and Barley

CLOOTIE DUMPLING

8-10 servings

A huge pot hung over the fire which leapt in a shining black-and-steel range. A black kettle stood on one hob, a brown teapot on the other. Steam rose gently from the kettle and thickly from the great black pot, whence also came a continuous 'purring' noise and the wonderful smell.

Jennifer Gowan
'Friendship is a Clootie Dumpling', Scottish Field, July 1966

This is a plain dumpling; the name comes from the use of a cloth 'clout' (pronounced cloot) which the pudding is boiled in.

To cook in the traditional way, it should be boiled in a large cloth. It can quite easily be cooked instead in a greased pudding bowl but the result will not have the 'skin', greatly loved by dumpling-eaters, which forms on the outside of the pudding.

4 oz/125 g suet, finely chopped (1 c)
8 oz/250 g self-raising flour (2 c)
1 teaspoon baking powder
4 oz/125 g breadcrumbs (1 c)
3 oz/75 g brown sugar ($\frac{1}{2}$ c)
8 oz/250 g currants/sultanas mixed ($1\frac{1}{2}$ c)
1 teaspoon each — cinnamon, ginger
1 tablespoon golden or maple syrup
2 eggs

Preparing the cloth

Half fill a very large pot with water and bring to the boil. Add a large piece of white cotton or linen cloth to the boiling water and leave for

a few minutes. Lift out with some tongs, allow excess water to drip off then lay out flat on table. Dust a layer of flour over the cloth (this forms the 'skin').

Making the dumpling

Dissolve the syrup in a little buttermilk and add with the eggs to the other ingredients. Mix to a soft dropping consistency. Put the mixture into the centre of the prepared cloth, draw up the edges and tie with some string, leaving some room for expansion.

Steaming

Put an inverted plate in the bottom of the pan and then add the dumpling. The water should come about $\frac{3}{4}$ of the way up the dumpling. Bring to simmering point, cover and cook for 3-4 hours. Check the water level occasionally. (Alternatively use a 3 pt/$1\frac{1}{2}$ L pudding bowl — English pudding basin, cover the top with foil or greaseproof paper and tie securely.)

To turn out

Fill up with cold water a basin large enough to hold the dumpling and have ready a bowl that the dumpling will just fit into. Also a large round heated plate or ashet. First dip the pudding into cold water for about ten seconds. This prevents the skin sticking to the cloth. Now put into the bowl and untie the string. Open out the cloth and hang over the sides of the bowl. Put the serving dish over the bowl, invert it and then remove the cloth carefully.

Drying off and Serving

Dry off in the oven or in front of the fire. Sprinkle with caster sugar and eat with cream or custard. Leftovers provide useful breakfasts fried with bacon, or slices may be wrapped in foil and re-heated in the oven.

SWEET OATEN PUDDING with raspberries

All old Scottish cookery books have versions of this pudding. Mostly, the recipes are for a kind of rich custard pudding which has been thickened with oatmeal and well-flavoured with nutmeg, mace, lemon and brandy. The mixture was usually boiled in a cloth but occasionally it was put in a pie shell and baked.

The following recipe is a modern adaptation using the original flavourings and ingredients, plus raspberries for colour and flavour, but changing the method to make a light cream sweet.

$\frac{3}{4}$ pt/450 ml milk (2 c)
2 oz/50 g medium oatmeal ($\frac{1}{2}$ c)
1 large egg, beaten
1 small lemon, zest and juice
2 tablespoons caster sugar
$\frac{1}{2}$ oz/15 g gelatine (2 envelopes)
$\frac{1}{4}$ pt/150 ml double cream, lightly whipped ($\frac{3}{4}$ c scant)
Blade of mace
A little grated nutmeg

Soak overnight

The oatmeal and blade of mace in milk (or at least for a few hours).

To make pudding

Put the oatmeal mixture into a pan and bring to the boil, simmer for 3-4 minutes. Pour into a bowl and add the beaten egg, grated lemon rind, grated nutmeg and sugar to taste. The heat of the mixture will thicken the egg. Put the gelatine and lemon juice into a cup and set in a pan of simmering water. Dissolve gelatine and allow to cool a little, add to the mixture then fold in the cream.

Serving

Put some fresh raspberries into individual glasses and pour mixture on top. When set, garnish with raspberries and cream or make a raspberry purée (p. 158) and pour a layer on top when set.

BUTTERED OATS

I changed the name of this very useful oatmeal mixture from 'Oatmeal Topping' (An Oat Information Council recipe), which reminded me too much of the 'dream' variety, to one that would more effectively capture the richness of its character. It can be made in quantity and stored in an airtight jar, making it handy as a 'crumble' top for cooked or uncooked fruits. Nuts can be added and it can also be mixed, Cranachan style, through cream and soft fruit. It is also good as a layer in the base of the tin when making particularly moist cakes. (See recipe for Cinnamon Apple Cake p. 223.)

I have used it mostly in layers with stewed apples, something in the style of the Danish Apple Cake, using buttered oats instead of breadcrumbs.

$1\frac{1}{2}$ oz/40 g butter
2 oz/50 g brown sugar (2 tbsp)
4 oz/125 g rolled oats ($1\frac{1}{4}$ cup)
Melt the butter in a pan and add sugar and oats. Mix well.
Spread out in tin and toast in a moderate oven till golden brown.

Apple purée

Peel, core and slice 4-5 medium cooking apples. Toss them in the juice of $\frac{1}{2}$ lemon and put into a casserole with a tight-fitting lid. Bake in a moderate oven till apples are soft and fluffy. They should take about 30 minutes. Beat up with sugar to taste. Cool.

Finishing the dish

Using a straight sided soufflé dish or any other suitable sweet-dish or pie-dish, arrange a layer of oats, then apples and so on till all are used up. Finish with a layer of oats and leave at room temperature for about an hour for the flavours to blend.

A SWISS/SCOTS BREAKFAST

A leading exponent of natural food, Anton Mosimann*, the Swiss chef at the Dorchester Hotel in London created this intriguing blend of fresh fruit flavours to a background of oats. As is often the case in the realms of food, similar traditions develop in different countries and the old-fashioned Scots Brose finds its counterpart in modern Swiss Muesli.

The recipe can be adapted to make a good ending to a meal by garnishing with cream, strawberries and brambles (blackberries) and decorating with pineapple leaves. Otherwise it makes a good start to the day.

Soak overnight

4 oz/120 g rolled oats ($1\frac{1}{4}$ c)
$\frac{1}{2}$ pt/300 ml milk ($1\frac{1}{4}$ c)

Add

1 grated apple
2 oz/50 g chopped hazelnuts ($\frac{1}{2}$ c)
Juice of 1 orange
Juice of 1 lemon
1 orange, segmented
1 banana, sliced
2 oz/50 g fresh pineapple, sliced ($\frac{1}{2}$ c)
Sweeten to taste with honey

For a sweet, garnish with

$\frac{1}{4}$ pt/150 ml double cream ($\frac{3}{4}$ cup)
2 oz/50 g brambles (blackberries) ($\frac{1}{2}$ c)
A few strawberries
Pineapple leaves

*Cuisine Naturelle, 1985.

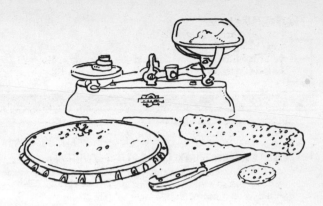

WALNUT AND OAT BISCUITS

A coarse-textured hearty biscuit, richly flavoured with walnuts, vanilla and oats.
Pre-heat the oven to 350F/180C/Gas 4.
Greased baking tray

Beat together till creamy

6 oz/175 g butter ($\frac{3}{4}$ c)
6 oz/175 g brown sugar (1 c generous)
4 oz/125 g granulated sugar ($\frac{1}{2}$ c)
1 egg
4 teaspoons water
1 teaspoon vanilla essence

Mix in

4 oz/125 g plain flour (1 c)
1 level teaspoon salt
$\frac{1}{2}$ teaspoon bicarbonate of soda
9 oz/250 g rolled oats (3 c)
4 oz/125 g walnuts, finely chopped (1 c)

Using some extra rolled oats on the board, roll out the mixture into a long sausage shape about 2″ (5 cm) in diameter and then put in a cool place for an hour to harden. Cut with a sharp knife into $\frac{1}{4}$″ (1 cm) slices and place on baking tray. Bake for 15-20 minutes till lightly brown.

Other Recipes using Oatmeal

Fresh Herring or Mackerel fried in oatmeal p. 56. Dulse Cakes p. 101. Minced Collops p. 127. Beef Olives p. 129. Cream Crowdie (Cranachan) p. 164. Oatmealed Potatoes p. 182. Sautéed Chicken and Leeks with Skirlie p. 187. Buttered Kale p. 195. A Cake with Apples in It p. 223. Mealie Candy p. 230.

CHAPTER TWO
FISH

There is an element of exotic interest in sea food which is perhaps not sufficiently exploited in this country.

A.D. McIntyre (Director. Marine Laboratory. Aberdeen)
The Sea and Fresh Waters. 1985

If you look through the window of the average Scottish fishmonger, you might get the feeling that the sea contains only about six varieties of wet fish — haddock, herring, mackerel, cod, sole and whiting. It is true that these are the fish that are most caught around Scottish waters, but according to fish landings in Scotland there are at least another 24 species which are also caught and landed. So where are they? Some, possibly, on the slabs of more enterprising Scottish fishmongers, and there are quite a few, but most will go to other markets in England and abroad.

Inbuilt tradition has restricted Scottish horizons and fishmongers need to feel confident that the consumer is keen on trying out the more unusual species. They also need to be willing to explain what is the best treatment for fish their customers are not familiar with.

It's not that Scots don't eat fish — they do. In 1983 the average household consumption of fish in Scotland was 22.3 lb compared with the reputedly fish-conscious London of 22.9 lb. Even more revealing is the fact that, of that amount the Scots ate 75% in a fresh state rather than frozen or processed, while the Londoners ate only 42% fresh.

All round our very long coastline there is evidence of an ancient fishing tradition which has encouraged the Scots to eat a lot of fish. Earliest fishing traditions are on the East coast, where there is an abundance of natural harbours, while West coast fishing was a later development when the people lost their lands and turned more to the sea for sustenance. In the Islands, the Hebrides, Orkney and particularly Shetland, the people were born and bred to a long tradition of fishing. Shetland fishermen went to the Faroes, Iceland and Greenland and established fishing in these parts long before fishermen from the rest of Scotland.

Off the Western Highlands and Islands there were tremendous shoals of herring, haddock, whiting and mackerel. There were also good supplies of salmon, cod, ling, eel, turbot and other flat fish as well as innumerable shellfish, including cockles, oysters, lobsters and scallops in plenty. Round the Hebrides and Orkney, whales and seals were eaten. Whale flesh was thought better boiled than roasted, while the liver was regarded as a great delicacy — 'It smells like Voilets, tastes pleasantly, and is very nourishing being salted.' Guy Miege, <u>The Present State of Great Britain and Ireland</u>, 1738.

While fishermen in those days had no concern for preservation of the fish stocks, today our established species, especially the top six, are under threat due to overfishing. Herring and mackerel stocks are particularly vulnerable (for reasons see p. 55) and stocks are now monitored by scientists and the fishing closed (as it was in 1977 for herring) when they reach a dangerous low. Though there is little or no control of these wild stocks of fish, the possibilities in the future of farming the sea may be one way of stabilising supply. The main fish being farmed in Scotland at the moment include turbot, Atlantic salmon and Rainbow Trout, but they make up only a very small percentage of the total fish production from Scottish waters and it seems unlikely that, for the moment, the yield will increase much, except for salmon.

I should like to have devoted much of this chapter to the other 24 varieties of fish which are caught and landed in Scotland and of which the Scots don't eat enough, but here instead is a list of them. And in addition two books which will help, firstly identify them, and secondly cook them.

Brill, Catfish, Conger Eels, Dabs, Dogfish, Dover Sole, Flounders, Gurnard, Hake, Halibut, Ling, Lythe, Megrims, Monkfish, Norway Pout, Plaice, Saith, Sand Eels, Shark, Skate, Torsk, Turbot, Witches, Sprats.*

<u>North Atlantic Seafood</u> by Alan Davidson (Macmillan, 1979/ Penguin, 1980).

<u>Fish Cookery</u> by Jane Grigson (International Wine and Food Publishing Company, 1973/Penguin, 1975).

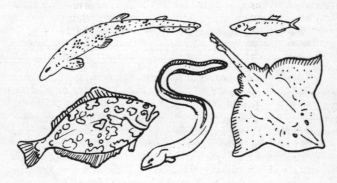

Atlantic Salmon (Salmo salar)

Life Cycle

Hatched in the purest of Scotland's fresh-water rivers, after two years or so they migrate to the sea, grow fat over several years, then return to their native waters, fight their way back upstream to where they were hatched and then spawn. The female lays her eggs on the river bed and the male fertilises them. By this time, both fish are badly run down and either die or go back to sea to return another year.

The terminology for the various stages starts with **Fry** which is just after the salmon hatch and come out of the gravel, on to **Parr** which is the two year period of growth in their home river. Just before they leave, they change physically to fit them for sea water and at this point are called **Smolts**. Salmon which come back after one year are called **Grilse** and weigh 2 lbs-8 lbs depending on the richness of their sea feeding grounds. Fish which come back after two, three or four years are **Adult Salmon** and the best quality are caught early in the season when still fat and flavoursome from the rich sea feeding grounds. They are likely to weigh from 8 lbs upwards to about 60 lb. When, and if, they reach their place of hatching the female spawns and the male ejects his milt on top of the spawn. After this, they either die from exhaustion and lack of food (**Spent Kelts**) or they make it back to sea (**Mended Kelts**) and return to spawn again. All Pacific salmon spawn and then die, whereas 5% of Atlantic salmon return to spawn. They usually spend two to three winters in the sea, maximum five. The oldest recorded salmon was caught on Loch Maree in Wester Ross and was thirteen years old and had spawned four times.

Wild Scottish Salmon

These are caught either at sea with nets, or by 'sport' fishing as they make their way up the river. Their superb flavour surpasses all other varieties and they are generally recognised as the finest. Scots who know and enjoy them, understand that their rich flavour should not be complicated with competing ones. They should be eaten with simple things like plain boiled floury potatoes, fresh green peas, with perhaps a little sharpness from some lemon to counteract the fat.

Season

Lasts from February to September with variations for rod-caught fish on some rivers. Most plentiful from May-July.

Farmed Salmon

West Coast salmon farming started in 1969 and the industry is still growing. In 1992, almost 38,000 tonnes of farmed salmon were produced. (600 tonnes of wild salmon were caught in 1992.) 80% of farmed salmon is now smoked. There have been many problems, not least coping with the effects of gales which break up the tanks. There are few really sheltered areas which are suitable on the West Coast but fish farmers have been studying the fish farming technology which has been developed by the Japanese.

The flavour does not compare with Wild Salmon, nor should it be expected to, given the entirely different life styles and feeding. Improved feeding has now greatly improved the flavour but the texture remains different from wild salmon and is the factor, before you actually taste the fish, which most easily tells the difference. Since the fish don't have the exercise of crossing the Atlantic, they tend to have flabbier, less well-developed muscles than wild fish, which means that the muscle flakes fall apart more readily when cooked. Smoking techniques differ from wild salmon. When smoked, the looser held-together muscles make very very thin slicing more difficult and therefore slices from farmed fish are slightly thicker. In recognising the need for the fish to exercise, fish farms are now allowing them much more room to move about.

Better farmed salmon is now being produced. As well as a good source of much needed local employment in remote and jobless areas of the Highlands it also produces a slightly cheaper form of salmon which is more available to a wider market.

Check, however, when you buy salmon from a fishmonger or in a restaurant whether it is Farmed or Wild. They ought to know.

Season

Available all year round.

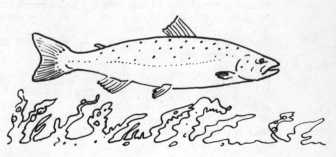

BAKED SALMON in butter

'Tibby was for cutting it in twa cuts, but I like a saumon to be served up in its integrity.'

Christopher North
Noctes Ambrosianae. 1822-1835

To do this is difficult if you don't happen to have a large enough fish kettle, which may have been Tibby's problem. Working in hotels has meant that I've usually had one available to cook the salmon whole. But it was in a hotel, not a mile from the finest salmon river in the area, that I first used this method which dispenses with the kettle, with no detriment to finished flavour or texture.

The whole fish is well buttered and then wrapped in foil and baked in the oven in its own juices. Cooking food in its own juices, like this, is an old and respected method which goes back to primitive practices like coating the food with a thick layer of clay and burying it in the embers of a fire. Gipsies liked cooking hedgehogs in this way and potters used their clay to wrap up meat and fish which they cooked in the kilns. Chicken 'bricks' and cooking foil are the modern development.

Don't let any of the moisture escape or the food will dry out.

To bake a whole or part of a Salmon or Salmon Trout in foil

Pre-heat the oven to 300F/275C/Gas 1-2.

Clean, gut and wipe salmon. Check that it will fit into the oven. If it is too large try removing the head (it can easily be put back on again). Otherwise cut off the head and a bit of the shoulders, the less the better. Use double-thickness foil, the thickest, strongest variety. Put foil on baking tray and brush liberally with melted butter, then place the salmon on top. Brush salmon liberally with more melted butter. Season lightly with salt and put some salt and a few lumps of butter into the body cavity. Now cover with a double layer of foil and secure, not too tightly, round the edges.

Place in a cool oven and bake. Allow 12 minutes per lb (500 g) plus 12 minutes.

If to be served hot, leave for 10 minutes before removing foil, otherwise leave in foil till cold. Skin and garnish with lemon and some greenery — the delicate, green feathery dill or fennel, if you have them, are lovely with pink salmon, but if not, good fresh parsley will do. Served on an old blue and white ashet: the dish needs no more adorning.

To cook in a fish kettle

If you do happen to have a large fish kettle and want to use it, the fish can be prepared as above, placed into cold water in its foil casing and brought to the boil. Give it about 30 seconds boiling, then turn off the heat. Leave to cool and finish cooking in the latent heat. Not suitable for serving hot.

GRILLED SALMON STEAK with parsley and lemon butter

All the ghillies I've known who fish salmon rivers have had an uncanny knack of cooking salmon to perfection. Most of the fish, mind you, was of the 'poached' variety but their favourite way of cooking, when the salmon was fresh and in prime condition, was by grilling.

Salmon has so much natural richness, especially early in the season, that grilling rather than frying preserves the flavour and texture best. For such a sensitive protein as fish (it coagulates so much quicker than meat and, when over-coagulated, the muscle fibres begin to squeeze the natural juices out of the fish thus destroying both flavour and texture), grilling is a more easily regulated method and the fish can be removed from the heat and the cooking stopped more quickly when it has just set.

All of the cook's art can be revealed in grilling fresh fish. One of the most respected and well loved chefs in Scotland, the late Ted Reynolds, used to test a restaurant out, not by some complicated dish needing a battery of sauces and garnishes, but by the degree of perfection of simply grilled fish.

To grill

Dip the steak in mild flavoured oil (sunflower or groundnut) and salt lightly. 1 steak = $1\frac{1}{2}$" (3-4 cm) thick. The best cuts for grilling are from the end of the belly opening towards the tail, giving a cut of uniform thickness and without the belly flaps.

Place on a very hot grill until it takes colour, turn, grill the second side. Remove the central bone and serve.

To make the butter

Melt 4 oz/125 g butter (1 stick) in a pan and add 1 tablespoon chopped parsley, juice of 1 lemon and salt and pepper. Beat with a wire whisk over a moderate heat for a few minutes till well blended and serve in a heated sauce boat with small steamed potatoes sprinkled with parsley and some skinned diced cucumber tossed in chives.

POTTED SALMON

2-4 servings

Early methods, like the one in Meg Dods (1826), baked the salmon first with butter, seasoning and spices, pounded mace, cloves, black pepper and allspice. Then it was drained and the pieces packed into 'potting cans', covered with clarified butter and kept in the larder for later use. There are few people nowadays who suffer from a surfeit of salmon to the extent that they would want to resort to this kind of preservation method. These are recipes for the days when salmon was the commonest and cheapest fish in Scotland. A highland laird travelling in the South of England in the 19th century recalls how he ordered salmon for his servant and beef for himself and was dismayed to find the salmon cost him more than the beef.

A more economical method uses left-over cooked salmon and butter.

If keeping for any length of time clarified butter is necessary for sealing, since because the air is expelled it makes a safer seal. Clarified butter can be used throughout, if you wish, though not essential.

To clarify the butter

Place the butter in a pan and heat gently — it is worth doing 1-2 lb/$\frac{1}{2}$-1 kg (4-8 sticks) at a time since it keeps well and can be used for frying for it has had the solids removed which normally cause it to burn. When melted, it will have divided into three parts:

(1) a foam on top
(2) a middle layer of pure clear butter
(3) sediment at the bottom.

Lift off the foam with a wide flat skimming spoon. Decant the clear butter into a bowl, leaving the sediment at the bottom.

Use the sediment and foam for flavouring soups but remember they are very salty.

Ingredients for potting

8 oz/250 g cooked salmon, skinned and boned
1 cup melted butter
Salt and pepper
Pinch of grated nutmeg
Clarified butter for sealing

Beat the salmon and butter together to a smooth paste, season and pack tightly into pots. Ones with a lid are best since the lid prevents the butter drying out and shrinking from the edges. Otherwise, cover with foil. Knock the pot hard to expel any air and cover with a very thin film of clarified butter. It will keep for several weeks in a cool place.

Serve for lunch or supper with fresh crusty brown bread and a light green salad. Or use small ramekins and serve as a first course at dinner with hot toast.

SALMON SOUP

8-12 servings

The delicate salmon-pink and varying shades of green make this an attractive soup. You must be careful not to overcook the greens and spoil their fresh green colour. It is a fairly substantial soup, good as a soup/stew at lunch. It also has the advantage of using up the head and trimmings of the salmon if you happen to have them. (Helpful fishmongers will keep them for you at little or no cost.)

Head, bones, skin and fins of the salmon
Bones from 2 whiting
6 oz/175 g fresh salmon or 4 oz/125 g cooked
2 sticks celery, finely chopped
1 medium onion, finely chopped
1 lb/500 g small diced potatoes
2 leeks, white and green finely chopped separately
2 oz/50 g butter ($\frac{1}{2}$ stick)

2 tablespoons double cream
Salt and pepper
Put all the fish trimmings into a pot, cover with 4 pts/2 L (10 c) of
cold water and bring to the boil. Skim and simmer for 20-30
minutes. Just before turning off the heat, add the fresh salmon and
leave to cook in the liquor. (Do not re-cook if the salmon is already
cooked.) When cooled, skim off any excess fat and strain stock.
Remove the salmon and break up into flakes.

Meantime, melt the butter in a pan and add the vegetables (the
white of the leek only). Gently sweat with the lid on, stirring every
few minutes to prevent sticking, for about ten minutes. Add the fish
stock and bring to the boil. Simmer gently till the vegetables are
tender, about 30 minutes. Add the finely chopped green leek and the
flaked salmon. Heat through for a few minutes, add the cream,
season and serve.

TAY SALMON in Pastry with Vermouth and Dill sauce

6 servings

Cutting through these crisp golden puff pastry envelopes reveals a pink
salmon layer topped with a creamy sole mousse. The delicate dill-
flavoured sauce which surrounds them, perfectly completes this
delightful combination, which is one of the ways David Wilson serves
salmon from the river Tay at the Peat Inn in Fife.

6 × 5-6 oz/150-175 g slices fresh Tay salmon
1 lb/500 g puff pastry
1 yolk of egg mixed with 1 teaspoon water
For the Fish Mousse
$\frac{1}{2}$ **lb/250 g sole**
1 egg
1 egg white
$\frac{1}{2}$ **pt/250 ml double cream (1$\frac{1}{4}$ c scant)**
Skin sole, chop roughly and liquidise or put in processor. Add whole
egg and egg white. Mix well. Refrigerate and when required add
cream.
To prepare the salmon
Pre-heat the oven 450F/230C/Gas 8.

Spread the fish mousse about $\frac{1}{4}$-$\frac{1}{2}$" on top of each slice of salmon.
Roll out the pastry almost paper thin and cut into 6 squares. The
size will depend on the shape of the salmon. Each piece of pastry
should be large enough to wrap round the salmon slice with about a
$\frac{1}{4}$" overlap and at the ends it should extend by about $\frac{1}{2}$". Place salmon
slice on pastry square, mousse side down. Wet edges of pastry and
fold over, making both edges just overlap slightly in the centre.
Press down to seal. Repeat with other slices. Brush with egg wash.
Place on baking sheet, reversing so the mousse side is up and bake
for about 10 minutes till the pastry is lightly brown and puffed up.

To make the sauce

> 3 fl oz/75 ml Chambray Vermouth
> ¼ pt/150 ml good fish stock (¾ c)
> Fresh or dried dill to taste
> 4 oz/125 g unsalted butter, softened (1 stick)
> Put the vermouth and fish stock into a pan and reduce by about
> half. Add the cream and gradually the butter in small pieces. Adjust
> consistency with more butter or fish stock. Add dill and taste for
> seasoning.

To serve

> Place salmon portions on warm plate and cut half way through the
> middle, open slightly, pour sauce round. Garnish with a fine
> julienne of vegetables on the side of the plate.

Smoked Scottish Salmon

All smoked salmon is not created equal. Most aficionados give
the nod to smoked Scotch salmon as the best. . . . It is as a rule
the least oily, the most subtly flavoured, has the firmest and
most pleasing texture and the least amount of salt. It is also the
most expensive.

New York Times, 1984

While Harrods and Fauchon may buy smoked salmon which has been
caught in Scotland, but smoked in England, connoisseurs who appreciate the subtleties of this delicacy prefer to buy from Scottish smokers
who are within easy reach of the best supplies. Prince Charles knew
what he was doing when he ordered two hundred and fifty sides of
smoked salmon for the Royal Wedding breakfast from a Caithness curer,
only a short distance from the Helmsdale river, who smokes only wild
salmon over peat.

This must surely be one of the foods with the widest divergence in
quality and yet there is no simple guide for consumers in the form of
information printed on the product to tell them exactly what kind of
smoked salmon they are buying.

The Scottish smoked salmon which you buy may very well be Atlantic
Salmon but caught in Norway; it may be farmed or wild; it may also be
Pacific Salmon rather than Atlantic but smoked by the Scottish method
of curing (described as Scottish cured). The demand for smoked salmon
is such that suppliers cannot meet requirements, and it is to satisfy this
market that Scottish curers are turning to other countries for fish, since
there are not enough caught in Scotland of either wild or farmed variety.

The current confusion could be solved if there was a system whereby it was indicated on every package whether the salmon was wild or farmed/Scottish or imported plus the formula for curing. 'Top quality wild fish, smoked in Scotland by experienced local smokers with distinctive cures, is to the mass produced product as "Chateau Bottled" is to "Vin Ordinaire",' says salmon curer Keith Dunbar, 'and it ought to be labelled as such.'

There may also be a further confusion in the future with a smoked salmon which has not actually been smoked (it is already on the market in small quantities). Food technologists, conscious of the possible hazards of ingesting certain smoke components, have been working from the 1950s on methods of producing a smoke solution which can be sprayed onto the fish (the fish can also be dipped in it). This is a technique which is now being quite widely applied in the bacon industry. According to the regulations laid down in the 'Preservatives in Food Regulations 1979' a food can be called smoked even if it is flavoured with a smoke solution. Smoking, after all, is no longer a necessary means of preservation, but rather a way of adding flavour to food.

Judging flavour is a subjective thing which must inevitably be left to the consumers. Will they be happy, though, to buy and enjoy smoke-flavoured salmon in the year 2000? If current trends are anything to go by, then they may still want their salmon, and other fish as well, smoked in smoke; and may be willing to campaign (as the ones for Real Bread and Real Ale have shown) for a flavour of food they like. One thing is sure, the smoke-flavoured herring, if it is to come, can never be called a kipper.

Buying

A side of Atlantic Salmon is longer and narrower, smaller and thinner than a side of Pacific salmon. Pacific salmon widen greatly towards the middle and are thick and meaty. It is difficult to tell purely by colour, but the Pacific fish is closer to deep coral in colour than the Atlantic fish. In flavour and texture the Atlantic has a much more delicate flavour and a finer more satiny texture, which allows it to be sliced to translucent thinness. Pacific fish have a coarser wider grain and a less subtle flavour.

Cures

The traditional Scottish cure is based on a process which begins when the boned side is dry-brined to stabilise the salt content of the side to about $2\frac{1}{2}$%. Other flavours may be added like Dark Rum, molasses or brown sugar (additives which traditional curers often prefer not to use). The side is then cold smoked by a heavy dense smoke over a short period, followed by gentle drying. The smoke is created by hardwood chips and is responsible for creating distinctive flavours. All kinds of combinations are used, though oak seems to be the most common. Peat is used in some cures, while one of the oldest established family firms of Smoke Curers in Scotland, S.L. Neil, use oak chips from the barrels which have been used for maturing whisky. The oak/whisky fragrance which you can smell from a handful of the dry chips intensifies as they are turned into smoke. In a survey of the quality of smoked salmon in nine New York stores, the New York Times (1978) decided that the S.L. Neil cure was one of the two best. 'It was a beautiful deep pink, with a woodsy flavour and just the faintest glow of sweetness counteracting the saline base. It sliced like satin.'

Fresh/Frozen/Vacuum-Packed

The 'fresh' fish will slice better and taste better but provided the frozen and vacuum-packed are carefully handled, there should not be too much loss of flavour or texture. To de-frost a vacuum pack take it out of the pack, then place uncovered in the refrigerator. This allows it to thaw slowly and excess moisture to evaporate instead of going back into the fish. Frozen fish will never slice as thinly as non-frozen. Vacuum packs will keep in good condition in the refrigerator for about two weeks at about 36F. Once opened they should be used within the week.

Sliced/Unsliced

While convenient, pre-sliced cannot compare in texture and flavour.

Colour/Appearance

The flesh should be a natural looking pink — beware of bright pink or orange: it may have been dyed. It should look firm and smooth, not torn or mottled and should have a natural sheen without looking oily. Smoked salmon does go 'off', when it will have a fairly obvious rancid odour.

Preparing

Ready sliced — the supplier should cut the slices wafer thin, almost transparent. For the full benefit of the flavour they should be served at room temperature or very slightly cooler, so remove at least 20-30 minutes before serving. Keep closely covered with cling film since they dry out very quickly.

Whole side — place on a wooden board and prepare by trimming round the edges, if necessary. With tweezers remove the 'pin' bones which run down the centre of the fillet. Use a sharp knife with a thin flexible blade. Special knives for slicing smoked salmon may be bought from specialist suppliers. They are about 10″ long and have a slightly undulating edge. Keep the knife flat while cutting and make long even strokes working towards the tail, making paper thin slices without tearing the flesh, which should be dense and resilient. The slices should be as large as possible, preferably one slice covering the entire plate. Do not slice more than 2 or 3 hours before use.

To serve

Smoked salmon lovers ask only that the fish and cure be of the finest quality; that it be cut paper-thin for the flavour fully to be savoured and that it be served simply with brown bread and butter and perhaps a little pepper. 2-3 oz/50-75 g should satisfy the most ardent palates though I have known some people consume 4 oz/125 g without any strain on their digestion.

What to drink with it is a matter of taste. Scandinavians drink chilled vodka or schnapps with Gravlax which is superb but somehow anaesthetises the palate for the more subtle flavours of smoked salmon. Champagne has its followers, others drink Muscadet or White Burgundy. Drink pundits agree that red wines compete too much, so sticking to a dry or perhaps medium-sweet white wine seems best if Champagne is out of your price bracket.

Sea Trout, Salmon Trout, Brown Trout (Salmo trutta)

This is a confusing species, which embraces the brown trout of rivers: the bull or lake trout of larger inland waters: and the sea trout, which is a migratory fish with a natural range from North Africa to Norway and Iceland.

Alan Davidson
North Atlantic Seafood, 1979

The sea/salmon trout has a similar life cycle to salmon; it also eats the same kind of food (among other things, pink crustaceans) and therefore has a similar pink flesh. It is different in size — smaller than salmon and with a more delicate flavour preferred by many. Fresh water brown trout are smaller, and their flavour is entirely dependent on the richness of their feeding grounds, which also applies to the farmed variety.

BAKED BROWN TROUT with herbs and lemon

4 servings

This is the same method as Baked Salmon — encasing the fish in foil and allowing it to cook in its own juices without drying out.

4 × ½ lb/250 g trout
2 tablespoons olive oil
Sea salt
Freshly ground Black Pepper
4 tablespoons dry vermouth
4 sprigs fresh herbs (either — dill, fennel, chives or parsley)
1 lemon
Pre-heat the oven to 450F/230C/Gas 8

Scale and clean the trout; cut off the fins and wipe with kitchen paper. Season the inside with salt and pepper and put in herbs. Cut 4 pieces of foil into oval shapes long enough to hold the fish plus 3" (7 cm). Brush the foil with oil and lay the trout up the centre. Brush the fish with oil, season with salt and pepper, pour over vermouth and place a slice of lemon on the fish. Bring up the sides of the foil to make a boat and pleat over the foil at the top to enclose the fish, pinching together with thumb and forefinger to make a scalloped edge like a Cornish Pasty.

Put on a baking sheet and bake in a hot oven for 8-10 minutes. Cooking time will depend on the thickness of the fish, so check one by opening up. Gently and carefully ease open the flesh at the thickest part along the lateral line right down to the bone. There should be no opaqueness. Serve as they are in foil, first making a small slit in the foil for easier opening.

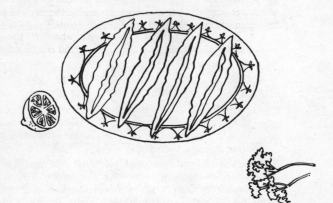

Herring

Of all the fish that swim in the sea
The herring is the fish for me.

Scottish Folk Song

Not only songs have been sung about this remarkable little fish; battles
have been fought over them and even towns established on the strength
of their availability.

The word 'herring' comes from the Teutonic word, 'heer', meaning an
army, which is a good description of the shoals of herring numbering
many thousands of fish which swim around together for protection.
This fact was, to some extent, the reason why in 1977 the Scottish
herring fishing was closed. Catches had been relatively stable up to
1963, but then they began to rise rapidly to a peak in 1969 when over a
million tons were caught. From then on there was a steady decline till in
1976 there was only two hundred thousand tons caught in Scotland. It
seems that with the introduction of the purse seine net, which could
catch a whole shoal of herring much more effectively than previous nets
and because there were improvements in fish detection, many more
whole shoals of herring were being caught more effectively than ever
before. Even if the whole shoal was not caught, the remaining fish could
not survive from predators without the protection of the large shoal.
Serious conservation methods of protecting the species are now in
operation with scientists monitoring stocks closely, setting quotas and
closing down the fishing in certain areas when the fish are under
pressure. The future of the herring in Scotland is safe at least for the
moment.

Seasons and Buying

I agree with Meg Dods (1826) when she says that herring should be
eaten 'almost alive'. They are like shellfish and deteriorate quickly when
dead. Having lived for some time in Ullapool, the principal herring
fishing port in Scotland, and having enjoyed the luxury of fresh herring
straight off the boats, I find it impossible to buy herring from city shops
when it has lost its 'bloom' from lying on the slab too long. The same
applies to mackerel. Look for firm bright fish as they have a flabby look
when past their best.

Herring are available all year round from different sources but
generally the heavier fatter summer fish have more flavour than the lean

winter ones. The amount of fat in the flesh varies throughout the annual reproductive cycle. There is a long period of starvation after spawning, followed by a time of intensive feeding while the milts and roes are developing. The fat content can vary from as little as 2% to as high as 20%, so it is important to look for the plump fish which have been feeding and have well developed roes. They have the highest fat content and therefore the best flavour.

The availability from certain areas around the Scottish coasts is, and always has been, unpredictable but each ground has its season and the fishery at any one place is rarely exploited outside these periods.

Fishing ground	Herring Season
Shetland	May to September
Peterhead	May to August
Clyde	All year round
Minches	May to March

FRESH HERRING fried in oatmeal

4 servings

One of the great Scottish combinations. The rich herring needs a coating with flavour and bite to it which the oatmeal provides.

Fish cooked with the bone left in have more flavour and herrings are no exception, but having seen some horribly mangled remains of whole fish with only half the flesh eaten, I believe it may be safer for the cook (or waiter) to remove the bone after it has been cooked.

A common breakfast dish when we lived on the East coast during the holidays with my grandmother was a large ashet piled with whole fried herring or flukies (flounders). She lived in a fishing village and from an early age children had to master the art of removing the bones from fish — or starve. She believed, along with the fisher wives, that removing bones before cooking removed half the flavour and, in any case, given the vast amounts of fish consumed, no one had any time for filleting.

4 fresh herring, whole or filleted
2 heaped tablespoons medium oatmeal, lightly toasted
Salt and pepper
Butter and/or a neutral oil for frying

To prepare whole herring

Slit up the belly and remove the gut, scraping up the backbone with your thumbnail to loosen the spinal vein starting from the tail up. Cut off the head if you wish, though this is not necessary. Cut off all fins with scissors and wash. Make sure all blood is removed from the belly cavity and salt inside.

To fillet herring

Place the fish which has been prepared as above on a board skin side up with the belly flaps spread out, skin side up and press with the base of your palm from tail to head along the back-bone. The fish will flatten out as you press and when it is fairly flat, without being squashed, turn onto flesh side and the bone will lift out; cut at the tail to release.

To fry

Heat the fat in a large frying pan. Mix the seasonings into the oatmeal and press the wet fish into it, coating both sides — it is not necessary to moisten the fish with anything. Shake off excess oatmeal and fry. Filleted fish should be placed flesh side down first. Whole fish will take longer to cook. Test by opening carefully with a sharp pointed knife at the thickest part right down to the bone: if the flesh still looks opaque leave for another few minutes. They should take from 5-10 minutes each side depending on the thickness of the fish.

To bone cooked fish

Removing the flesh is quite simple once you have found the lateral line which runs from the middle of the gill flap to the middle of the tail. Cut with a sharp knife through the skin and right down to the bone in a straight line the length of the fish. Now gently ease away the fillets on either side. If the fish is correctly cooked they should come away cleanly, exposing the bone. Now lift the tail and release the skin and flesh at the very end. Then with your knife hold down the flesh on the plate and prise off the bone, gradually working upwards towards the head. When you reach the head it should come away easily attached to the bone. Before you discard it, do not forget to pick out the cheeks — a delicacy often overlooked.

'FRESH HERRINGS AS DRESSED AT INVERARAY (and the Highland Sea-Lochs)'

The best herrings are obtained in these localities almost alive. Cut off the head, fins, and tails; scale, gut, and wash them. Split and bone them or not, dust the inside with pepper and fine salt. Place two herrings flat together, the backs outmost, and dip in toasted oatmeal and fry them for seven minutes. Serve hot. They are delicious; and, in the summer, add much to the breakfasts on the steamers on the Clyde, and round all the north-east and west coasts of Scotland.

Meg Dods
The Cook and Housewife's Manual, 1826

A useful method for small herring, the two flesh sides fuse together making a moist juicy centre which contrasts with a crisp outside.

OPEN ARMS HERRING with Drambuie butter

4 servings

Using fresh local herring, Chef Douglas, of the Open Arms Hotel in Dirleton, combines traditional Herrings in Oatmeal with a Drambuie flavoured hard butter and lifts them out of a common everyday dish with this simple touch. He mostly serves them as a starter dish though they may also be eaten as a main coarse.

4 herrings, fried in oatmeal (see p. 56)

Drambuie Butter

4 oz/125 g unsalted butter (1 stick)
2 teaspoons lemon juice
1 tablespoon chopped parsley
3 tablespoons Drambuie

Soften the butter slightly without melting. Beat in the other ingredients. Roll into a sausage shape 1″ (2½ cm) in diameter. Wrap in foil or greaseproof paper and leave to harden slightly. Cut in slices and serve two on each fish just before serving. Garnish fish with lemon wedges and watercress. To store left-over butter for future use, cut all the butter into slices. Place on tray and freeze, then put in small freezer bags and keep frozen till required. Do not keep for more than a few weeks since the Drambuie flavour will begin to deteriorate in time.

GRILLED HERRING with mustard

4 servings

There are many interesting varieties of mustard being made in Scotland. The Islay mustard made by the Arran Mustard company is a smooth tasting blend using whole mustard seeds, balanced with an oatmeal base which is excellent with both fried and grilled herring or mackerel or you may wish to make a Store Mustard (see p. 238).

4 whole or filleted herring
2-3 tablespoons medium oatmeal, lightly toasted
Salt and pepper
2 oz/50 g butter (½ stick)

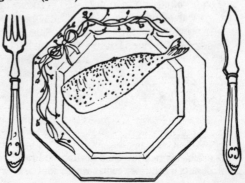

For whole herring

Slash the skin diagonally about three times on either side: this opens up the flesh and makes it cook more evenly. Salt the inside of the fish. Mix the seasonings through the oatmeal. Now press both sides into the oatmeal and place in grill pan. Put pats of butter on top along the centre line and place under a hot grill. Cook on both sides for 5-10 minutes and serve with mustard (see p. 238).

For filleted herring

Press the wet fish into the seasoned oatmeal, shake off excess. Place under a hot grill skin side up and dot all over with butter. Grill on both sides about five minutes.

Serving

Serve with mustard. Serve also with plain boiled floury potatoes skinned, sprinkled with chopped chives and with plenty of butter. Mashed Scottish turnips (known as Swedes in England; Rutabaga in North America) are good with fried or grilled herring. This can all be mashed together and served as Orkney Clapshot.

SOUSED OR POTTED HERRING

6 servings

Try potting them whole. If they are cooked slowly for four to five hours the vinegar dissolves all the small bones and the cooking liquor becomes quite thick and full of flavour. A little of it should be served with the fish. Make sure you use good fatty herring. Poor quality herring will not stand up to the long slow cooking, nor will they survive the strong spicy flavours which characterise this method of cooking herring.

With the season's first Loch Fyne herring, gleaming silver fish, plump and full of fat and flavour — once experienced, never forgotten.

6 fat herring
$\frac{1}{2}$ pt/300 ml malt vinegar (1$\frac{1}{4}$ c)
$\frac{1}{4}$ pt/150 ml water ($\frac{3}{4}$ c)
1 teaspoon salt
$\frac{1}{4}$ teaspoon ground black pepper
6 cloves
2 blades of mace
1 bay leaf
12 peppercorns
1 oz/25 g butter ($\frac{1}{4}$ stick)
1 cayenne pod
Pre-heat the oven to 425F/220C/Gas 7 — 30 minutes.
Reduce to 250F/130C/Gas $\frac{1}{2}$ for 4 hours.

Clean the herring and remove the heads (optional) and fins. Season the belly cavity with salt and pepper. Lay the fish, heads to tails, in a large casserole with the spices and seasonings in between. Pour over the vinegar and water. It should almost cover them. Cover very tightly and place in a hot oven for 30 minutes till the liquid begins to bubble, then reduce the heat to the lowest possible and leave for 4-5 hours. Leave to cool in the liquid.

To pot filleted herring

6 servings

6 herring
Salt and pepper
$\frac{1}{4}$ pt/150 ml malt vinegar ($\frac{3}{4}$ c)
$\frac{1}{4}$ pt/150 ml dry cider ($\frac{3}{4}$ c)
$\frac{1}{4}$ pt/150 ml water ($\frac{3}{4}$ c)
2 bay leaves
10 peppercorns
2 blades of mace
$\frac{1}{4}$ teaspooon grated nutmeg
4 oz/125 g clarified butter (1 stick) (see p. 48)
Pre-heat the oven to 350F/180C/Gas 4.
Clean and fillet the fish. Season flesh surface with salt and pepper.
Roll up from head end to tail and place in shallow casserole closely
packed together with the tails sticking up. Sprinkle spices on top
and cover with vinegar, cider and water. Cover and bake for 45
minutes. Leave to cool in the liquor. Drain and serve.
Note: To pot correctly, the fish should be drained well, then packed
into an earthenware pot and covered with clarified butter. They will
keep in a cool place for at least four weeks if treated in this way.

SWEET SPICED HERRING

Use good fatty herring for this spicy, sweet/sour cure — lean winter
herring will be totally overpowered by the spice. They are good served
slightly chilled with a grated Beetroot Salad (see p. 66) and some sliced
raw mushrooms and spring onions for garnish.

Put in a pan and simmer gently for a few minutes to infuse then leave to cool
8 fl oz/250 ml pickle vinegar (see p. 239) or wine or cider vinegar
(1 c)
1 medium onion thinly sliced
6 oz/200 g granulated sugar ($\frac{3}{4}$ c generous)
1 tablespoon allspice berries
1 tablespoon black peppercorns
3 small bay leaves

To prepare the herring
1 lb/500 g fresh herring
Clean, gut and fillet the herring (see p. 56). If possible, skin the fish.
If it is in good condition this should be quite easy. Loosen the very
thin papery skin at the head end and then push your fingers under
it. When you have enough loosened to get a good grip, pull
downwards towards the tail and it should all come off in one piece.
Separate the two fillets, trim and place flat in an earthenware
casserole. Pour over cooled spice vinegar and leave at least overnight
but preferably for 2-3 days before use. Keeps well for at least a
month in a cool place.

Atlantic Mackerel
(Scomber scombrus)

A powerfully muscular fish with a streamlined body which is similar to herring in many respects. From the fishing aspect it also swims in very large shoals which makes it more liable to over-fishing. From the cooking aspect it also spoils rapidly and like herring has a rich oily flesh which also fluctuates according to season. It differs in flavour and in the texture of the flesh which is firmer and freer of fine bones found in herring.

Traditional recipes serve mackerel with acid fruit sauces, gooseberry being the most common though it is good with other sharp fruits like rhubarb (Irish), cranberries or raspberries.

Season — They spawn throughout the spring, early and late summer and stop feeding during the winter, so are at their best from April through to November.

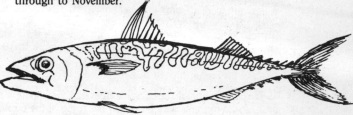

Hot smoked mackerel

They lend themselves to this method of smoking and they can be eaten cold or heated gently under the grill. They are also excellent potted with lemon and garlic.

POTTED MACKEREL

10 oz/275 g skinned and boned mackerel
5 oz/150 g unsalted butter (1¼ sticks)
1 clove garlic, crushed
Lemon juice to taste
Salt and pepper
Clarified butter to cover (see p. 48)
Soften the butter and place in liquidiser or processor or beat by hand for a slightly coarser result, with the mackerel and garlic. Blend to a smooth paste. Taste and season with salt and pepper and lemon juice. Put into individual pots and cover with clarified butter. Serve with hot toast for High Tea or Supper or as a starter course for Dinner.

Kipper

Although kippers are not a Scottish invention they make up about a quarter of all the processed fish eaten in Scotland today and there are some fine Scottish cures.

In the 1840s, when the kipper was first developed in Newcastle, a much less perishable product was wanted than we need today. The original kipper was much saltier, much drier and a different colour to the modern one. It was coloured naturally from the smoke to a dark brown colour. During the last years of the 1914-18 war a vegetable dye was used in kippering which meant that the smoking time could be reduced without loss of colour or weight. By the 1930s there were no big manufacturers of undyed kippers left and today most of the kippers we eat are of the dyed variety with a subsequent loss of keeping quality and flavour. There is, however, still a demand for undyed kippers which are produced by the smaller curers. The undyed kipper is a paler silvery brown kipper easily distinguished from the richer brown of the dyed variety. It has the advantage of being free from the unnecessary Brown 'FK' kipper dye and its possible harmful effect on health. Kippers with the bone removed have a consequent loss of flavour and especially so if they are frozen.

Buying

For the best flavour and keeping qualities look for kippers which have a glossy sheen to them, which is partly the result of the brining process but also indicates a good fat content, essential for a well-flavoured kipper. There are many companies making kippers in Scotland with a wide range of qualities and types.

POTTED KIPPER

4-6 servings

It is essential to use a well flavoured fatty kipper.

2 medium to large kippers should give approximately —
   8 oz/250 g kipper meat
4 oz/125 g butter (1 stick)
2 tablespoons whisky
4 anchovy fillets
2-3 teaspoons lemon juice
Cayenne pepper

Put all the ingredients into a liquidiser or food processor and reduce to a fine paste. This will break up all the fine bones in the kipper flesh.

Adjust lemon, cayenne and whisky flavourings to taste. Salt may not be necessary with the anchovies. Serve with oatcakes which have

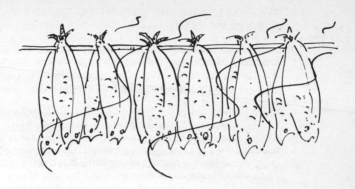

been slightly warmed in the oven or with hot toast. A good dry cider is excellent with this and other kipper dishes.

Note: I have tried using some of the more interesting peaty malt whiskies but they tend to lose their distinctive characteristics. A good blended whisky will give that faint taste of whisky which is all that is necessary.

TO COOK KIPPERS

All kipper addicts have their favourite way of cooking. If it is left to the cook, however, she will make sure that they are cooked in such a way that the whole kitchen, and all the utensils used, do not smell of kipper for days.

Grilled Kipper

This is a good method since it concentrates the flavour well, though the grill should be well lined with foil. It is not necessary to baste with butter — there should be enough natural fat in the kipper to keep it from drying out. The head and tail can be cut off before grilling. Place under a medium hot grill, flesh side up and cook for about ten minutes, (depending on size) on the flesh side only.

Frying

Not a popular method with cooks, since they can't protect the frying pan with foil. It also coats an already fatty fish with another layer of fat. If intent on frying, use the merest film of oil in the pan, just enough to prevent sticking, and place the kipper in flesh side down. Cook for five minutes on either side and serve.

Jugging

This is a popular method for cooks and kipper lovers alike since it doesn't involve any cooking as such, and the utensil used is easily cleaned. Place the kipper in a heated jug which is deep enough to hold it, and fill the jug with boiling water. Alternately use a deep pot, but make sure it is well heated. Cover well, and leave for at least 10 minutes. Remove the kipper and serve immediately. Some of the flavour and fat is obviously lost in the liquid but the fish retains its plumpness and the texture of the flesh is soft and juicy.

Baked

Another method favoured by both cooks and eaters. The whole fish is wrapped in a foil parcel, placed in a moderate oven 350F/180C/ Gas 4 for 15-20 minutes. Wrap the fish individually and serve in the parcel to preserve the full aroma till it is opened.

Uncooked

Philip Harben (one of the first cooks to have a television series in the 1960s) was an early advocate of this way of eating kipper. He suggested it should be boned, sliced thinly and covered in a marinade of oil and lemon juice for several hours before eating. More recently Jane Grigson has suggested that the thinly-sliced raw fillets should be 'arranged in strips round the edge of some well-buttered rye bread, with an egg yolk in the middle as sauce'. (<u>Good Things</u>, 1971). A deeply chilled glass of vodka or schnapps goes well with this.

Salt Pickled Herring

Ironically, this is the cure which made Scotland famous for many years as the world's greatest herring-producing country, but is the one we eat least of today. About ninety per cent of the cured fish was exported so perhaps it is not surprising that Scots have not continued to eat it in any great amount. The Scandinavian countries, to which much of the herring was exported, have maintained a liking for it and still eat pickled herring in large quantities. They have developed an amazing range of ideas for dealing with this fish, while the Scots are more or less left with Tatties and Herring.

Buying

Most good fishmongers will have a barrel of salted herring. The herring should be big and fat. The longer they have been in the pickle the saltier they will be.

Eating

I have seen fishermen eat them raw on the bone, they stimulate the digestive juices like no other food I know, but I prefer, if eating them raw, to have the flavour slightly modified in a sweet vinegar pickle. The raw fish can also be cut in strips and used in the same way as for anchovies.

TATTIES AND HERRING

Remains a popular dish, particularly in Highland areas, the salty fish and the bland potatoes making the sharp contrast in flavours which is so much part of its charm.

To salt herring

1 small wooden barrel or large plastic bucket
Coarse salt
Fat fresh herring

Begin by removing the gills and long gut from the fish, leaving on the heads. Begin with a good thick layer of salt then set the fish in the layer with their backs uppermost, but slightly on their sides. Put in the next layer of salt, then the fish lying in the opposite direction. Continue in layers till the barrel is full. Put a plate on top to keep weighted down when the brine forms. Cover well and store in a cool place.

To cook

Wash fish and soak overnight in cold water. They may be cooked in the same pan as boiled potatoes. Usually they are laid on top of the boiling potatoes, or they may be cooked separately well covered with water and simmered for about 10 minutes and then eaten with boiled jacket potatoes.

To eat

Tatties and herring are traditionally dished up into an 18" shallow square dish used specially for the purpose called a 'clar' in Gaelic. They were then picked up and eaten with the fingers which were then washed in a large communal finger bowl.

MARINATED SALT HERRING

4-6 servings

I understand from a Finnish friend that herring is seldom eaten fresh in Finland but instead the Finns consume vast quantities of the salted variety. They appreciate the fact that, once dead, the fish deteriorates so quickly, and instead prefer to eat it preserved by a method which intensifies the character of the fish.

Finns as well as other Scandinavians have a highly developed tradition of salt herring dishes which I have learnt to make and enjoy. This is one which they describe as Everyday Herring. The Scots have obviously made something similar, according to F. Marian McNeill The Scots Kitchen (1929). It was called a 'Pickled Herring' and the salted herring were simply marinated in vinegar, brown sugar and onions.

This must be made with an acetic acid based condiment (as they use in Scandinavia) and not Vinegar of any kind, which is too harsh and completely spoils the flavour. If the Spirit Condiment (also called Non-brewed Condiment) is not available then chemists sell concentrated acetic acid which can be diluted to taste.

8 salted herring
3 tablespoons sugar
3 medium onions, sliced
2 carrots, thinly sliced
Bay leaf
1 tablespoon allspice
1 tablespoon peppercorns
3 cups non-brewed spirit condiment
Bone and skin the herring. Slice into bite-sized pieces and arrange in a dish with sugar, spices, onions and carrots layered in between.

Pour over condiment to cover.

Leave overnight in a cool place. To serve, garnish with some fresh onion (red onions are very good if you can get them) and plenty of chopped fresh dill. Eat with thickly buttered rye bread and ice cold schnapps or chilled lager.

SALT HERRING SALAD with Beetroot and Mushrooms

4 servings

Rich dark beetroot, shining strips of silvery herring, creamy white mushrooms and green spring onions make a stunning visual impact. You may arrange them as you wish. The flavour combinations are equally powerful.

8 salt herring
2 lb/1 kg beetroot, boiled
2-3 tablespoons wine vinegar or Red Umeboshi
**   (Japanese Plum vinegar)**
4 tablespoons olive oil
Salt and pepper
4 oz/125 g mushrooms, sliced
4 spring onions, chopped
4 tablespoons soured cream (not essential)

Bone and skin the herring and slice into bite-sized pieces. Grate the beetroot finely and mix with the oil and vinegar. Taste for seasoning.

To assemble

Arrange the beetroot on the dish. Place the herring on top, then a spoonful of soured cream and finish with raw mushrooms and spring onion. Serve with thickly buttered Oatmeal Bread (see p. 32) or Barley Bannocks (see p. 29) and chilled lager.

Haddock, Cod and Whiting

In Scotland more haddock is caught and eaten than any other white fish. Cod comes next, and then whiting. These, and other demersel fish, have different habits from the herring; swimming around in much smaller shoals at the bottom of the sea, they are less in danger of having large amounts wiped out with one net and therefore less likely to be seriously over-fished.

The chemical composition of the haddock flesh is similar to that of cod and other members of the cod family and therefore it is quite practical in recipes to interchange fish of this type.

Seasons and Buying

Plump and firm, top quality **North Sea Haddock**, are available from November through to February and are best during these months. After February, they spawn and from April to June the fish are soft and poor quality, but from about July onwards they begin to recover and after September the flesh firms up rapidly. The cycle for fish from more northern waters is the same but occurs about a month or so later than in the North Sea.

Other White Fish

All these fish are available all year round but for spawning reasons, they are a better quality fish during the following months.

BRILL — June to March
COD — October to February
FLOUNDER — August to November (also known as Flukie)
HALIBUT — August to April
HAKE — May to February
LEMON SOLE — December to March
LING — November to April
MEGRIM, ABERDEEN SOLE — August to April
PLAICE — May to December
SAITH — September to May (also known as Coalfish, Sillock, Coley and Green Cod)
TURBOT — September to March
WITCH — September to May (also known as Witch Sole or Long Flounder)
WHITING — November to March

Treatment and recipes for Haddock may be applied to other White Fish, even small cuts of larger fish such as brill or turbot.

HADDOCK AND CHIPS

4-6 servings

I know that batter fried fish and chips are the sacred domain of 'Chippies' (Fish and Chip shops). They have a mystique all of their own — the smell of the fried fish and vinegar mingling together as it filters through the newspaper: warming and comforting food for cold Scottish winter nights, which has not been displaced, despite strong competition from all kinds of new fast-food developments. This is not an attempt to recreate the genuine article at home but just instructions for those not fortunate enough to live near a genuine 'Chippie'.

Beer Batter

This is a light crisp batter. The yeast in the beer has a leavening effect if left for up to 24 hours when the batter will have expanded and the flavours amalgamated. It can be used sooner but should be left for at least 1 hour minimum.

Sift into a bowl

4 oz/100 g plain flour (1 c)

Add

2 egg yolks (reserve whites)
1½ teaspoons salt
2 tablespoons oil
4 fl oz/125 ml beer (½ c)
Pepper

Beat with a wire whisk till well mixed and free from lumps. Cover and leave for 1-2 hours or overnight.

To fry the chips

Heat the fat or oil to 375F/190C. Peel 1-2 lb potatoes and cut into even sized chips. Pat dry in kitchen towel. Immerse chips in a basket in the heated oil and cook, tossing occasionally, till they have just cooked through without taking any colour — known as blanching. Remove from the oil and drain. Repeat the process if they have to be done in two lots. Leave aside till the fish is cooked when the fat should be reheated to 400F/200C. Plunge the chips into the very hot oil, they will brown very quickly. Remove basket, shake off excess oil and drain on crumpled kitchen paper for a few minutes. Salt lightly before serving.

To fry the fish

1½ lb/750 kg firm-fleshed haddock fillets
Oil for frying

Heat the oil to 375F/190C.

First beat egg whites fairly stiff and fold gently into batter. Cut each fillet into two up the centre back line to make pieces of roughly the same size and drop three or four pieces into the batter at a time. Gently shake off the excess. Make sure they are well coated before lowering gently into the hot oil. Fry for about five minutes depending on the size and thickness of the fish. Test by removing a piece and gently prising open with a very sharp knife. Turn with a slotted spoon a few times. When cooked drain on kitchen paper to absorb excess fat and repeat the process with the rest of the fish. Keep hot until the chips have been browned off and serve with salt and malt vinegar. To disperse the vinegar evenly it is necessary to have a shaker. A fairly large salt cellar filled with vinegar will do.

FRESH HADDOCK in a light creamy mustard sauce

4 servings

This was a popular Victorian breakfast dish which adapts well to lunch, supper or high tea. Mustard with fish is an old combination.

1 lb/500 g fresh haddock fillets
1 tablespoon seasoned flour
4 fl oz/125 ml clarified butter or oil ($\frac{1}{2}$ c)
1 teaspoon Mustard Store Sauce (p. 238) or other made mustard
8 fl oz/250 ml single or double cream (1 c)

Heat about half of the butter in a frying pan. Coat the haddock in butter/oil and then in flour. Put into the pan and seal quickly on both sides without browning. Add cream and simmer gently till the fish is cooked. Remove some of the cooking liquor and mix with the mustard. Return to the pan and mix through but do not cook any longer since mustard loses its flavour very quickly when cooked. Serve the fish and pour over sauce. Serve with Buttered Kale (see p. 195) sprinkled with toasted oatmeal.

RIZZARED HADDOCK or Blawn Whiting

The small whiting, hung up with its skin on, and broiled without being rubbed in flour, is excellent. A wooden frame, called a 'hake', is used for drying fish. In Orkney cuiths (which in Shetland they call piltocks and in the Hebrides cuddies) are prepared in this way, care being taken that the fish are perfectly fresh, newly gutted, and thoroughly cleaned, and that the salt is rubbed well in along the bones from which the guts have been removed. They may be either boiled or brandered — if boiled, they are eaten with butter, melted. They are particularly good with buttered bere bannocks or wheaten-meal scones and tea.

F. Marian McNeill
The Scots Kitchen. 1929

4 whole fresh haddock (medium size, about $\frac{1}{2}$ lb/250 g each)
8 oz/250 g sea salt (1 c)
2 tablespoons seasoned flour
2 oz/50 g melted butter/oil ($\frac{1}{2}$ stick)

Gut and clean fish, remove eyes. Place fish in an ashet and sprinkle over salt. Put plenty in the body cavity and rub well into the skin all over. Leave in a cool place for about 12 hours.

Remove and wipe dry. Hang up in a cool place where there is a good draught, threading a wire through the eyes or tie in pairs tied by the tail for another 12 hours.

To cook — make about three slashes into the skin across the thickest part of the flesh about an inch apart. Brush with butter and roll in seasoned flour. Grill till lightly browned on both sides. Serve.

GRILLED FRESH HADDOCK
served with Lemon and Parsley Butter

4 servings

> 1 lb/500 g fresh haddock fillets
> 4 fl oz/125 ml clarified butter ($\frac{1}{2}$ c)
> 4 oz/125 g breadcrumbs (1 c)
> Salt and pepper

Mix the seasoning through the breadcrumbs. Pass the haddock through the butter, drain off any excess and then press into the breadcrumbs. Place on a buttered tray which will fit under the grill and sprinkle the fish with melted butter. Grill gently till golden brown.

Serve with Lemon and Parsley Butter

> 4 oz/125 g butter (1 stick); 2 teaspoons lemon juice; Pinch of cayenne pepper; Salt to taste (the butter may be salty enough); 2 tablespoons finely chopped parsley. Soften the butter slightly without melting and beat in the other ingredients. Roll into a sausage shape and slice $\frac{1}{4}$" thick. These can be deep frozen on a small tray and then stored in small freezer bags.

Finnan Haddock

A good breakfast as usual in Scotland, with Findon Haddocks, eggs, sweetmeats (preserved blackcurrants formed one) and honey.

Robert Southey
Journal of a Tour in Scotland in 1819

This amazing Scottish cure makes up about a quarter of the total amount of processed fish produced in Scotland today. Its ancestry stretches far back at least to the 16th century when they are mentioned in the household book of James V. They are a direct descendant of the 'speldings' which Robert Fergusson refers to in his poem, <u>The Leith Races</u>, 1773 — 'Guid speldins, fa will buy?' and in the same year James Boswell in his diaries describes them as: 'salted and dried in a particular manner, being dipped in the sea and dried in the sun, and eaten by the Scots by way of a relish.' He also says that you could buy them in London.

Speldings were a hard, salted, unsmoked haddock distinguished from the modern Finnans which are only lightly salted and smoked. The smoking development was something they were particularly good at in the village of Findrum and it is from this fishing village six miles south of Aberdeen that the smoked cure took its name. The advent of the railways in the late 19th century was responsible for changing a rock hard, heavily smoked fish into a much more perishable product with obvious improvements to the eating quality. The old cures 'fell into disuse as transit improved' said a fish curer in 1882.

Today, more than a hundred years later, curers are preserving and continuing a tradition which provides us in Scotland with a superb delicacy known and appreciated around the world. The main cures available can be divided into 'cold' smoked and 'hot' smoked.

Cold Smoked Finnan Haddock

This is a whole haddock, head removed but bone left in, split open, brined and smoked to a pale straw colour or darker. No dye is used in the brining. These are the ones with the finest flavour and most character.

With a few pats of butter on top and a hearty grinding of pepper, and put under a hot grill, they make a feast of a meal for a minimum of effort.

Variations

Local variations of the basic cure are the **Pales** whose brining and smoking times are shorter than for the Finnan. They are made mainly from smaller haddock and include the Eyemouth cure and the Glasgow Pale. Some Pales are so lightly smoked that they have only the slightest smokey flavour and almost no yellow colour.

The **Golden Cutlet** is made from a fillet of haddock or whiting with the skin removed. It is lightly brined and lightly smoked so has much less flavour than any other cure; it also has some dye added to the brine bath which gives it a brighter less natural colour.

Smoked Fillet: this is the single fillet from a medium or large haddock. The skin is left on to hold the fish together during a longer curing process than the cutlet. It may be dyed slightly but frequently is not. The flavour is better than the cutlet. Sometimes it is known as an <u>Aberdeen fillet</u>.

FINNAN HADDOCK with melted CHEESE AND EGGS served in a ramekin with toast

4-6 servings

For the Cheese and Egg Mixture

Put $\frac{1}{2}$ lb/250 g (2 c) grated Galloway Cheddar in a pan with 1 teaspoonful of cornflour which has been mixed into 6 tablespoons milk. Heat, stirring constantly, for five minutes till the cheese melts. Beat 3 egg yolks together lightly then spoon some of the hot cheese mixture into the eggs and beat well. Pour back into the pan and continue cooking over a low heat till the mixture thickens slightly then add 8 oz/250 g cooked finnan haddock. Season with salt, pepper and/or cayenne. Pour into heated ramekin dishes.

BAKED SMOKED HADDOCK with Cream and Poached Egg

4 servings

Served for breakfast, lunch or supper with oatcakes or bread and butter or with boiled floury potatoes, baked tomatoes or buttered spinach.

$1\frac{1}{2}$ lb/750 g smoked haddock*
8 fl oz/250 ml double cream (1 c)
Freshly ground black pepper
Small piece of butter for greasing
4 poached eggs

Pre-heat the oven to 350F/180C/Gas 4.

Grease a shallow gratin dish with butter and place the fish skin side down. Pour over cream and grind some pepper on top (salt should not be necessary). Bake for 20-30 minutes giving it a shake in the middle of the cooking to re-coat the fish. Serve with the cream which will have reduced slightly and thickened and a poached egg.

*Either smoked fillets, Aberdeen fillet with the skin still on or Finnan Haddock on the bone may be used — allow an extra few ounces/grammes if the bone is still in.

SMOKED HADDOCK FLAN

When I was visiting Killiecrankie Hotel recently, Chef Paul Booth was busy in the kitchen making this superb fish pie for lunch and he kindly shared the recipe with me. It is richly flavoured with cheese and smoked fish but topped with a thick layer of creamy potatoes by contrast. It can also be made into a fish pie by omitting the pastry flan and putting the mixture into a pie dish.

For the pastry

(see p. 136 for origin)

6 oz/175 g plain flour ($1\frac{1}{2}$ c)
2 oz/50 g lard ($\frac{1}{2}$ stick)
2 oz/50 g butter or margarine ($\frac{1}{2}$ stick)
2 fl oz/50 ml boiling water ($\frac{1}{4}$ c)
2 oz/50 ml grated cheese ($\frac{1}{2}$ c)
Seasoning

Pre-heat the oven to 350F/180C/Gas 4.
Size of flan tin — 9″ (22 cm) round by 2″ (5 cm) deep.
Cut the lard and butter into a bowl and pour over the boiling water. Beat with a wire whisk till the fats are melted and the mixture creamy. It does not matter if it separates. Sift in the flour and salt and pepper and add the cheese. Mix thoroughly and put in the refrigerator for at least one hour to harden. Roll out and line flan tin, bake blind.

For the filling

1 lb/500 g smoked haddock
1 tablespoon plain flour
1 tablespoon butter
$\frac{1}{2}$ pt/300 ml milk ($1\frac{1}{4}$ c)
2 oz/50 g Red Galloway Cheddar ($\frac{1}{2}$ c)
2 hard boiled eggs
2 lb/500 g creamed potatoes
1 oz/25 g grated Red Galloway Cheddar ($\frac{1}{4}$ c)
Seasoning

Place the haddock in milk and poach gently till the fish is almost cooked. Cool, remove the fish and flake. Melt the butter in a pan and add the flour, cook for a few minutes and then strain in the milk gradually, stirring as it thickens. Add the haddock and season.

To assemble the flan

Slice the cheese thinly and put a layer in the base of the flan. Cover this with a layer of thinly sliced hard boiled eggs and then pour the sauce on top. Leave this to cool and set before putting the potato on top. This can be done with a piping bag or simply spread over and forked up. Cover with a layer of grated cheese and heat through in a hot oven 425F/220C/Gas 7 for 10 minutes or until top is lightly brown. Serve with a light salad for lunch or supper.

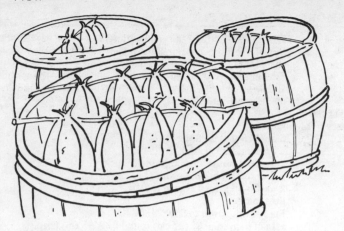

Hot Smoked Arbroath Smokie

These are whole haddock, but unlike Finnans are not split open. They have been known as 'Closed' fish though the guts and head have been removed. They are tied in pairs by the tails, lightly brined and smoked till cooked.

I can remember seeing rows of blackened barrels dotted along the cliff top edge of the village of Auchmithie in the 1950s when I was taken there as a child. The lovely wood smoke mingled with the cooking haddock as it wafted along the cliff tops and gave Auchmithie an exotic fascination for me. The haddock, which were hung up inside the barrels, had a dark, tarry appearance, a powerful aroma of smoke and a very strong flavour. When we took them home, they were eaten for tea heated through in the oven, and served with lots of melted butter. Smokies today are less heavily smoked and are more of a light copper colour on the outside and the flesh inside is golden near the skin, paling to a creamy white near the bone. Requires no cooking.

BAKED ARBROATH SMOKIE served with Baked Potato

4 servings

> **2 pairs Smokies**
> **2 oz/50 g melted butter (½ stick)**
> **Freshly ground black pepper**
> Pre-heat oven to 350F/180C/Gas 4.

Place each Smokie on a piece of buttered foil, brush well with butter on both sides and brush foil. Grind a few turns of pepper over each one. Wrap up, or omit foil and place in a shallow dish with a tightly fitting cover; or cover with foil. Bake for 15-20 minutes. Serve in individually wrapped parcels or remove from foil, split open along the backbone and remove the bone. Place a pat of butter in the centre, close up and serve with Lemon wedges and Baked Potato.

ARBROATH SMOKIE poached in milk

4 servings

This traditional way of cooking sometimes has the milk thickened slightly, though in fishing communities it is more often left plain.

4 Smokies
Boiling water
½ pt/300 ml milk (1¼ c)
Pepper
1 teaspoon cornflour

If the fish are freshly smoked, the skin will peel off quite easily. Otherwise pour boiling water over the smokies, drain and peel off the skin.

Put in a pan with the milk and heat through. Remove fish to warmed serving dish. Blend the cornflour with some of the milk, add to the sauce and boil up to thicken. It should not be too thick. Pour over the fish and serve.

POTTED ARBROATH SMOKIE with oatcakes

4 servings

2 medium Smokies (approximately ½ lb/250 g flaked flesh)
4 oz/125 g softened butter (1 stick)
Salt
Cayenne pepper
Lemon juice
Clarified butter (see p. 48)

Remove the skin (as above with boiling water if necessary). Take the flesh off the bones and place in a bowl. Add softened butter and beat together to a smooth paste. This can be done in a processor which makes the texture a uniform smoothness. Beating by hand produces a roughness without being too coarse. Season with salt, pepper and lemon juice. Pack into individual pots or into one large pot. Knock to remove any air and cover the top with a thin layer of clarified butter. Cover with a lid or foil and store in a cool place. They will keep for at least a month.

Serve with slightly warmed oatcakes or hot toast and butter.

CHAPTER THREE

SHELLFISH
&SEAWEED

Very early in the spring, long before the cold east winds of March have gone, the women take up their positions. Each one has an improvised table, consisting frequently of an orange box, on which are placed saucers containing shellfish, together with the necessary condiments.

J.H. Jamieson
'The Edinburgh Street Traders and their Cries',
in the <u>Book of the Old Edinburgh Club</u>, 1909

Three things have combined to influence the amount of shellfish eaten by the Scots today. Firstly, industrial pollution has destroyed shellfish beds in Lowland waters which at one time provided taverns in the nearby cities with cheap and plentiful supplies. A single Edinburgh tavern in the 19th century could account for ten thousand oysters in a week. Remnants of this trade survive, though not with oysters, but in the mussels, whelks and clabbies (horse mussels), which you can enjoy on a Sunday morning from the shellfish stalls and shops at the Glasgow 'Barras'.*

Equating the eating of shellfish with direst poverty is the second factor which has continued to inhibit some Highlanders, in particular, from eating shellfish. While camping some years ago on a beach on the island of Rhum we cooked a huge potful of mussels for a meal and some curious local children came to join us. They returned the next day, sent by their parents, with food for the 'starving' people on the beach. This attitude to shellfish as a 'last resort' food is not universal, however, and there are many other Highlanders who are extremely knowledgeable and avid shellfish and seaweed eaters.

The third factor is that in the last twenty years or so the Scots have discovered the 'buried treasure' which lies beneath their seas.

In the money making race, shellfish are well out in front as a top earner for Scottish fishermen. The world wants Scottish shellfish in

*Sunday Street Market, i.e. — Barrows.

unlimited quantities — and is willing to pay a good price for it but unfortunately for Scots, this has had the inevitable effect of making some of the more highly prized species too expensive for them to eat themselves.

Everywhere round the Scottish coast there is evidence of the increasing prosperity of the shellfish trade with small labour-intensive units handling these highly perishable fish. Much is transported around Scotland in a live state to discerning markets which demand the top quality fresh shellfish, while the rest is processed and frozen for markets further afield. Although it seems that there are plenty of shellfish at the moment there is always the possibility that they could be overfished and marine scientists predict that there is little room for expansion at the moment. Note: Because shellfish are sometimes commonly described by the wrong name (eg. a periwinkle called a 'whelk' or a Norway Lobster called a 'prawn' or 'crayfish') I have given the generic name for correct identification.

Molluscs — Scallops

 Their beautifully decorative shell gives them a charm in outward appearance which is only matched by the subtle and delicate flavour of the contrasting creamy muscle and orange coral inside. They call for the simplest methods of cooking since their elusive flavour is easily lost in complicated dishes.

Now a major Scottish shellfish catch with higher landings than any other mollusc, their importance has increased steadily since the 1960s and scallops are now fished all round the coast, though the early fishery was in the Clyde.

Identification

There are two types of scallops in Scottish waters, the **Great Scallop** (Pecten maximus) whose shell is up to 6" (15 cm) in diameter and the **Queen Scallop**, caught in deeper waters, (Chlamys opercularia) whose shell is only 3-4" (6-10 cm) diameter. Scallops have a highly developed white muscle in the centre of the shell and an orange roe, both of which are edible. The 'frill' round the edge of the shell, which is in fact the eyes, should be removed.

Buying

Scallops are often sold ready prepared, but if possible try to obtain live ones and open them yourself at the last minute. Those which have sprung open have been out of the sea too long and should not be eaten. They can also be bought smoked.

SCALLOPS SAUTEED IN BUTTER with shallots

Cooking quickly and lightly in a little good butter preserves their full flavour. Served in their shell, their natural visual attraction speaks for itself and needs no embellishments.

16 scallops (24 Queens)
2 oz/50 g unsalted butter (½ stick)
4 shallots, finely chopped
Salt and pepper

To open scallops

Slide the blade of a knife under the flat lid of the shell and cut through the muscle, keeping the blade hard against the shell so that the muscle is removed in one piece. The shell will then open. Scoop out the scallop attached to the hollow shell. Separate the white part and the orange coral, discard the frilly membrane and any brown parts.

Reserve 4 good shells, clean well and put to heat through in the oven with a small nut of butter and the white of a chopped shallot in each shell — the shallot should soften slightly. Cut the white parts of the scallops into two horizontally.

Cooking

Heat the oil and butter in a frying pan. Add the white parts and sauté for a few minutes then add the corals and continue for another minute. Season. Put into shells, pour over pan juices, squeeze over a few drops of lemon juice. Garnish with the green shallot finely chopped. Serve with crusty bread or hot toast and a chilled Muscadet or very dry cider.

STEAMED SCALLOPS in a creamy white sauce

8 servings

The flavour of the scallops comes through strongly when cooked in a creamy white sauce, while the breadcrumbs on top make an important texture contrast.

16 live scallops (24 Queens)
2 oz/50 g butter (½ stick)
½ pt/250 ml milk (1 c)
1 tablespoon butter ⎫ **Kneaded butter**
1 tablespoon flour ⎭
2 tablespoons cream
Salt and pepper
2 oz/50 g lightly browned breadcrumbs (½ c)

Cooking the scallops

Prepare the scallops as in the previous recipe. Use a double boiler or steamer or plate on top of a pan of hot water. Season the scallops with salt and dot with nuts of butter. Pour over milk and cream. Cover the pan, place it on the heat and bring to the boil. Remove and leave for five minutes with the lid on.

Making the sauce

Drain off the cooking liquor and put into another pan. Bring to the boil and reduce slightly. Work the flour into the butter to make a smooth paste and drop very small nuts into the boiling liquid to thicken very lightly. Season.

Serving

Put scallops into heated shells and pour over sauce. Cover with browned crumbs and serve.

Oysters

A genuine oyster-eater rejects all additions, — wine, eschalott, lemon, etc., are alike obnoxious to his taste for the native juice.

Meg Dods
The Cook and Housewives Manual, 1826

Unlike most other shellfish which we harvest and eat today, oysters have been eaten with great relish in Scotland for centuries. James Hogg (1770-1835) known as the Ettrick Shepherd and an avid oyster-eater, complained that 'a month without an R has nae right being in the year'.

They were the central feature of oyster parties in Edinburgh taverns of the 18th and 19th Century. Genteel Edinburgh ladies, with a taste for excitement, frequented the less genteel subterranean Oyster Cellars for dishes of oysters and pots of porter. This over, they regaled themselves with 'a large bowl of brandy punch' to finish the night! So cheap and plentiful were oysters that cooks threw handfuls into sauces, soups and stews (sixty or so at a time) which makes it difficult for us to imagine the kind of flavours they must have created. These were the large native oysters, mentioned by Martin Martin in his Description of the Western Islands of Scotland (1709) as growing on 'rocks and are so big that they are cut in four pieces before they are ate'.

Identification

There are two types of oyster — the wild and the cultivated, but many different species. The original indigenous oyster beds in Scotland were European native oysters (Ostrea edulis). When pollution was destroying the oyster beds at Prestonpans in the Firth of Forth, oyster spat (eggs) was taken from Scotland to Brittany, so that French oysters today have a Scottish pedigree. There are still some natural oyster beds of native oysters around the coasts but most were overfished when discovered and are now extinct. European native oysters are being commercially cultivated in oyster beds round the Scottish coast.

Pacific oysters (Crassostrea gigas) are being farmed on the West Coast but because the water is too cold they do not breed and are therefore sold all year round. Breeding oysters retain their eggs and taste unpleasant, though not poisonous, during the breeding season, which is from May to August. Oysters farmed on the West Coast of Scotland are a particularly good flavour since they grow naturally in the very pure sea water in an area which is free from industry and shipping and which has only a sparse population. They are therefore taken straight from the sea for sale, which retains the natural fresh flavour and do not have to go through sterile water tanks to make them safe for consumption.

Native oysters are fan shaped, almost circular; one half of the shell is flat, the other cupped. The shell of the Pacific oyster is more deeply cupped, rougher and more elongated than the native. Most of the West Coast oysters are of this variety. All show wide variation in colour and texture according to their origin.

Buying

Reject an oyster which is not tightly shut; if buying in a restaurant remember that a 'good' oyster is full of liquid and looks alive. The bad one is shrivelled and dried up. They must be the most talked about erotic food, though there is no scientific evidence that they are aphrodisiacs. (Clement Freud has been known to complain to his favourite oyster bar that of the six oysters he had eaten there the previous day, only four had worked!). Flavour depends on feeding grounds so there is great variation. Discriminating oyster-lovers have their own favourites. Once the oysters have come out of the water they should be kept in a cool place, the salad section of the refrigerator is a good place, under a damp cloth. They will stay fresh for four to five days but should be eaten sooner if possible since their juices will dry up on keeping.

Opening

Hold the oyster in a cloth in your left hand with the round side in the palm so that the juice is not lost. Insert a strong knife with a short rounded blade at the hinge end which should be towards you and give a quick upward turn, cutting through the muscle at the hinge. Remove any shell fragments.

Eating

Oysters are best eaten raw on the half shell. Serve in the deep half to reserve the juice and place on a bed of ice. Serve with brown bread and butter and a chilled very dry white wine such as a Muscadet or Sancerre. Between 8-10 are usually regarded as a portion, though a dozen used to be common when they were cheap and plentiful. (Lemon juice, cayenne pepper, chilli sauce or Tabasco are matters of taste.)

Other Ways of eating oysters

This very much depends on the type of oyster since some species are large and tough and lend themselves to cooking. Almost every chef has his own ideas, and whole recipe books have been written on the subject, but I particularly like the combination of oysters and whelks which the Troisgros brothers suggest in their book, <u>The Nouvelle Cuisine</u>, 1977. Scottish whelks are of such superb quality that most of those to be found in Billingsgate market in London are from Scotland.

OYSTERS WITH WHELKS

4 servings

If oysters are too expensive then **Clabbie Dubhs** are excellent in this recipe. Their flavour combines well with whelks and their very large deep shells hold the sauce nicely. If the clabbies are large then two per person should suffice. Steam them open first (see recipe 84).

24 oysters (8 clabbies)
12 doz whelks (1 pt/1$\frac{3}{4}$ lb/2$\frac{1}{2}$ c), washed and steeped overnight in fresh water

For cooking the whelks

2 carrots sliced
1 onion sliced
1 stick celery sliced
1 sprig of thyme
1$\frac{3}{4}$ pts/1 L water (4$\frac{1}{2}$ c)

For the sauce

8 oz/220 g butter (2 sticks)
2$\frac{1}{2}$ tablespoons distilled vinegar
Juice of half a lemon
Salt, freshly ground pepper
Open the oysters over a small pan, catching all the liquid. Detach the oysters and put them into the pan with their liquid. Place the hollow shells in two ovenproof dishes. Put carrots, onions, celery, thyme and vinegar into a pan, add the water and bring to the boil — cook for 15 minutes to develop the flavours. Add the whelks, bring back to the boil and cook for 3 minutes. Take the pan off the heat and let the whelks cool in the liquid. Strain off liquid, reserving about 5 tablespoons. Pick out whelks, remove the eyes and put the whelks into a bowl.

To make the sauce

Strain the five tablespoons of the whelk cooking liquid into a small saucepan and place over a fierce heat. Add the butter in very small pieces, working up with a whisk till you have a smooth sauce. Taste for seasoning, add lemon juice.

To finish the dish

Heat the oysters gently without boiling, about 2 minutes over a medium heat. Heat the empty oyster shells in the oven and put the oysters into their shells. Arrange six whelks in each oyster and cover lightly with the sauce. Place on a bed of coarse sea salt, garnish with a little parsley and add a few whelk shells for decoration.

Mussels

These are not yet important commercially but are being increasingly grown on ropes in sheltered areas around the coast. Also harvested from natural rocks, they reach maturity at about three years when they are two inches long.

Identification

Usually from 2-3″ (5-8 cm) in length, they have lovely blue-black shells, paler blue turning to pearly white inside with a contrasting orange muscle.

Buying

They should be bought live, all shells tightly shut. Discard any open ones.

Preparing

Leave overnight in fresh water then scrub clean and remove beards — the tuft of fibres projecting from the shell which anchors it.

MUSSEL STEW with crusty bread and butter

It's simple and quick to cook and serve mussels in their shells. Piled high on plates their steaming aroma captures all the essence of the sea.

4 lb/2 kg mussels in their shell, well scrubbed and cleaned
½ pt/250 ml water or white wine (1 c)
1 medium onion, finely chopped
Sprig of thyme
1 bay leaf
1 handful chopped parsley
2 oz/50 g butter (½ stick)
Freshly ground black pepper

Put the water or wine, onion, thyme and bay leaf into a very large pot. Bring to the boil and add mussels. Cover well and cook over a high flame, shaking frequently until the shells begin to open. This will only take a minute, even less if the mussels are small. Remove from the heat, keep the lid on. The remainder of the mussels will

open in the latent heat — it is important not to overcook. Pile the mussels high in soup plates. Strain cooking liquor, taste for saltiness and adjust with boiling water if necessary and stir butter in. Season with a few grindings of pepper, add the parsley and ladle over mussels. Serve with crusty bread and butter.

Using cooked mussels — Mix through a creamy scrambled egg or warm them through in a little butter and fold into a soft omelette. Add to the sauce with Roast Lamb (p. 142).

MUSSELS grilled in their shells with wine and butter

4 servings

This is how some French friends who were visiting us in the Highlands cooked and served mussels gathered from rocks in the loch. The method of eating is the same as for raw oysters but the shells in this case are filled with mussels, wine and butter, which keeps the mussels plump, juicy and full of flavour.

4 lb/2 kg mussels, well washed and scrubbed
½ pt/250 ml white wine (1 c)
2 oz/50 g butter (½ stick)
1 handful chopped parsley

Cooking mussels

Put a large open pan on to heat, put in about ¼″ (½ cm) water and bring to the boil. Add the mussels and cook over a high heat, stirring and tossing all the time till they open. Remove and take out of shells.

Serving

Remove beards and split shells. Place half shells on cooling rack or wire rack and put a mussel into each shell. Fill up shell about three quarters full of wine and add a knob of butter and put under a hot grill for a minute. Sprinkle over some chopped parsley and place (still on rack) on a tray in the centre of the table. Eat with the fingers with crusty bread and butter.

Horse Mussels, Scottish — Clabbie Dubhs

These are known in Scotland by their Gaelic name Clab-Dubh meaning large black mouth. Their flavour is more robust than the small mussel and they are very filling. Small young ones have a more delicate flavour than the larger variety. Latin name — Modiolus modiolus.

Identification

Similar in shape and colour to the smaller mussel but about 6-8" (15-20 cm) long.

Buying and Preparation

As for smaller mussels

CLABBIE DUBHS with leek and tomatoes

This excellent soup/stew is well flavoured with tomatoes, garlic and leeks. It can be adapted either way or made as a stew one day, then thinned down with stock and with some more vegetables as a soup for the next day.

8 clabbies
1 pt/500 ml water (2 c)
1 leek, finely chopped
3 tablespoons olive oil
6 oz/175 g long grain rice brown or white, well washed (1 c)
3 medium tomatoes, finely chopped
2 cloves garlic, crushed
Salt and freshly ground pepper

Preparing

Cook the clabbies in water till they just open. Strain the cooking liquor. Take clabbies out of their shells and remove beards. Cut into two or three pieces depending on size.

Cooking

Melt the oil in a pan and add the white of the leek, cook for a few minutes and then add tomatoes and garlic. Stir in the rice and then start adding the cooking liquor. Add about half, and simmer gently, uncovered till it is absorbed, stirring from time to time. Add more stock as needed without making the mixture too wet. If making into a soup, all the stock can be added at once. Brown rice will take about 40 minutes to cook, white will take less.

Now add the green leek, stir through till softened and finally add the chopped mussels just before serving. Season well.

Periwinkles — Scottish Whelks

Scottish Whelks are now collected in quite large numbers round the coasts by local pickers. I disagree with those who say that the 'joy of winkle eating lies wholly in the challenge of getting the things out of their shells'. The best Scottish whelks from the richest feeding grounds are plump and juicy morsels with a unique flavour. Market demand for them has been growing steadily in the last decade as their popularity increases.

Identification

This is the dark grey, black little shell, Latin name — Littorina littorea and not the true Whelk (Buccinum undatum) which has a whiter shell and flesh and is known to Scots as the Dog Whelk and not generally eaten, since it is tough and lacking flavour compared with the black variety. Winkles are also known as Buckies in some parts of Scotland.

Preparation

Steep overnight in fresh water to remove sand, etc.

Cooking

Place in boiling water to cover and simmer for 2-3 minutes. Drain, save liquid for using as stock.

Eating

Serve with a large pin to pick out the meat. Discard the mica-like plate, 'the eye', at the mouth of the shell.

Other Scottish Molluscs — Limpets, Cockles, Clams and Razor Shells

These are common on Scottish sea shores though not as widely used or sold as others. **Limpets** have an interesting flavour but rather tough muscle. Chip them off the rocks with a sharp knife or knock them with a sharp stone. They are boiled in the usual way and can then be added to Stovies (p. 180). The liquid which they have been cooked in has lots of flavour and should be used as stock for making fish sauces and soups. Small limpets are more tender and once boiled, can be fried with bacon. **Cockles** live in sand and must be raked out and must be steeped in fresh water with a handful of oatmeal or flour to remove the sand. They may be eaten raw or cooked as for mussels. **Clams** are usually cooked, but very small ones can be eaten raw. **Razor shells — Scottish Spoots —** are a highly esteemed delicacy among coastal communities who catch their own seafood. Difficult to find, they are often in reasonable numbers at the very edge of the lowest tides and especially where there are spent shells to be seen. Digging with a long pronged fork is the only satisfactory way to get them out. They should be boiled very briefly simply to open the shells and then the liquid used to make broth. Remove the stomach bag and add the meat chopped finely just before the soup is served. Long cooking toughens the muscle.

Crustaceans — Edible Crab or Common Crab — Scottish Partan

Crabs are an under-rated and under-exploited Scottish shellfish, though their importance has been growing steadily in the last few years. In 1982, 4,000 metric tons were landed compared with only 1,686 metric tons in 1975 (Scottish Sea Fisheries Statistical Tables, 1982).

Identification

Reddish brown colour, tinted with purple, legs reddish and claws black. Legal minimum size is $4\frac{1}{2}''$ (11 cm). Size across the back up to 12″ (30 cm). Latin name — Cancer pagurus.

Buying Crab

Preferably buy live: they should smell fresh and sweet with no hint of ammonia and they should be reasonably lively. Lift the crab by its back to check that it is a good weight for its size. Male crabs are a better buy since they have a better quality and higher proportion of white meat than females. They can be distinguished from the female by a smaller tail flap on the underside. They are available all year round but are best from April to September.

Boiling Crab

Put live crab in boiling salted water, press down with tongs for a few minutes and then reduce to a simmer and cook for about 10-15 minutes. Remove from the pan and leave to cool.

To remove meat before serving

1. Remove the claws and legs close into the body shell. Crack the shell of each claw with a wooden mallet without damaging the flesh. Remove the flesh and separate the bony cartilage. Break open the legs at the joints and pick out the flesh with a skewer.
2. To open the crab, pull off the tail flap and discard. Hold the crab in both hands with two thumbs hard against the base at the bottom of the tail flap and press hard. The whole central part should come out, but if it does not, loosen with a knife round where the legs were attached and then press again. Pull central part free and remove the elongated gills (deadmen's fingers) along the edges and discard. Cut down the middle and use a skewer to pick out the flesh from the many crevices on both sides.
3. With a teaspoon, scoop out the meat from inside the shell and reserve it, but remove and discard the small stomach sac which is just behind the crab's mouth.
4. To open out the shell, press round the outer edge where there is a weak line: it should break cleanly. Wash the shell.

To serve plainly

Mix the brown body meat with the meat from the centre part of the shell. Season and return to the shell on either side, leaving a space in the centre for the claw and leg meat. Garnish with chopped parsley and serve with a lightly flavoured mayonnaise, brown bread and butter.

PARTAN PIES

4 servings

The crab shell acts as a useful container for all the meat extracted. The strongly flavoured body meat is enlivened with nutmeg and red wine following a traditional recipe. It is packed into the sides of the shells, while the white claw meat forms a strip in the centre. Good eaten hot or cold.

4 medium crabs
2 tablespoons soft breadcrumbs
$\frac{1}{4}$ pt/125 ml red wine ($\frac{3}{4}$ c)
4 oz/125 g butter (1 stick)
$\frac{1}{4}$ grated nutmeg
$\frac{1}{2}$ teaspoon made mustard (p. 238) optional
Salt and pepper
1 handful of chopped parsley

Boil the crabs and remove all meat from claws and body, clean out shell thoroughly, break off pieces of shell on either side of eyes with thumbs. They should come cleanly away to open up the shell more.

Keep the two meats separate. Put the soft body meat in a pan and add the wine, breadcrumbs, half the butter, nutmeg and mustard. Heat through and season to taste. Pack this mixture into the sides of the shell. Mix the other meat with softened butter, season and place in the centre. Cover with foil and heat through in the oven. Serve hot or cold garnished with chopped parsley.

PARTAN BREE

serves 4

The crab flavour comes through strongly in this creamy soup which is thickened with rice. It is also good made with razor fish. Bree means liquid or gravy.

1 large cooked crab (see p. 87)
2 oz/50 g rice ($\frac{1}{4}$ c)
1 pt/600 ml milk ($2\frac{1}{2}$ c)
1 pt/600 ml cooking liquor from boiling the crab ($2\frac{1}{2}$ c)
$\frac{1}{4}$ pt/125 ml single cream ($\frac{3}{4}$ c)
Salt and pepper
Garnish — finely chopped chives

Remove all the meat from the crab but keep the claw meat separate. Put the rice into a pan with milk and water and cook till tender. Liquidise this with the brown body meat from the crab and then add the white meat. Add cream and re-heat. Taste for seasoning. Adjust consistency with more milk if necessary. Serve garnished with some fresh green finely chopped chives.

Lobster — European

Lobster stocks have been in some danger recently with the East coast area from the Borders to Moray under intensive exploitation. In Orkney and Shetland, landings have been down, as have landings on the West coast. In order to conserve stocks a minimum landing size was introduced in 1984 of 85 mm (approx 3½″) carapace length (upper body shell).

Identification

Bluish black shell, thick round body and two large forward claws. Length up to 18″ (45 cm). Weight varies from ¾ lb (375 g) to 2¼ lb (1¼ kg). Latin name — Homarus gammarus.

Buying Lobster

Choose a live lobster which looks lively, i.e. when prodded it thrashes about with some vigour. If it is sluggish in reacting, then it has probably been kept for several days out of water and without food, with a consequent loss of weight. Lift up the lobster by the back: it should feel heavy for its size.

Available all year round but best and most plentiful in the summer.

Killing Lobster

Method 1 — Dealing with a live lobster at home may be a problem. If possible, ask your fishmonger to kill it for you. There are various methods, one is to cut through the spinal cord. Keeping your hands clear of the claws, hold the lobster underside down on a board and using a heavy sharp knife pierce the shell firmly in the centre of the cross-shaped mark behind the head. Press down heavily and cut along the body and tail to halve the lobster. Then cut the head in half.

Method 2 — To kill and cook the lobster fill up a large pot with boiling salted water and plunge the lobster in. Hold it under the surface with tongs for two minutes. Turn down the heat, cover the pan and simmer the lobster, allowing 12 minutes for the first 1 lb (500 g) and 10 minutes for the next pound and 5 minutes for each additional pound.

GRILLED LOBSTER

This method ensures that no flavour is lost in the cooking. It is important not to overcook and dry out the flesh.

2 × 1½-2 lb (¾-1 kg) live lobsters
Salt
4 oz/125 g unsalted butter (1 stick)
4 fl oz/125 g double cream (½ cup)

Preparing the lobster

Split the lobster in half lengthwise through the stomach shell and the hard back shell. Remove the sand sac, the red coral and any external roe. Discard the white gills and the intestinal canal which runs down the middle of the tail.

Grilling

Place lobsters on a baking or roasting tin cut side up. Brush liberally with melted butter and put under a hot grill. Grill for 3-4 minutes and then turn. Brush shell with butter and grill for another 3-4 minutes. Turn again and pour in plenty of butter onto cut sides. Continue grilling till the flesh is just cooked — this will depend on the thickness of the lobster. Place them on the serving dish. Heat cream in a pan, pour the residue from cooking the lobster into the cream and reduce till a good consistency and flavour. Pour over lobster, crack the claws and serve.

BOILED LOBSTER
How to prepare a boiled lobster for serving plainly

1. Remove the lobster when it is cooked and leave to cool. Snap off the eight legs close to the body. Break legs at joints and pick out meat with a skewer.

2. Remove each claw close into the body, and bang with a wooden mallet to crack the shell. Pull away the shell and remove the meat. Remove the cartilege that runs through each claw.

3. Lay the lobster on its back and cut with a heavy sharp knife close to the hard outer shell along its entire length on either side. Pull away the bony covering on the underside. Starting at the tail, prise away the tail meat in one piece. Strip off the brown-grey feathery gills.

4. The soft grey-green liver will remain in the shell. Scoop it out with a spoon and save. Lift out the inedible gravel sac (stomach) and discard.

5. Lay the tail meat on a chopping board and slice into pieces about ¾" (2 cm) thick. Scrape out any remaining meat in the lobster shell.

To serve

Clean the empty tail shell and fill with the meat. Arrange the remainder attractively on a large white plate with the liver and coral (if there is any) as a garnish. Decorate with some cooked and buttered mangetout peas. May be served with a lightly flavoured lemon mayonnaise and brown bread and butter. Chilled dry white wines or Champagne are best with cold lobster.

LOBSTER SOUP

Crushing the shells finely extracts every last ounce of flavour from the lobster with excellent results.

To prepare the lobster

Use $2 \times 1\frac{1}{2}$ lb ($\frac{3}{4}$ kg) live lobster and kill by either Method 1 or 2. Take off the tails and claws, split the head part lengthwise down the middle and remove the stomach sac and discard. Take out the coral, which is green in raw lobster, and put in a bowl. Crack the claws and season all with salt and pepper.

Heat in a large saucepan

2 tablespoons oil

1 oz/25 g butter ($\frac{1}{4}$ stick)

When very hot add lobster and cook, turning all the time, till the pieces are a good red colour.

Add

1 medium onion, finely chopped

1 shallot, finely chopped

1 carrot, finely chopped

3 fresh tomatoes, chopped

1 tablespoon tomato purée

Cook over a low heat for about five minutes. Add $\frac{1}{4}$ pt/150 ml white wine ($\frac{3}{4}$ c) and 1 pt/600 ml fish stock or water ($2\frac{1}{2}$ c). Cover and simmer for about ten minutes.

Remove the pieces of lobster. Take the meat out of the tails and claws and dice for garnish. Marinate in 2 tablespoons cognac. Put the tails and heads in a liquidiser or food processor to crush. Return to the pan and cook for another 10 minutes.

Work the coral to a paste with 1 tablespoon softened butter and mix into the soup. Add 5 tablespoons double cream and bring to the boil. Strain through a fine conical strainer rubbing soup through. Season with lemon juice, salt and cayenne pepper.

To serve

Place the diced meat and cognac in the base of a heated soup tureen. Pour over hot soup and serve immediately. This richly flavoured soup can be served with a cool, young, relatively light bodied red wine.

Norway Lobster

Of all Scottish shellfish this is the one which has 'taken off' most dramatically in the last twenty-five years. In the early 1950s it was completely unknown commercially, compared with landings of 14,000 metric tons in 1982 — the highest landing for any shellfish. It is caught in deep muddy waters on the East and West coast, particularly in the Firth of Forth, the Moray Firth, the Minch and the Clyde.

Terminology

Known by many names, and causing much confusion, their generic name is **Nephrophs norvegicus**. A species of the Lobster family, their name has been confused with prawns initially by the fishermen who refer to the 'prawn-boats' and the 'prawn-fishing'. This comes from the habit in Dublin of calling them Dublin Bay Prawns which is the first name they were popularly known by in the United Kingdom. The qualifying words were dropped and they became known as 'prawns' which is unfortunate since the Norway Lobster is really nothing like the common prawn (Leander senatus). Perhaps the important point to remember is that Nephros Norvegicus is in fact a true lobster with all the characteristics which distinguish the common lobster of the genus Homarus to which the European and American lobsters belong. (They are known to the Italians as Scampo and the French as Langoustine.)

In Scotland, they are also referred to in the fish trade and sometimes on hotel menus as **Crayfish**. This is correctly a freshwater crustacean (Astacus fluvuatilis) no longer common in Britain but a great delicacy in Scandinavia. Yet another misnomer, adding to the confusion when the same name is applied to different species. (French — Ecrevisse.)

Identification

Whole, they look like small lobsters. They are pale, orangey pink and when raw the claws are striped with white. Sometimes they are sold alive and this is the best way to buy them. Also sold pre-boiled. Flavour and texture deteriorate with freezing.

Buying

You can expect an average of 6-8 whole per pound.

For 4 servings depending on course and other accompaniments — approx. 2 lb/1 kg tails in their shells; 1 lb tails shelled; 3-4 whole per person for a starter, double for main course depending on size. Available all year round but best in the summer months.

Preparing and Cooking

Boil in salted water for three to four minutes, depending on size, with a few bay leaves and juniper berries — drain. They need little preparation if being served in the shell. If they are whole and have been pre-cooked, first pull off the head and claws. Then cut with a sharp knife through the bony cartilage on the underside, but do not cut through the tail meat. Open out and remove the whole tail, pick out spinal cord. Crush the claws with a wooden mallet and pick out the meat with a skewer.

Serving

These very pretty pink-orange shelled creatures need no fancy garnishing.

To serve hot in their shells

They may be tossed in butter for a few minutes till thoroughly heated through then served in the centre of the table in the saute pan or on a heated ashet and garnished with some colourful fresh fruits — Kiwi fruit, pineapple (use leaves to decorate), mango, strawberry. (As served by Nick Ryan at his Seafood Restaurant in Crinan Hotel, Argyll, and described as Jumbo Prawns Corryvreckan.)

To serve as a cold salad

They may be left in their shells or removed and used to decorate a large, preferably white, plate. Use salad vegetables to complement the pink-orange colour. Greens of varying shades are lovely but reds clash. Serve with Shellfish Sauce (see p. 96).

NORWAY LOBSTER in a cream sauce with sherry

1 lb/500 g cooked meat (tails and claws)
4 tablespoons medium dry sherry (or Madeira)
2 egg yolks
$\frac{1}{4}$ pt/150 ml double cream ($\frac{3}{4}$ c)
1 oz/25 g butter ($\frac{1}{4}$ stick)
Salt and pepper
4 oz/125 g boiled rice
Handful of chopped parsley

Melt the butter in the pan and add the cooked meat. Toss for a few minutes and then add the sherry or Madeira. Continue tossing for about five minutes. Add egg yolks and cream, draw to the side of the stove and heat through to thicken without boiling. Thicken with more butter if wished. Season and serve inside a ring of boiled rice. Garnish with parsley and serve.

93

Other Scottish Crustaceans — Spiny Lobster
(Crawfish — French, Langouste).
Brown Shrimp, Common Prawn, Squid

These are available from Scottish waters in varying quantities. Least available are the **Spiny Lobsters**. Their most noticeable feature, in comparison with lobster, is that they do not have claws. They are reddish-brown in colour with yellow and white markings for cooking and they can be treated in the same way as Lobsters. (Scottish fishermen also catch 'spinies' or Squat Lobsters — $\frac{1}{4}$-$\frac{1}{3}$ size of Norway Lobsters.)

Both **Brown shrimps** and **Common Prawns** are harvested from Scottish coasts. Of the catch, only about 7% is Brown Shrimp. About the same amount of Common Prawns are landed as Lobsters and **Squid**. While there is evidence of both shrimps and prawns having been eaten by Scots in the past there seems no history of the use of squid despite the fact that good and abundant supplies are available. It has been left to the ethnic communities in Scotland to make full use of squid, but some enterprising natives also see its potential.

ORKNEY SQUID

4 servings

Good supplies of small tender squid are available in Orkney and Norma Hasham serves them as a local feature at the Foveran Hotel in Kirkwall. They are lightly cooked in a rich tomato sauce and colourfully finished with parsley and chives. Served with some lemon and a local beremeal bannock they are a unique taste of the islands.

4 small squid
1 medium onion, finely chopped
2 tablespoons oil
4-5 large tomatoes, skinned and chopped
1 clove of garlic, crushed
3 tablespoons red wine
Salt and pepper
Chopped parsley
Chopped chives

Heat the oil in a pan and add the onion; cook till soft then add the tomatoes and reduce slightly. Add the wine, squid, garlic, and simmer gently till the squid is just cooked. Stir in plenty of parsley and chives. Taste for seasoning and serve with lemon and Beremeal Bannock.

Other Shellfish recipes

ARISAIG SEAFOOD PASTRY

6-8 servings

At the Arisaig Hotel in Inverness-shire Janice Stewart makes this seafood pastry with whatever seafood is fresh and available from local boats at Mallaig. Usually the selection includes Norway Lobster, Prawns, Salmon, Clams, Monkfish, Halibut or Turbot, Crabs and Lobster when they are plentiful and cheaper, and also squid.

1 lb/500 g puff pastry
2 lb/1 kg selected seafood, shelled
6 oz/175 g butter (1½ sticks)
2 oz/50 g well flavoured Scottish cheddar, grated (½ c)
1 egg yolk mixed with 1 teaspoon water for glaze
Salt and pepper
Pre-heat the oven to 450F/230C/Gas 8.

For the sauce

3 oz/75 g flour (¾ c)
3 oz/75 g butter (¾ stick)
1½ pt/850 ml milk and fish stock (3¾ c)

To make the sauce

Make a roux with the flour and butter and then add the milk gradually and cook till thick.

To bake the pastry

Roll out the pastry to ⅒" thick into strips about 3" (8 cm) wide. Brush top with egg glaze and bake till golden and risen.

To assemble the dish

Melt the butter in a pan and add the seafood. Sauté lightly till cooked. Mix into the white sauce and add cheese, taste for seasoning. Split the pastry through the middle and fill the bottom half with the seafood. Cover with lid. Slice and serve hot with lemon and green salad.

SHELLFISH BROTH

The smaller crustaceans, taken as a group, have diverse shapes and colours from the dark blue of the mussel to the lovely bright orange of the scallop coral. To assemble them simply, plainly boiled in their cooking liquor, has a stunning visual effect. Serving can be done in two ways. Either pile all the shellfish in a very large deep ashet in the centre of the table and serve the broth separately in a tureen with a ladle, or arrange the shellfish in large round deep soup plates and pour over the hot broth just before serving.

Selection of shellfish from the following

(1) Mussels, whelks, cockles
   — Clean well, scraping shells if necessary
(2) Norway Lobster, crawfish
   — Wash well and remove any roe
(3) Scallops, oysters
   — Open shells, loosen them from the shells and reserve the juice in a bowl.

To cook the shellfish

Put the mussels into a pan with about $\frac{1}{2}"$ of boiling water in the bottom. Keep moving till they open, then remove from the heat. Cover and keep warm. Cook the cockles in the same way — reserve cooking liquid and keep warm. Cook the whelks in boiling water for about 5 minutes. Reserve liquid and keep warm.

If not already cooked, boil the Norway Lobster and crayfish in boiling water, reserve liquid and keep warm.

Cook the oysters gently in their own juice and a little water. The scallops only take a couple of minutes; the oysters about 30 seconds. Return to shells and keep warm.

To make the broth

Sauté the onion in butter till yellow and soft then add the cooking liquor from the shellfish to make up to 2 pts/11.5 dl/5 c. Some will be saltier than others so balance the combination accordingly. Add chopped parsley. Pour over shellfish in plates or put into tureen. Finish by throwing a handful of freshly chopped parsley and a healthy grinding of pepper over the shellfish and serve.

SHELLFISH SAUCE for serving with all cold shellfish

Left-over shells still hold an amazing amount of hidden flavour, which can be extracted by making this lovely sauce to serve with any cold shellfish.

For the stock

2 lb/500 g heads of either lobster or Norway Lobster
1 tablespoon cognac
$1\frac{1}{2}$ tablespoons dry white wine
1 tablespoon neutral oil
$\frac{1}{4}$ pt/150 ml fish stock ($\frac{3}{4}$ c)

For the sauce

$\frac{1}{4}$ pt/150 ml whipping cream ($\frac{3}{4}$ c)
1 tablespoon wine vinegar
1 teaspoon smooth Arran mustard
Salt and freshly ground black pepper

Crush the shells in a liquidiser or food processor. Melt the oil and sauté them for 5 minutes. Add the cognac, flame and then add the white wine followed by the fish stock or water and tomato purée. Simmer for 20 minutes.

Strain through a conical strainer pressing the shells firmly with the back of a spoon to press through all the flavour.

Return to the pan and reduce to about 4 tablespoons. Remove from pan and allow to cool. Mix the mustard, cream, vinegar, salt and pepper in a bowl. Whisk together and then start adding the shellfish stock gradually. Season.

Seaweeds

In the North, and in many other places on the coast of this country, people feed upon Sloke, that is, the sea lettuce; they make Broath with it, and sometimes serve it up with butter, Some of them eat dils; . . . and some eat that sort of Sea Tangle. It is a pleasant taste betwixt salt and sweet; it's eaten as a salade.

R. Sibbald
Provision for the poor in Time of Dearth and Scarcity. Edinburgh, 1709

'Dulse and Tangel' was a favourite Leith Street cry a hundred years ago with a Midlothian drawl on the 'el'. For a country surrounded by seaweed the Scots are, today, more cautious of it than in the past. I only made the mistake once of telling a friend in advance that I wanted to try out some seaweed recipes: now I serve up seaweed in all sorts of disguises. Most are intrigued, none can ever say exactly what it is, but all agree that carefully combined with other flavours it adds a unique taste experience. Carragheen gelatine is after all an unseen additive in many commercial soups, ice-creams and quick-setting jellies.

In the East, seaweed is an important food supply. Both China and Japan have progressed further in the utilisation of seaweed as a food than any other countries. They eat the raw weeds as salads, mix them with a kind of roasted nut which has been finely chopped and keep this mixture in glass jars for months to serve with bread and butter, cold meat and fish. Some of the larger species are used in every household as noodles, toasted, served with rice or in soup. Smaller species are dried.

Their nutritional value is interesting as they are very low in fat, almost calorie free, while at the same time containing more minerals than any other kind of food. Approximately 30% of the mineral content is lost to the soaking water, so use the water whenever possible.

Gathering/Buying

Seaweeds have seasons of growth like other plants. They produce shoots in the spring, grow quickly in the summer and wither in the winter. The best months to gather are May and June.

The new young shoots have the best flavour and texture. Remove the overlying seaweed and gather the tiny plants from beneath. Do not take too far down the stem since if enough is left the weed will regenerate. Before cooking, wash in fresh running water to remove sand, shells, etc. It is easy to dry and store. Simply lay out in a good cold current of air till thoroughly dry and store in an airtight container. Dried seaweed can be bought in specialist whole food shops and there is now a wide variety available including some from Japan.

Carragheen (Chondrus crispus)

Named after the village of Carragheen near Waterford in Ireland where it abounds. It usually grows on a boulder-strewn shore near the low water mark of spring tides, so that sometimes it could be collected only about two hours each side of the low water for a few days each fortnight. Carragheen is high in vitamin A and iodine and it also contains B vitamins and many minerals. It is an important source of vegetable gelatines (alginates) which are used commercially for thickening soups, emulsyfying ice-creams and setting jellies.

Identification

Having spent fruitless hours, with frozen hands and feet, gathering, by mistake, Batter Frond which is very similar in appearance to Carragheen but produces no jelly, I recommend that you either buy some so that you can positively identify it, or take along someone from the area who knows where to find the right weed. The branched fronds can be up to 6″ (15 cm) long, their colour varies from purple to brown to a bleached browny white when exposed to light. These have a distinctly flat stalk, and branch repeatedly into a rough fan shape. Batter Frond is different since it has a concave surface with the sides of each segment tending to roll inwards, and older specimens have tiny pimples.

CARRAGHEEN CHOCOLATE PUDDING

Children in Ireland enjoy this pudding. Carragheen has a bland flavour which can do with some pepping up. In its natural state it was eaten mostly by invalids who were unable to cope with other food and Highlanders still make a natural Carragheen Jelly for the sick. To make this, omit all the other flavourings except the sugar, though without it, the true flavour of the seaweed can be appreciated and some people prefer to eat it like this with lots of whipped cream, even if they are not ill.

½ oz/15 g dried carragheen (¼ c)
1 pt/600 ml milk (2½ c)
1 tablespoon sugar
1 egg
2 oz/50 g bitter chocolate
Almond or vanilla essence or Angostura Bitters

Wash the carragheen in cold water to remove any grit etc. Put into a bowl and just cover with hot water — about ¼ pt/150 ml (¾ c). Leave for 15 minutes. The seaweed will have softened and the liquid become jellyish. Put into the milk. Bring to the boil and simmer gently for about 10 minutes or until the mixture is quite thick — about 20 minutes. Strain. If the seaweed is very young and tender much of it can be pressed through the sieve, though this obviously gives a stronger carragheen flavour. Melt the chocolate over a gentle heat and add the mixture with the sugar, egg yolk and flavouring, stirring well. Beat the egg white till stiff and fold in. Pour into a mould or four small dishes and leave till set. Serve with cream.

CARRAGHEEN for thickening soups and stews

To add to soups and stews, soak in cold water for a few minutes and remove from the water leaving behind the grit, etc. Chop the carragheen finely or put some of the soup or stew liquid into a liquidiser with the carragheen and blend till smooth. Carrragheen gives nice body to a soup or stew; the delicate flavour is not obvious.

Dulse and Tangle

Dulse (Rhodymenia palmata) is a broad-leaved seaweed, dark reddish purple in colour, which can grow up to 12″ (30 cm) long. The young fronds are thin and papery. Tangle is a variety known as Laminaria saccharina, often found attached to small stones on muddy sandy flats. Pepper Dulse (Laurencia pinnatifida) can be a variety of colours from yellow-green to red-brown and is up to 7″ (18 cm) long. This is the one which Scots like to chew for its pungent flavour (Poor Man's Tobacco). It is the kind of eating experience which begins in childhood, beach-combing with parents who encourage the idea of eating seaweed and a lifelong liking, even craving, is developed, as many Highlanders will testify. Dulse contains the highest concentration of iron in any edible food source, as well as being rich in potassium and magnesium.

Uses

Dulse has a more definite flavour than Carragheen and it combines well with lamb and with most root vegetables. It has an affinity with white fish like haddock, cod and whiting, rather than the stronger flavoured oily fish and is good with shellfish, particularly sliced very finely in accompanying salads. It is also good added to Stovies. Soak for 15

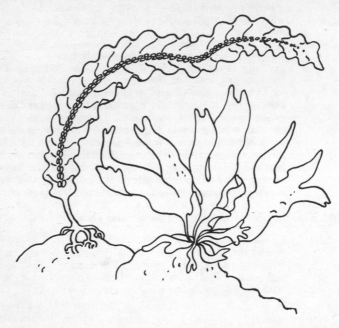

minutes then drain. Chop finely and add with the potatoes and meat. (Recipe p. 180).

DULSE BROTH with lamb or mutton

This is one of the very obvious ways in which you would expect Scots to use dulse. Other meats can be used but mutton seems more common. The dulse soup which I have eaten has always been made with mutton, sometimes even the salted variety.

2 lb/1 kg neck of mutton
1 onion, finely chopped
1 medium carrot, diced
3 sticks of celery, diced
2-3 medium potatoes, thinly sliced
1 oz/25 g butter or 1 tablespoon oil
2 oz/50 g dulse (1 c loosely packed)
4 pts/2 L water (10 c)
Salt, freshly ground pepper
Handful of chopped parsley

Place the neck in a pan and add water. Bring to the boil, skim and simmer till the meat is tender. Strain cooking liquor, remove excess fat. Cut off all the edible meat from the neck and dice finely.

Melt the butter in a pan and add the onion. Cook till the onion is soft and yellow. Add all the other vegetables and dulse and gently sweat, tightly covered, for five to ten minutes, stirring occasionally to prevent sticking. Add the stock from the mutton and seasoning, bring to the boil and simmer gently till the vegetables are cooked.

Just before serving, add the meat and parsley and adjust the seasoning.

DULSE CAKES

I first came across this idea in Roger Phillips' Wild Food (1983). I have used Scottish yellow turnip rather than parsnips partly because it is a more common Scottish vegetable but also because I think it combines better with the very distinctive flavour of the dulse. I make them in four round flat cakes rather than in the eight croquettes recommended by Roger Phillips, mainly to save time. Croquettes will need more oats for coating and according to Roger Phillips should be deep fried, which I think might be tricky with such a loosely-held-together mixture.

8 oz/250 g carrots
8 oz/250 g turnip
3 oz/75 g rolled oats (1 c)
1 oz/25 g dulse ($\frac{1}{2}$ c)
2 tablespoons olive oil
Salt and pepper

Boil the carrots and turnip in water till tender, drain and mash together.

Rinse the dulse and then steep in cold water for 10 minutes. Drain and chop finely. Add to rolled oats, mix thoroughly. Put half this mixture into the vegetables, season and mix in. Shape into four round cakes. Coat with remaining oat mixture, fry on both sides in hot oil till lightly brown.

Serve as a vegetable with roast lamb.

Sloke

This is the Scottish/Irish name for what the Welsh call Laverbread. Latin name — Porphyra purpurea. It is a reddish colour which turns bottle green when cooked. Rinse the weed well to remove all sand and dirt, then steep overnight in fresh water with a handful of salt. Drain. To make a purée, put in a pan with a little sea-water. Bring to the boil and simmer for a few minutes, beat well and then repeat the process till reduced to a pulp. Season with pepper and butter — salt may not be needed — and serve hot with mashed potatoes.

According to Alan Davidson writing in North Atlantic Seafood (1979) — 'The Welsh remain the great enthusiasts for laverbread, although their formerly abundant supply has dwindled and much of what is sold in Cardiff market now comes from Scotland.'

CHAPTER FOUR

GAME

> . . . Game was so plentiful, red deer, roe, hares, grouse, ptarmigan and partridge; the river provided trout and salmon, the different lochs pike and char; the garden abounded in common fruits and common vegetables; cranberries and raspberries ran over the country, and the poultry yard was ever well furnished.
>
> Elizabeth Grant of Rothiemurchus
> <u>Memoirs of a Highland Lady</u>, 1797-1827

Game is not an exotic food, or an exclusive delicacy of the rich. First eaten by prehistoric man, whose survival depended on his ability to hunt and catch wild animals, it continued to be eaten throughout the centuries as a central part of the everyday diet of the people.

The association with the aristocracy and landed gentry, which gave it an exclusiveness, came when other animals were domesticated and game meant sport and hunting rather than necessity. In England, game reserves were set up and game laws passed to protect the animals. Laws also applied in Scotland but with so much wild country, game parks with high fences and walls were not practical, and it seems that the common people continued to catch and enjoy what had always been part of their diet. Sir Frederick Eden writing in 1797 on 'The State of the Poor' says that of the opportunities of the Scottish crofter to catch game — 'there is no restraint, but 'tis every man's own that can kill it'.

Today, some of this attitude to natural food supplies in remote areas continues, with owners turning a 'blind eye' to local poaching purely for domestic use. (Commercial poaching, though, is a different and serious problem.)

Game dealers and butchers (there are about two hundred of them in Scotland) now make available a variety of game so that it is not only those who hunt who can enjoy the merits of this rich and varied food supply. According to an economic survey carried out by the Standing Conference on Countryside Sports in the early 1980s — 'Almost half of the annual bag and catch is sold', while the remainder is consumed on the estates. The Director of the Game Conservancy, Richard Van Oss, estimates that of the amount sold, about 80% of venison and 70% of fish and game is exported, which means that most of the game and venison not exported is consumed on estates while only a small percentage (possible 10% of venison and 15% of fish and game) actually reaches the consumer in Scotland.

It provides exciting meat for the cook though, with such a huge range of subtle flavours reflecting the creatures' varied diet and in sharp contrast to the more predictable flavours of domestic meat and poultry. While it lends itself to rich sauces of cream, wine and spirits it is important not to forget that its unique flavour should be allowed to speak for itself. When well cooked and in prime condition it gains nothing from being smothered in competing flavours.

In Scotland there is so much land that is free from urban pollution that the quality and range of game is unrivalled in the rest of Britain and most of the rest of Europe.

Venison

. . . Dined sumptuously upon venison, a piece of Roe, dressed partly in Collops with sauce, and partly on the grid-iron.
Robert Forbes
Diaries 1708-1775

Venison originally meant the flesh of anything which was hunted. It comes from the Latin 'venatio' meaning hunting, and was used for the flesh of hare and rabbit and for other game meats. The change in terminology seems to have been gradual over several centuries until the 19th century when it was exclusively applied to the meat from any kind of deer.

About 40,000 **Red Deer** are sold commercially in Scotland each year to registered game dealers who export about 80% of this to West Germany, which continues to offer the highest price for Scottish venison. The trade with West Germany started in the late 1940s and has grown steadily ever since, with Scottish venison very highly regarded for quality and flavour.

The remaining 20% of venison available is sold through the game dealers, some to other countries besides West Germany, so it is difficult to establish exactly how much venison is eaten in Scotland. Some good game butchers are now marketing it in a much more positive way, providing the housewife with manageable pre-packs of certain cuts and giving valuable information on how to cook. The Red Deer Commission have tried to interest large food manufacturing companies in marketing venison in Scotland, but since venison comprises a mere 1% of the total meat eaten, an expensive advertising campaign is not a commercial proposition. So it seems that, for the moment at any rate, West Germans will continue to eat and enjoy most of our venison.

Roe Deer are sold commercially in much smaller numbers, about 13,000 a year, though this does not include those killed on private shoots which are not sold. There are only a few small herds of Sika Deer and only about 400 a year are sold to dealers, while only 21 Fallow Deer were sold in the year 1982/83. These figures all come from the '82/83 period and are gathered annually by the Red Deer Commission who say that numbers do not vary much from year to year.

Farmed Venison

This is the modern equivalent of the early Deer Parks which controlled stocks and allowed for selective breeding. While there are up to fifty people who keep deer on their farms in Scotland, only a handful of them are actively selling the meat commercially. The herds of deer on these farms are fairly small, the largest is about three hundred, so that while satisfying local needs the impact on the game market of farmed venison is not great. Scottish members of the British Deer Farmers Association, whose Secretary is Martha Crawford of Beauly, sell their venison to the Deer Producers Society who retail it for them, but it is also available at the farms with some of them, like Rediehill in Auchtermuchty, developing a considerable trade for both raw meat and made up sausages, burgers and pies etc.

Like farmed salmon, the meat from farmed deer should not be compared with the wild variety, it is an entirely different product. The main differences are in flavour, almost entirely dependant on feeding but also affected by hanging times and temperatures, and texture which is more tender than the wild. The farmed venison which I have eaten has always been extremely tender,with a more delicate flavour than the wild variety and cooking methods obviously have to be adjusted since heavy rich sauces and strong marinades are unsuitable.

Red Deer

The commonest variety in Scotland inhabits rough wild hill country. A Stag weighs about 14-16 stone (cleaned): Hind $7\frac{1}{2}$-11 stone.

Scottish Season for stags — 1st July-20th October
for hinds — 21st October-15th February
Best time for eating stags — early autumn: for hinds — December to February.

Roe Deer

Inhabits forests, weighs about 4 stone.

Scottish Season for bucks — 1st May-20th October
for does — 21st October-28/29th February
Best time for eating bucks — October: for does — December to February.

Fallow Deer

Inhabits forests and parklands, weighs about 12 stone.
Scottish Season for bucks — 1st August-30th April
                    for does — 21st October-15th February
Best time for eating bucks — October to November: for does —
December to February.

Sika Deer

Stag weighs 6-7 stone: Hind $4\frac{1}{2}$-5 stone.
Scottish Season for stags — 1st August-30th April
                    for hinds — 21st October-15th February

Buying

The lean meat should be dark red and close grained, the fat should be
firm and white. The **Haunch** or **Leg** is a prime cut for roasting or slicing
into collops (steaks). The **Saddle** is also a prime cut for roasting and it
includes the fillets. The ribs may be divided into loin chops for frying or
grilling. The **Flank** may be boiled or stewed or minced for sausages. The
Shoulder may be cut up and stewed or braised in a piece. **The Neck** may
be stewed or boiled for soup. The **Head** may be used for broth. A good
Liver is a great delicacy and can be fried or used for a venison haggis
along with the **Heart**, and flank. **Kidneys** may be fried. Venison **Tripe** has
a very good flavour but must be removed from the animal and washed
out thoroughly within half an hour of killing, otherwise the stomach
continues to digest the contents and the flavour of the tripe is spoiled.
This can be difficult if the beast has been shot on top of a mountain —
farmed deer do not cause the same problem.

Age and hanging time greatly affect venison meat. Older animals will
be tough, sometimes very tough, and possibly also dry, and should be
braised or stewed rather than roasted. The person who butchers the deer
will know exactly the likely tenderness of the meat by signs of age on the
animal. If you only have the joint to go by, it is possible to tell by the
development of the muscles, and the size, also the fat on a younger beast
is whiter. But these are all tests which you will only learn by experience.
If in doubt, play safe and braise rather than roast.

To develop a good gamey flavour the animal should be hung for at
least two weeks — in hot humid weather this may be shorter while in
cold dry weather, longer.

BRAISED SHOULDER OR HAUNCH OF RED DEER with Sloe Gin

The taste and aroma of sloes, juniper and gamey wild venison combine
with admirable results. The sloe gin was not a sweet one — I have also
made it with ordinary gin and some port. The idea of using gin comes

from the Germans, who are well practised at cooking venison, one of their favourite meats.

4 lb/2 kg shoulder or haunch, boned and rolled
2 medium onions, finely chopped
2 rashers bacon
2 sticks celery, diced
1 tablespoon crushed juniper berries
¼ pt/150 ml sloe gin (¾ c)
1 cup sloes from the gin
2 tablespoons oil
Salt and freshly ground black pepper
Pre-heat the oven to 300F/150C/Gas 2.

Browning the meat and vegetables

Melt the oil in a heavy pan which will go into the oven and which will contain the meat snugly. Put in the meat and brown it on all sides. Remove. Add the onions, celery and bacon and cook till a light brown colour. Add the juniper, sloe gin and sloes, scrape up the pan residues and then put the browned meat on top.

Cooking the meat

Sprinkle the meat with salt and add enough water or stock to come half-way up the meat. Set the pan over a high heat till the liquid comes to the boil. Cover with a buttered paper and then a tight fitting lid. If necessary put a layer of foil under the lid, twisting it down the sides of the pot to ensure that moisture does not escape. Put into the oven and cook for about 2 hours, testing for tenderness after an hour and a half.

Finishing the dish

Remove the meat to a baking dish and keep warm. Strain the cooking liquid into a wide pan. I worked with a chef once who reduced all his sauces in a large frying pan. It is a good idea since the greater the surface area the faster the reduction. Reduce to a syrupy consistency — it should be a rich mahogany colour by now. Taste for seasoning. Remove the string from the meat and pour the sauce over it.

Carve the venison into thick slices and serve with broccoli, new potatoes, some Spiced Damsons (see p. 236) and a robust red wine.

ROAST SADDLE OF VENISON with brandy and claret sauce

6-8
servings

The important thing in roasting venison is to make sure that it has enough fat/oil basting it during the cooking time. I do not find it necessary to either marinade or lard cuts of venison for roasting which are from prime young animals. If it needs either of these treatments, then it ought not to be roasted but cooked by some moist method which will prevent it drying out and at the same time tenderise it. It will then have plenty of time to absorb the flavours from wine during the longer cooking time.

The saddle is the part that lies between the top of the hind legs and the first ribs. Roasting on the bone protects the meat, prevents it drying out and improves the flavour.

4 lb/2 kg saddle of young venison
3 tablespoons olive oil
2 oz/50 g butter ($\frac{1}{2}$ stick)
3 tablespoons brandy
5 tablespoons claret
$\frac{1}{4}$ pt/150 ml game stock ($\frac{3}{4}$ c)
Salt and freshly ground pepper
Pre-heat the oven 450F/230C/Gas 8.

Preparing the meat

Place the saddle, back uppermost, on a board and starting at one side of the flank loosen the tough layer of fat and pull back towards the spine. When you reach the spine on one side free the fat from the other and then cut away the whole sheet of fat from the backbone. Now slide a very sharp knife under the tough membrane which covers the muscle and pare away carefully, trying not to cut the meat unnecessarily. Put the meat in a dish and rub in olive oil to all surfaces. Grind some black pepper on top.

Roasting

Weigh the saddle and allow a roasting time of 15 minutes per pound (500 g) for underdone pink meat. Heat the butter in a roasting tin and put in the saddle. Turn it in the butter and cook, basting frequently. Remove and keep warm on heated ashet covered with some buttered greaseproof paper or foil.

Making the sauce

Drain off the excess fat from the pan, add the brandy and then the claret, scraping up all the residues from the pan and simmering to reduce and concentrate the flavours. Now add the stock and continue reducing, stirring all the time. Some juices will, by now, have dripped out of the saddle and they should be poured into the sauce. When the sauce has a good consistency and flavour, season with salt.

Carving and Serving

Carve down the centre back on either side of the bone, keeping close into the bone. Then, holding the knife parallel with the board, take thin slices of meat with the grain making slices into long strips. Continue to carve horizontally on both sides. Turn the saddle over and slice out the small fillets — carve at a slant across the grain to give thin escallops. Slice the flank pieces into neat strips and arrange pieces of each type meat on each plate.* Serve with the sauce and some Rowan Jelly.

*Serve on very hot plates since venison fat congeals at a higher temperature than other fats and if you have been eating or drinking something cold previously, the fat may actually congeal in your mouth with less than delicious results.

VENISON COLLOPS with lemon and port

A tender, young haunch of venison is essential for this very old Scottish way of serving venison. Red Deer from Scottish moors have a special flavour, dependent on the heather and other plants which they eat. Deer from Rannoch Moor, one of the wildest and most desolate parts of the Highlands, were used for this recipe which I first tasted at the Moor of Rannoch Hotel in Perthshire. It is a much simplified version of Venison Collops. Mrs McLintock's recipe (1736) called for 62 shelled oysters for the sauce along with some red wine. The meat was coated in lemon, mace and nutmeg flavoured breadcrumbs, and fried.

In this recipe the collops are quickly grilled with lemon and port poured over just before serving. A good method for tender farmed venison.

4 × 6 oz/175 g $\frac{1}{2}$" (1 cm) thick steaks cut from a boned haunch
2 oz/50 g melted butter ($\frac{1}{4}$ stick)
   or 4 tablespoons olive oil
Salt and freshly ground black pepper
Juice of 1 lemon
4 tablespoons port
Brush steak with butter or soak in oil for an hour before grilling. Season with salt, pepper and a few drops of lemon juice and place in a baking tray under a very hot grill. Cook both sides, basting and turning frequently, about five minutes each side. Just before serving pour over port and return to the grill for a minute. Serve with the juices poured over and some Red Currant or Rowan Jelly.

May also be served with Raisin Chutney (see p. 238).

VENISON PASTY with claret or port

6 servings

A modern pasty is made of what does not roast well. as the neck. the breast. the shoulder. The breast makes the best pasty.

Meg Dods
Cook and Housewives Manual. 1826

Some people use pork fat with venison but I have always followed Meg Dods' recommendation and used lamb or mutton fat, mainly because I think the lamb improves the flavour. Mutton, if you can get it, would be even better. On the question of marinading meat she says — 'Some cooks marinade the meat in the wine and other seasonings for a night, or for some hours previous to baking. This, no doubt, imbues the venison with the flavour of the seasonings, but at the same time drains off the juices, and hurts the natural flavour of the meat, so that we discountenance the practice.'

3 lb/1$\frac{1}{2}$ kg neck, breast or shoulder

$\frac{1}{2}$ lb/250 g firm fat from the neck or leg of lamb or mutton
2 onions, finely chopped
2 tablespoons oil
Salt, freshly ground pepper
$\frac{1}{2}$ teaspoon ground mace
$\frac{1}{2}$ teaspoon ground allspice
$\frac{1}{4}$ pt/150 ml good venison stock ($\frac{3}{4}$ c)
$\frac{1}{4}$ pt/150 ml claret or port ($\frac{3}{4}$ c)
2 tablespoons wine vinegar
8 oz/250 g puff pastry
For brushing — 1 egg yolk, 1 teaspoon water
Pre-heat the oven to 400F/200C/Gas 6 for the first 20 minutes.
Then turn down oven and cook for a further 80 minutes at
325F/170C/Gas 3.

Cooking the meat

Heat the oil in a stewpan and brown the onions. Add the meat and
brown lightly. Mix in the seasonings then the stock, claret or port
and vinegar. Pour into an oval 2$\frac{1}{2}$ pt/1$\frac{1}{4}$ L pie dish. Season and leave
to cool slightly.

Making the pastry

Place a pie funnel in the centre of the dish. Roll out the pastry about
1″ (2.5 cm) wider than the rim of the dish. Place dish on top of
pastry and cut round. Use extra strip for round the rim of the pie
dish. Wet the pie dish edge well and press on. Wet pastry edge and
put pastry on top. Press down well to seal the edge. Decorate the
edge and also the top of the pastry with scraps. Make two holes for
steam to escape. Brush with egg yolk and bake.

VENISON LIVER

An old keeper friend, Peter MacIntosh, was well practised in cooking
liver since the innards are always the keeper's perk. He only fried the very
best liver (the quality of the liver is a good guide to the health of the animal and must be inspected by a vet before export). His test of quality was
to put first finger and thumb on either side of the liver and press
together. If there was a lot of resistance then the liver was too old and
tough, but if your finger and thumb came together easily then it was
good for frying. This is Peter's way of cooking. His timing was always
excellent and the liver served up just pink in the middle and well
browned and crisp on the outside. He ate it with oatcakes and butter,
usually for high tea or for breakfast with crisp fried bacon.

4 rashers of bacon
4 slices venison liver about $\frac{1}{2}$″ (2.5 cm)
3 tablespoons milk
1 tablespoon seasoned flour
Put the bacon into a hot pan and fry till crisp. Remove and keep
warm. Meanwhile soak the liver in milk for a few minutes then coat
in seasoned flour. Fry in hot bacon fat very quickly.

VENISON TRIPE (Pocha Buidh — Yellow Bag)

This is another of Peter's specialities and, along with venison liver, one of the great eating experiences associated with venison.

The tripe should be cleaned (see p. 104) then soaked for 24 hours in cold salted water. Rinse out thoroughly and then simmer for 6-8 hours in plenty of water. Drain and cut into squares. Fry about 4-5 medium onions, finely sliced, in 4 oz/125 g butter (1 stick) till soft and yellow. Add 4 oz/125 g flour (1 c) and cook for a few minutes. Gradually add 2 pt/1 L milk (5 c), then the tripe and seasoning, and simmer for about an hour, adding more milk if necessary. Serve with hot toast.

Red Grouse (Lagopus Scoticus)

Red grouse live on the high heather moors eating, besides heather, a number of other herbs and grasses which give them a very special flavour. Native to these wild Scottish moors, they do not survive well in other lands.

Also in the grouse family, though less well known, are the Black Grouse (Blackcock); Wood or Great Grouse (Capercaillie) and the White Grouse (Ptarmigan).

Season — 12th August to 10th December.

Judging age

One method is to look at the two outer primary feathers. If the bird is young they will be pointed, whereas old birds have more rounded, tattered and sometimes faded feathers.

Another method which is recommended by the Game Conservancy is the Bursa test. The Bursa is a blind-ended passage on the upper side of the vent. In all young game birds it becomes much reduced or may close completely when the bird reaches sexual maturity. The presence of a normal Bursa is a certain test for a young bird. Insert a matchstick which is burnt at one end, so that it is narrow but not too sharp, or a quill.

Yet another guide is to look at the claws. Adult grouse shed their nails between July and September so that if a nail is in the process of shedding then it is an old bird. If it has already been shed there may be a transverse ridge where the old nail was attached, which again indicates an old bird though this may fade after a month or two.

Hanging

Young birds can be shot and eaten the same day (as they always are at the opening of the grouse season on the Glorious Twelfth). They should not be hung for more than 2-4 days, depending on temperature and humidity. Their flavour is spoiled if they become too gamey.

ROAST YOUNG GROUSE

4 servings

> **4 young grouse**
> **8 slices of fat bacon or piece of pork fat**
> **2 tablespoons oil**
> **4 oz/125 g softened butter (1 stick)**
> **Salt and pepper**
> Pre-heat the oven to 450F/230C/Gas 8.

Preparing the grouse

Divide the butter into four pieces and insert into each bird. Lay the pieces of bacon or pork fat on the breasts and truss the bird with a needle and string, securing the fat in the process.

Roasting

Heat the oil in a roasting tin and when hot, add the birds, turning them to coat thoroughly. Roast for about 15 minutes. Remove the birds from the oven, cut the trussing strings and remove the fat. Return to the oven for about 10 minutes to brown the breast.

Serving

Grouse is usually served on a round or square of bread sometimes spread with a liver paste (the grouse liver may be used or other livers). Meg Dods serves her grouse on 'buttered toast soaked in the dripping pan' and recommends that the toast is first sprinkled with a little lemon juice. However you decide to serve, the bread under the bird is a good idea since it catches the natural juices which continue to drip out of the meat.

Grouse legs which have been roasted tend to have a bitter flavour which spoils the more delicately flavoured breast and so they are often removed (not essential) after roasting and used in other ways, in pies, stews and stocks where longer cooking moderates the bitterness. To remove the legs, open up the bird cavity and cut with a sharp heavy knife through the backbone behind the legs so that they are still joined together by the backbone when removed. Place the trimmed birds on a serving dish and garnish with watercress.

GROUSE SOUP

6-8 servings

> But, oh! my dear North, what grouse-soup at Dalnacardoch.
> You smell it on the homeward hill, as if it were exhaling from the
> heather. . . . As you enter the inn the divine afflatus pene-
> trates your soul. When upstairs, perhaps in the garret, adorn-
> ing for dinner, it rises like a cloud of rich distilled perfumes
> through every chink on the floor, every cranny of the wall.
>
> Christopher North
> Noctes Ambrosianae, 1822-35

I make this with the debris from roast grouse legs, etc. or with older
birds. The same method can obviously be used for other game birds,
singly or in combinations. It is easily the best way to extract every last
ounce of flavour from game bones and meat.

Making the stock

3 grouse (or the bones and legs from 4-6)
4 pts/2 L water or poultry stock (5 c)
6 crushed juniper berries
Bundle of fresh herbs including parsley
2 sticks of celery

Remove the breast meat from the grouse if using whole birds. Put
them into a pan, cover with water/stock and add herbs and celery.
Bring to the boil, cover and simmer gently for at least 1 hour, 2 if
possible. Strain, leave to cool and skim off any excess fat. Remove
any edible meat from the carcasses and chop finely for adding to the
broth at the end. Discard the carcasses.

Finishing the soup

2 tablespoons oil*
1 oz/25 g butter (1 tablespoon)
2 rashers of bacon, finely chopped
2 medium onions, finely chopped
4 stalks celery, finely diced
4 shallots, finely chopped
2 tablespoons long grain polished rice, washed and drained

Melt the oil and butter and begin by sautéing the onions and bacon.
When the onions are soft and yellow and the bacon just crisp, add
the other vegetables and the rice. The grouse breast meat, chopped
finely, may be added at this point or it may be kept for a separate
dish. Cover and sweat over a very low heat for ten minutes, checking
that it is not burning.

Add the strained stock, bring to the boil and simmer until the
vegetables are just tender and the rice cooked. If there is any other

*Or use some of the excess fat from the stock — it will have much more flavour than oil.

edible grouse meat from the carcasses, chop finely and add at this point. Taste for seasoning and add parsley. Serve with boiled potatoes.

Pheasant

It was called the Phasian Bird when it lived beside the river Phasis in Greece, but the Greeks took it to Rome and the Romans took it with them as their empire expanded and eventually it arrived in Britain — the Pheasant. It doesn't frequent the high moorland or eat very much heather so its flavour is milder and less distinctive than grouse. Nevertheless if well hung it has a pleasantly mild gamey flavour which is actually much stronger when eaten cold. It is cheapest to buy during the height of the season and is more generally available than grouse.

Season — 1st October to 1st February.

Judging age

The Bursa test (p. 110) can be applied to both the cock and hen bird. In young birds the Bursa will be approximately 1″ (2 cm). In old birds it may be closed completely.

Hanging

Pheasant should be hung by the head and the time will depend on your own taste, the age of the bird and also the weather. I find pheasant which has not been hung long, lacking in flavour but that is a matter of taste and mainly because most of my early pheasant training was with a cook who never cooked pheasant till the body was just about to separate from the head. These were usually quite mature birds which needed the long hanging (at least two weeks) to tenderise them and develop the rich gamey flavour which I associate with pheasant.

ROAST PHEASANT with fresh herbs

2-3 servings

The secret of keeping this dry bird moist and succulent is to roast quickly and keep turning the bird so that it self-bastes. Most of the roasting time should be on its breast so that the juices are running into it, rather than out. Ideally it should be roasted on a spit. All problems of basting and turning, particularly these smaller birds which dry out so quickly, vanish if you are lucky enough to have one, while the results are the best ever.

1 × 2½-3 lb/1¼-1½ kg young pheasant, hung for 4-5 days
4 oz/125 g butter (1 stick)
4 large sprigs of parsley
4 sprigs of fresh tarragon (2 teaspoons dried)
Sheet of fresh pork fat for barding or 2 rashers of bacon
Pre-heat the oven to 375F/190C/Gas 5.

Preparing the bird

Put two sprigs of parsley and two of tarragon in the cavity with about half of the butter. Spread the remaining butter over the breast. Put the remaining herbs on top and cover with pork fat. Truss with a needle and string, tying on the pork fat well.

Roasting

Put the pheasant on its side on a rack in a shallow roasting tin and roast for 10 minutes. Turn onto other side, baste and roast for another 10 minutes. Now turn onto its breast, baste and roast for about 20 minutes. Remove from the oven, take off the barding fat and return to the oven for another 5 minutes to brown the skin. It should take about 45 minutes in all. To test the pheasant for doneness, pierce the meat near the thigh and leg joint. If the juices which run out are pale pink the bird will be juicy but slightly underdone. If the juices are clear then it is thoroughly done. This may take up to an hour, so be prepared to continue with the basting since the breast meat loses its juices very quickly if overcooked. Serve with a gravy made from a reduction of the pan juices and a little chicken stock or water and with some oyster mushrooms (ordinary ones will do if they are not available) sliced, sautéed in butter and garnished with chopped parsley and tarragon.

BRAISED PHEASANT with whisky and juniper

2 servings

This is a recipe for a mature well hung bird. I use a well flavoured malt, most recently Auchentoshan, with excellent results, but other malts and blends will all add the essence of their own distinctive flavours.

$1 \times 2\frac{1}{2}$ lb/$1\frac{1}{4}$ kg pheasant
2 tablespoons oil or butter
1 medium onion, finely chopped
$\frac{1}{4}$ pt/150 ml game stock or water ($\frac{3}{4}$ c)
1 tablespoon juniper berries
4 fl oz/150 ml whisky ($\frac{1}{2}$ c)
4 fl oz/150 ml whipping cream ($\frac{1}{2}$ c)
1 teaspoon lemon juice
Salt and pepper
Pre-heat the oven to 375F/190C/Gas 5.

Braising the bird

Melt the fat in a cast iron enamelled casserole and brown the pheasant on all sides. Remove and add onions and cook till golden brown. Return the pheasant to the pan and pour over half the whisky. Flame, and when the flames die down, add stock and juniper berries. Cover well, and bake in the oven for 45 minutes or until tender. It could take up to an hour depending on the age of the bird. Remove the bird and cut into 4 joints (2 legs and 2 breasts).

Finishing the dish

Keep the joints warm and covered in their serving dish while finishing the sauce. Strain the sauce and then return to the pan. Now add the remaining whisky, cream and lemon juice and reduce to a good consistency. Taste for seasoning and serve round the pheasant.

Hare

Not so highly regarded as a game meat, Scottish hares are more often of the Blue variety and tend to have exercised well on the mountains. Their flesh needs a long slow wet method of cooking which allows their rich flavour to develop to its full potential. Hare is available in season from good game butchers or dealers.

Season — no close season but may not be sold March to July inclusive. The best time for eating is October to January.

Judging age

A young hare will have soft thin ears which tear easily and white sharp teeth whereas an older hare will have tougher ears and larger, yellower teeth. The coat of an older hare will be rougher.

Types

Brown Hare — weighs up to 7 lb/3 kg. **Mountain Hare** or **Blue Hare** — weighs between 5-6 lb/2-2.4 kg. It has the same open season as the Brown hare but it is not suitable for roasting and should be stewed or braised or made into soup.

Hanging

Hares should be hung head downwards, ungutted, for 1-2 weeks, again depending on the weather, taste and toughness of the hare. Place a bowl with a teaspoon of vinegar in it (this stops the blood congealing) underneath the head to catch the blood.

Skinning

Make a circular cut through the fur just above the back heel joints. Make a lengthwise cut along the inside of the leg on both sides and pull the skin off both legs. Tie the paws together and hang up somewhere. This is not essential but makes the skinning job easier and means that the blood is collecting at the top end and is therefore less likely to spill out all over the place when the belly is opened up.

Make a slit at the base of the tail from the top of one hind leg to the top of the other. Peel the skin back gently, turning it inside out and leaving the tail attached to the body. Now peel the skin down over the body and forelegs to the shoulders. Make a circular cut through the fur on the front legs just above the paws and then slit the skin along the inside of the leg. Peel back the skin on both legs. Peel the skin from the neck and then over the head as far as the ears, cut off the ears at their base and pull away the rest of the skin. It may be necessary to loosen round the eyes and mouth.

Lay the hare on its back and with a very sharp knife open up the belly. Draw out and discard all the intestines leaving the liver, heart, lungs and kidneys. Now take out the kidneys; remove the liver carefully, remove the gall bladder and discard. Put the liver into a bowl with 1 teaspoon of vinegar. Position the bowl underneath the body and make a slit in the diaphragm at the base of the chest and allow the blood to run out. When you have collected the blood, pull out the heart and lungs and place in the bowl.

BAWD BREE

A mature, well hung hare is essential for this traditional soup/stew or 'mouthful soup'. It is aptly described in <u>The Household Book of Lady Grisell Baillie (1692-1733)</u> among her menus as — 'Hare soup with Hares in it'. 'Bawd' is the old Scots word for hare and 'Bree' simply means gravy, juice or liquid in which something is cooked.

3-4 qt/3-4 L cold water
1 hare
Bundle of fresh herbs
4 sticks celery, chopped
3 carrots, diced
1 small piece turnip, diced
1 large onion, finely chopped
2 tablespoons flour

2 tablespoons butter or oil
3-4 tablespoons port
Salt and freshly ground black pepper

Preparing the hare

Skin and clean reserving the blood, liver, heart, kidneys.
Remove the fleshy pieces from the back and legs and cut into neat
pieces. Place the remainder of the carcass in the cold water and leave
overnight.

Making the stock

Bring the carcass and water to the boil, skim and then add the
herbs. Simmer for 1 hour and then add the vegetables. Cook for
another hour. Strain and remove the vegetables. They may be diced
or sieved into the stock.

Finishing the dish

Flour the hare flesh. Slice the kidneys and heart and flour. Melt
butter in a pan and fry till lightly browned. Add to the stock and
simmer gently till the meat is tender. Add diced vegetables and any
edible carcass meat.

Press the liver through a sieve and mix with the blood. Mix the
blood/liver which has had vinegar added at the cleaning out stage,
with the remaining flour and gradually add some of the hot cooking
liquid. Pour back into the pan and heat through to thicken. It
should not boil. Add the port. Taste for seasoning. Serve in wide
deep soup plates with a boiled mealy potato in the centre of the
plate and Rowan Jelly on top.

Rabbit

Rabbits were widely eaten in Scotland before myxomatosis. Today, good
well-flavoured rabbits are available and are sometimes a more interesting flavour than some modern chicken. They are best eaten fresh
though they can be hung. They should be skinned first (see instructions
for Hare p. 116).

Buying

Look for soft ears and sharp teeth which indicate a young rabbit. They
should be plump with a smooth fur. There is no close season. They can
weigh from 1-3 lb ($\frac{1}{2}$-1$\frac{1}{2}$ kg) — 2 small or 1 large for 4 servings.

RABBIT WITH ONIONS

4 servings

Lowland Scots ate more rabbit than Highlanders and the most popular
way of cooking was with onions. They also made potted rabbit using the
same method as for potted hough and including hough with the rabbit.
They roasted young rabbit; made a minced rabbit which was sometimes

shaped into a meat roll with pork and onions; made soup with it and also pies.

Rabbits were cheap and plentiful since they were always making a nuisance of themselves by eating crops. When my father worked on a farm in an Angus glen, his first job in the morning was to go round the rabbit snares. On his return for breakfast the farmer's wife, Elsie Mac-Lean, was daily presented with an armful of rabbits which constantly stretched her culinary imagination. This is Elsie's way with rabbit and onions.

1 rabbit, skinned, cleaned and jointed
Seasoned flour
Roast dripping
1 medium onion
Salt and pepper

Melt the dripping in a pan and brown the onions. Coat the rabbit with flour. Brown the rabbit well. Add seasoning and enough water to cover. Simmer gently for 1-1½ hours or until the rabbit is tender. Taste for seasoning and serve.

HONEYED RABBIT

3-4 servings

Heather honey, tomatoes and a hint of garlic lift this rabbit stew out of the ordinary.

For the sauce

1 medium onion, finely chopped
3 tablespoons oil
1½ lb/¾ kg tomatoes, skinned and chopped
4 tablespoons milk
4 tablespoons heather honey

Heat the oil in a pan and add the onion, cook till soft without colouring then add the tomatoes, milk and honey and simmer to reduce. When it is a good thick consistency, add 1 clove of crushed garlic, salt and pepper to taste.

Finishing the dish

2 oz/50 g flour (½ c)
1 rabbit, cleaned and jointed
4 tablespoons oil
Salt and pepper

Heat the oil in a pan and dip the rabbit joints into the tomato sauce (this helps to make more flour stick and gives a better crust) then into the flour. Brown the rabbit in the oil on all sides and then add the sauce. The liquid should almost cover the rabbit. Cover with a lid and simmer gently till tender, adding more stock or water if necessary. Taste for seasoning and sprinkle over plenty of chopped parsley before serving.

RICH GAME STEW garnished with brambles and Choux Pastry

4 servings

I first met the combination of Game and Choux pastry when Peter Fulton, a New Zealander with a great flair for utilising Scottish natural resources in an original and imaginative way, won a gold medal at a Salon Culinaire for his **Amulree Grouse**. The grouse was roasted with a stuffing of brambles* which had been soaked in whisky and then served with choux pastry nests, made in fluted patty tins, the hollowed out centres filled with whisky-marinaded brambles. From a more practical point of view, anyone who has cooked in a sporting area will appreciate that game meat is much more frequently old and tough rather than of the young roasting variety, and the challenge is to turn it into something delicious.

At the Log Cabin Hotel in Kirkmichael, high on the grouse and venison moors of Perthshire, Elizabeth Sandell has many years of experience — 'making delicious meals out of old boots. The secret,' she claims, 'is to give the said footwear a long soak in a well flavoured marinade of oil, wine, vinegar, chopped onions, celery, carrot, bay leaf, rosemary, garlic, fresh black peppers, salt and crushed juniper berries'. She uses this for more than one marinading process, then finally it forms the liquid base for casseroling venison, old grouse, pheasant, partridge, hare, rabbit, pigeon and wild duck.

To make the Choux Pastry

$\frac{1}{4}$ pt/150 ml water ($\frac{3}{4}$ c scant)
2 oz/50 g butter ($\frac{1}{2}$ stick)
$2\frac{1}{2}$ oz/65 g plain flour ($\frac{1}{2}$ c generous)
2 medium eggs
Salt and cayenne pepper

Pre-heat the oven to 400F/200C/Gas 6.
Bring the butter and water to boil in a pan. Draw off the heat and quickly tip in the sifted flour and seasoning. Stir vigorously till the mixture comes away from the sides of the pan. Beat the eggs in one at a time till the mixture is smooth and shiny. (This can also be done in a processor. Put the flour and seasoning into bowl and switch on adding the liquid in a steady stream through the feed tube until a smooth dough is formed. With the machine still on, drop in eggs one at a time.)

To make the stew

2 lb/1 kg game meat, cut in roughly 1" (2 cm) squares
$\frac{1}{2}$ pt/300 ml strained marinade ($1\frac{1}{4}$ c)
$\frac{1}{2}$ pt/300 ml game stock made with the carcasses ($1\frac{1}{4}$ c) (see p. 112)
2 tablespoons Redcurrant, Rowan or Crab Apple Jelly
2 tablespoons port
2 tablespoons claret
Salt and pepper

*Blackberries

Put the meat, marinade and stock into a pan and cook till the meat is tender. Strain off liquid and put the meat into a shallow gratin dish. Cover and keep warm while finishing the sauce. Add port and claret and reduce to a good consistency. Finally add enough of the jelly to give a slightly sweetish flavour. Some jellies are much sweeter than others so add gradually, tasting as you go. Season and pour over meat.

Finishing the dish

Pipe or spoon the pastry round the edge of the dish, sprinkle browned crumbs over the stew and bake for about 20 minutes or until the pastry is crisp and well risen. Serve with a thick sprinkling of chopped parsley and some brambles.

Other Scottish Game

Seasons and sizes supplied by the Game Conservancy, Fordingbridge, Hampshire. *All dates inclusive.*

Duck

MALLARD $2\frac{1}{2}$-$2\frac{3}{4}$ lb (1.1-1.3 kg), 2-3 servings. Season — below high tide mark, 1st September to 20th February. Elsewhere — 1st September to 31st January.
TEAL 11-13 oz (300-370 g), 1 serving. Season — as for Mallard.
WIDGEON $1\frac{1}{2}$-2 lb (700-900 g), 2 servings. Season — as for Mallard.

Goose

PINK-FOOTED 6-7 lb (2.7-3.2 kg), 6 servings. Season — as for Mallard.
GREYLAG 8-10 lb (3.7-5 kg), 6 servings. Season — as for Mallard.

WOODPIGEON 1-$1\frac{1}{4}$ lb (500-600 g), 1 serving. No close season.
BLACKGAME 3-4 lb (1.4-1.8 kg), 3 servings. Season — 20th August to 10th December.
PTARMIGAN 1-$1\frac{1}{4}$ lb (400-600 g), 1 serving. Season (Scotland only) — 12th August to 10th December.
CAPERCAILLIE 6-12 lb (2.7-5.5 kg), 1 serving. Season — 1st October to 31st January.
PARTRIDGE Cock 13-15 oz (350-450 g); Hen $12\frac{1}{2}$-$14\frac{1}{2}$ oz (400 g), 1-2 servings. Season — 1st September to 1st February.
COMMON SNIPE $3\frac{1}{2}$-$4\frac{1}{2}$ oz (100-130 g), 1-2 per person. Season — 12th August to 31st January.
WOODCOCK 8-14 oz (230-400 g), 1 serving. Season — 1st September to 31st January.

CHAPTER FIVE

BEEF & LAMB

Beef

Scotland's hill and upland farms provide ideal breeding grounds for beef cattle and sheep that come to maturity on the lush pastures of the Scottish lowlands.

Scotch Quality Beef and Lamb Association

Cattle ran wild, like game, in the forests and hills of Britain seven hundred years ago, give or take a century. Six wild bulls are mentioned in the feast given when George Neville was installed as Archbishop of York in 1466 and according to C. Ann Wilson writing in <u>Food and Drink in Britain</u>, 1973, 'by Elizabeth's reign forest cattle had retreated from lowland Britain but were still to be found in the remote parts of Wales and Scotland.'

The history of cattle in Scotland from then to the present-day is an astonishing one. Firstly domesticated, they then became an important part of the Highland economy in Scotland, with thousands sent yearly to markets in the South along ancient drove roads until the '45 Rebellion; the Clearances and the introduction of steam ships and railways put an end to this tradition.

Early in the 19th century, cattle were mostly replaced by sheep in the Highlands, but in the North East some enterprising Scottish farmers, who knew a good thing when they saw it, began the process of moulding together the most valuable characteristics from the native black-polled variety. From the obscurity of the hills and glens of North East Scotland they produced a breed of cattle, in the space of a hundred years, which has become the supreme beef breed throughout the world — Aberdeen Angus.

Three men were principally responsible — Hugh Watson (1780-1865) of Keillor in Angus; William McCombie (1805-1880) of Tillyfour in Aberdeenshire and Sir George Macpherson Grant (1839-1907) of Ballindalloch in Banffshire. Being practical Scotsmen, they kept a sharp eye on the utilitarian qualities, while they were building up their families of cattle. Hardiness was important, so also the ability of the cattle to convert simple rations into high quality, well-flavoured beef more efficiently than other breeds. Other plusses which they appreciated were the fact that it was an advantage to have an early maturing breed and also a carcass which has a well marled flesh and firm white fat.

And so the pioneering work of these early producers of the Aberdeen Angus breed is continued by the modern Scottish farmer who has inherited the skills of animal husbandry from his forefathers. He aims, through the introduction of new breeds and blood lines, to produce the high quality meat that is in demand, always taking into account the needs of the consumers who at present are looking for a much leaner meat than they did twenty years ago. More muscle and less fat is the cry, and breeders have taken up the challenge.

The beef-breeding herd in Scotland, of nearly half a million, is largely composed of cross-bred animals of the five native breeds. Until recently these cows were mated with Aberdeen Angus, Shorthorn and Hereford bulls, but in the 1960s continental breeds were introduced with a leaner fleshier carcass, initially the Charolais but later the Simmental and Limousin, and breeders now cross them with native breeds to produce the leaner less fatty meat which is more in demand. These continental breeds are now well established in Scotland. Because they have been crossed with native breeds and because they have been fed differently, they no longer taste or even look like their continental counterparts.

Qualities of the other four native breeds besides Aberdeen Angus have been significant in this cross-breeding process which will continue to play an important part in the search for quality. The variously-coloured Shorthorn, prized for its robustness and beef quality and noted particularly for its ability to improve the poorer breed by crossing; the Galloway, of slower growth, but hardy; the Luing breed, officially recognised in 1966, and noted for producing good beef in the poor, wet conditions of the North West; and the picturesque Highland cattle renowned for their hardiness.

At present Scotland produces more than one third of the total beef produced in Britain, and between one fifth and a quarter of the beef produced in Scotland is exported. A large quantity goes to the London market, and the remainder overseas to many of the leading hotels in Europe — some as far afield as Saudi Arabia.

Cuts of Beef

Variations in cuts of meat from one part of the country to another are so complicated that it is possible to find 27 different names for the same cut — there are even variations in Glasgow between one side of the city and another. The simplest solution is — when in doubt, consult the butcher. Tell him how you want to cook the meat and he will advise the best cuts.

BOILED BEEF

This universal dish has many variations around the world from the sophisticated Austrian Tafelspitz, made with sirloin and served with chive mayonnaise and apple purée mixed with grated horseradish; to the more ordinary English Boiled Beef and Carrots.

Combining soup and meat courses in one pot is central to the Scottish culinary tradition. A North East farmer's daughter, Ethel McCurrach, recalls how on Sundays 'a 14 pint pot was used, that meant there was enough for Monday (Yavils)* and Tuesdays (Ley)*, as well as half a turnip plus a few carrots as well as the beef. Now if a dumpling was needed for the dinner (12 noon) it was tied in a cloth and boiled in amongst the broth, if not a mealie pudding mixture was tied tightly in a cloth and boiled amongst the broth. All that was then needed to finish off a full three course meal was a pot of boiled potatoes. Two pots for a three course meal that would last three days — it would be a 'pot man's' dream in a hotel kitchen today.'

In the North East the meat was usually removed from the pot and served first while hot. It was sliced by the master of the house. Farm servants didn't seem to have knives or forks. They ate the meat with their fingers, taking pieces from the central platter. Then the broth was served into wooden bowls and they supped it with their horn spoons.

For boiling a whole piece of beef

8-10 servings

Use a pot which will hold the beef and vegetables neatly. It is important not to have too large a pot with too much water since the flavour of both vegetables and meat will end up diluted in the liquid.

4-5 lb beef brisket, nineholes, silverside or hough
Cold water to cover
1 onion stuck with cloves
1 bay leaf
1 stick celery, cut in four
1½ tablespoon salt
1 teaspoon freshly ground pepper
1 teaspoon rosemary
6 carrots
1 large turnip
1 leek
12 even-sized potatoes, washed but unpeeled

Place the meat in a very large pot, cover with cold water and bring to the boil. Remove the scum. Add onion, bay leaf, celery and leek. Add salt, pepper and rosemary. Cover and simmer until the meat is just tender — approximately 1-2 hours depending on toughness of meat. Add carrots and turnips and cook for about 25 minutes till tender. Boil potatoes separately.

*Refers to the farming system of 2nd and 3rd year corn rotation.

To serve

Arrange the meat on a large ashet and carve in fairly thick slices. Surround with vegetables and pour a little of the broth on the meat to keep it well moistened. Give each person a cup of broth. Serve with Mustard (p. 238), Apple chutney (p. 237) or any other sharp pickles and some coarse salt.

Dumplings

These may be added to the pot about 20 minutes before serving.

Mix together

4 oz/125 g plain flour (1 c)
2 oz/50 g shredded suet
1 teaspoon baking powder
Cold water to mix
Salt and pepper

Drop in spoonfuls on top of meat and vegetables, cover and simmer gently till they are well risen.

For boiling pieces of beef

8-10 servings

This is Geordie Kelly's 'b'il't' beef'. He was the Scots/Irish cook on the 'Clara', a coal-carrying puffer sailing the Hebridean coasts in the 1920s. His recipe is described by Victor MacClure, who sat in the galley with him shelling peas and scrubbing carrots while gazing out to the islands of Colonsay and Mull, and learning the art of boiling beef.

'"Boiled" beef,' Geordie said, 'is a misnomer. You only drop your meat into boilin' water to give it a skin that'll keep it sappy*. If it was put into the pot in one piece like the Frenchies do it, you might need to give it five minutes real boilin'. But it's quite enough, when it's in bits like this, to bring it back to the boil for a jiffy. An' that's all the actual boilin' you ever give it. All it wants after that is as much heat as'll just keep the liquor saying 'plup!' six to twelve times a minute. In the piece you would allow about twenty minutes for each pound-weight and twenty minutes over. You can hardly spoil the meat by simmering too long, except that in the piece it'll likely fall to bits when you try to carve it. But *simmering*, mind! If you *boil* meat — that's to say at the heat of water for makin' tea — you'll get somethin' as tough and tasteless as cahootchy. (Indiarubber) An' nothin' in the world'll make it worth eatin' again.

'Of course,' Geordie went on, 'a certain amount o' the meat juice leaks out into the liquor. That's what makes the broth. An' when you come to put in the vegetables, somethin' o' their

*sappy — moist

juice gets into the meat, helpin' its flavour. But the notion is to
keep all the virtue you can in the beef, so you don't do anything
to encourage it to give its juices out. That's why you don't salt
your liquor until meat an' vegetables are nearly ready.'

Victor MacClure
Good Appetite my Companion, 1955

4 lb/2 kg brisket or other boiling cut
4 pts/2 L boiling water
Bunch of parsley
Few peppercorns (my additions — not Geordie's)
Bay leaf
Sprig of thyme
Cut the meat up into portion-sized pieces and put into the water
with parsley, peppercorns, bay leaf and thyme. Bring to the boil and
then skim. Reduce the heat to a very gentle simmer. Cover and cook
till almost tender.

Add

12 medium carrots, sliced
12 white turnips, sliced
Simmer for half an hour

Finally add

4 lb/2 kg fresh peas (summer)
4 leeks (winter)
4 shallots, finely chopped
Salt and pepper
Shell peas or chop leeks finely. Taste and season. Simmer for five
minutes and serve with Mealy Boiled Potatoes (see p.179).

SCOTCH BARLEY BROTH

Bit id's sorroo and grief if there's no bilan' beef
An, ye canna hev broth, on 'e Sunday.

Donald Grant
Broth on 'e Sunday, 1961

This traditional broth occupies the high ground between soups on the
one hand and stews on the other. Meg Dods describes this and a variety
of other substantial Scottish soups as 'Soup and Stew or Mouthful
Soups'.

For some reason Broth Making holds a fascination for the Scots'
male, and many men who otherwise find cooking something of a chore,
will turn their hand to a pot of broth. Such was Old Andra, an ex-Glasgow
shipwright whose magnificent Scotch Broth was something of a legend

and the highlight of the week for Madeleine Gibb when she was a teen-age apprentice during the depression in the 1920s to Andra's dress-maker daughter. Monday they had 'stovies' made from the leftovers of the Sunday roast, Tuesday was 'cooheel' but on Wednesday it was Andra's Special. Cooled and reheated overnight, the flavour developed and tasted even better on Thursday. He was ever ready to reel off the recipe for the broth which was made in a huge iron pot (probably hold-ing 14 pts) over the kitchen range. The procedure started at nine o'clock by filling the pot with cold water.

'Intae this,' commanded the receipt, 'fling a sma' haunfie o' coorse saut. Whan it biles pit in yer beef, a guid, fat, twa-pun piece. Then hauf-a-pun o' weel-washed baurley and twa pun o' well-soakit peas.' About ten-thirty Andra added 'wan guid swede turmut, fower carrots, eicht guid leeks and a wee tait o' sugar.' Before departing for his 'bit dram' he added 'twa guid haunfies o' choppit greens and eicht tautties'; and on his return — exuding the rich and heady perfume of the Special, he stirred in another 'haunfie' — this time of parsley which, with canny forethought — he had chopped before setting forth.

Madeline Gibb
Scotland's Magazine, December 1960

Earlier recipes from the more affluent 19th century have a much higher proportion of beef and much less peas and barley but the basic ingre-dients remain the same, as do the three basic stages.

Cooking the meat/barley/peas

If possible, use about 1 lb/500 g of beef to 2 pts/1 L of cold water. The cheapest cut is usual, something like nineholes (thick flank) or hough (shin), though other cuts suitable for boiling, and larger or smaller pieces, can obviously be used. 1 oz/50 g barley (rice is recommended as a substitute in some recipes) and $\frac{1}{2}$ oz/15 g split peas which have both been steeped in hot water for a few hours or overnight with a small nut of butter will give the broth a good lithing (thickening). All of this should be put on to boil with a little salt and a bunch of sweet herbs for at least an hour before the vegetables are added.

Note: Since it is difficult to know exactly the toughness or tenderness of the meat I boil the meat till tender and then remove and keep warm. If the vegetables are finely chopped they will not take long to cook, though if some are to be served in larger pieces with the meat as a vegetable then they must obviously be added sooner.

Adding the vegetables

The ones which take longest to cook should be added first and the additions so organised that all vegetables are just cooked through

without being overcooked when you are ready to serve the broth.

The proportions and the combinations are a matter of taste except that almost everyone would agree that carrots and turnips (Swedes), leek or onion and parsley are essential. Only Mrs Cleland, writing in 1759, varies widely from this when instead she uses 'four or five heads of celery washed clean and cut small (this was to 12 pts of water) and a few marigolds. Let this boil an hour. Take a cock or large fowl, clean picked and washed, and put into the pot; boil it till the broth is quite good, then season with salt, and send it to table, with the fowl in the middle.'

Potatoes were sometimes cooked in the broth, as in Andra's version, or cooked separately but served with the broth.

Use a medium-sized carrot, a quarter of a medium sized turnip and two leeks or two medium onions to the 2 pts/1 L (5 c) water. Peel and dice the carrot and turnip and add first. Chop the leek and/or onion and add (leek white only) when the carrot and turnips are about half cooked. Add a teaspoonful of sugar at this point.

Finishing the broth

When all are tender, finish with a good handful of chopped parsley and the green of the leek, very finely chopped. Season well with salt and pepper and serve with the meat as a separate course or with the meat chopped finely or coarsely and added to the broth. It is often eaten with a large mealy potato making an island in the centre of the soup plate.

MINCED COLLOPS (Mince and Tatties)

4 servings

A popular everyday Scottish dish always eaten with potatoes and commonly known as 'Mince and Tatties'. Collops is a term for thin slices of meat of any kind usually taken from the leg but with no bone. This version is based on a simple recipe given by Mrs Dalgairns in 1829, which depends for flavour on a very thorough browning of meat and onions. Scottish housewives use the best steak they can afford for mince and will choose their steak first, then have the butcher mince it for them.

1 lb/500 g stewing steak, minced (2 c)
1-2 onions, finely chopped
2 tablespoons oil/fat for browning
Salt and pepper
½ tablespoon vinegar (optional)
1 tablespoon medium oatmeal (optional)

Begin by melting the oil/fat in a pan and when it is quite hot add the onions. Cook slowly till a good rich dark golden brown then add the mince. Break up with a fork and keep stirring while it is browning. This should be done slowly (takes about 10-15 minutes). After this the meat is really cooked and simply needs moistening and seasoning before serving. Add about ½ pt/250 ml water or stock (1¼ c), boil up, add oatmeal, season, add vinegar and simmer for about 5-10 minutes. Usually served with creamed potatoes ('tatties'), and sometimes with triangles of hot toast.

Note: For convenience, carrots and turnips are often cooked in mince which lengthens the cooking time once the liquid has been added but at the same time they bring additional flavour. They should be very thinly sliced to reduce cooking time.

SCOTCH COLLOPS

4 servings

As soon as the collops were ready. Cluny gave them, with his own hand, a squeeze of lemon. . . . They are such as I gave His Royal Highness (Prince Charles Edward Stuart) in this very house.

Robert Louis Stevenson
Kidnapped. 1886

This dish appears in many old Scottish cookery books, and some English ones too. In at least one book they are referred to as 'Scotched' collops. Scotching is a term for cutting in a criss-cross pattern which does appear as part of the method of dressing the steaks before cooking in some recipes — it is just possible that the name refers to the method rather than the Scots. Nevertheless, they are very much part of the Scottish tradition.

This recipe is based on the one in Mrs MacIver's Cookery and Pastry (1773), the book she wrote for her students at one of Edinburgh's first cookery schools.

4 × 6 oz/175 g veal escallops
2 oz/50 g butter (½ stick)
½ pt/250 ml stock (1¼ c)
Slice of lemon peel
Few pieces of whole mace
Glass of white wine

Kneaded butter

½ oz/15 g butter
½ oz/15 g flour

Liaison

Yolk of egg; 3 tablespoons double cream

Garnish

Sliced lemon

Beat out veal and brown in butter. Add stock, lemon peel, mace and white wine and simmer for a few minutes. Remove escallops, continue simmering, reducing slightly then strain. Return sauce to pan and bring to the boil, thicken with the kneaded butter adding a little at a time. (Pickled oysters were added at this point in the original recipe.) Finish with egg yolk and cream taking care not to let the sauce boil, season and add a 'scrape of nutmeg'. Pour over the veal and garnish with sliced lemon.

BEEF OLIVES

4 servings

Rolls of thinly sliced beef or veal are stuffed to make this economical dish. Butchers in Scotland use a cut called Beef Ham to make their own sausage-stuffed beef olives. Although a name originally applied to Salted Beef, it now refers only to the very thin slice from some part of the leg of the animal — different butchers use different cuts but all cut it very thinly sometimes on a machine.

Skirlie (see p. 32) and Haggis make good stuffings; since both are crumbly it is better to spread them over the meat and roll up swiss-roll-style. This is a traditional breadcrumb-based stuffing sharply flavoured with lemon and herbs.

For the stuffing

4 oz/125 g fresh breadcrumbs (2 c); 2 oz/50 g finely chopped suet (½ c); 1-2 tablespoons chopped parsley; 1 tablespoon chopped lemon thyme; grated rind of 1 lemon; salt and pepper and 1 egg to bind together; 1-2 tablespoons lemon juice.

For the olives

1 lb/500 g rump steak, cut thinly or Beef Ham
2 tablespoons oil
1 medium onion, finely chopped
¾ pt/400 ml water (2 c)
Salt and pepper

Cut the steak into strips about 2″ (5 cm) wide. Place a spoonful of forcemeat on each piece; roll up and skewer with cocktail stick. Heat

oil and brown onion then add olives and brown. Add water and
seasoning and bring to the boil. Simmer gently till tender. Remove
meat and reduce cooking liquor to a rich glaze. Serve with olives.

CHARCOAL GRILLED BEEFSTEAKS with whisky and shallot butter

serves 4

Lucky Laing* . . . contrived to make her shop in the gloomy old
Tolbooth a cosy little place, half tavern, half kitchen, whence
issued pretty frequently the pleasant sounds of broiling beefsteaks, and the drawing of corks from bottles of ale and porter.

Marie W. Stuart
Old Edinburgh Taverns, 1952

The taste for simple old-fashioned meat dishes served at steak bars is as
much a part of our eating out scene today as it was more than two
hundred years ago. Beefsteaks were then, as they are now, one of the
commonest restaurant dishes.

The Rules for the Beefsteak Club which was established in 1734 were
— 'Pound well the steak till all the fibres are broken. Don't spare the coal.
Turn it frequently. Take care the fat is more done than the lean. Take
care the juice is allowed now and then to fall in the dish. Butter the steak
but do not season till dished.'

4 × 6-8 oz/200-250 g grilling steaks
Oil for brushing
Whisky and Shallot Butter
4 oz/125 g softened butter (1 stick)
1 tablespoon parsley, finely chopped
1 tablespoon shallot, finely chopped
2 tablespoons whisky
Salt and freshly milled pepper
Beat together

*She was a guidwife who had a basement tavern in South Bridge Street about the beginning of the
19th century. Her 'pièce de resistance' was a stew which she called 'Golli Gosperado' and which
she conveniently placed beneath the iron gratings in the pavement so that the aroma wafted
upwards and advertised the dish to the passers-by with enormously successful results. Unfortunately there is no record of her recipe.

To grill steaks

Brush steaks with oil and place over charcoal. Burn a criss cross
pattern on the meat with a red-hot skewer. Turn frequently, till
required degree of doneness. When ready, spread the meat with the
butter and serve.

Note: A hot grill may be used instead of charcoal.

SPICED BEEF

Dry Spicing

A method of preservation which adds a rich mellow flavour to beef. Early
methods simply involved burying the meat in dry salt in a stone trough
during the winter months; spices were added but the proportion of salt
was high and therefore it dominated the flavour of the meat. Today there
is less need to use so much salt and more modified versions depend on
subtle blends of spices. As the natural fluids of the meat drain out they
blend with the flavourings to make a rich form of marinade.

Cuts

It is not really worth spicing anything under 4 lb/2 kg since the whole
point is to have enough to last for several weeks. A 6-10 lb/3-5 kg piece is
best. The choice of cut really depends on how much you can afford.
Prime cuts like a middle rib of roast carefully cooked make superb spiced
beef, so also do silverside, rump and 'Salmon' cut, but equally successful
are the cheaper brisket and nineholes.

There should be a good mixture of fat and lean. The fat is necessary to
keep the meat moist during cooking, but also fat is a good absorber of
flavour during the spicing process. The meat should have all bones
removed and may be spiced rolled and tied, or unrolled. Penetration of
the spices is quicker and more thorough in unrolled meat. Also, because
the meat is flatter, more of it is sitting in the spicing liquor. It is important from this point of view to have a bowl or dish which fits the meat
neatly. Pieces which are a fairly uniform shape like the salmon cut or
silverside will not need rolling or tying before cooking but rib roast,
brisket and nineholes will need some tying.

Spicing

Put the meat into a fairly closely fitting dish and cover with 4 oz/ 125 g (1 c) brown sugar. Cover well and leave for 2 days in a cool place turning each day.

Pound together in a mortar — 1 oz/25 g allspice; 1 oz/25 g juniper berries; 1 oz/25 g black peppercorns; $\frac{1}{2}$ oz/15 g coriander seeds; $\frac{1}{2}$ grated nutmeg; 2-3 crushed cloves of garlic. Experiment with spice combinations — I do not like using cloves since I think they dominate the more subtle juniper and coriander too much, though Meg Dods uses $\frac{1}{2}$ oz/25 g in similar proportions. The spices may be ground coarsely in a grinder but they should not be powdered or it will be difficult to remove them from the outside surface of the meat at the end of the spicing, especially important if it is to be baked.

Mix with 4 oz/125 g salt ($\frac{1}{2}$ c scant) and rub into the meat. Put on cover and rub and turn meat every day. The length of time the meat should be left depends on how heavily or lightly spiced you like the meat. I left a 5 lb piece of silverside in the above mixture for a fortnight on one occasion and it was so strongly spiced no one would eat it. Nearly all old recipes recommend a month minimum — palates were more robust in those days. The pickling time also depends on the thickness of the meat — flat brisket will be quite well spiced in five to six days while a thick piece of rump will need about nine.

Cooking

For boiling — Wipe off excess spice and put in a pot of boiling water, bring to the boil and skim well. Add 1 stick of celery; an onion stuck with a few cloves; 1 carrot; 1 small piece of turnip; bunch of parsley and thyme; a tablespoon peppercorns. Bring back to the boil, skim and simmer very gently, allowing 30 minutes per lb plus 30 minutes till tender.

For braising — Wipe off the excess spice. Melt 2 tablespoons oil in a pan and add 2-3 chopped carrots; 1 small turnip and 1 medium onion, chopped, and sauté till lightly browned. Place the meat on top — cover with a skin of fat if necessary. Add enough water to cover the vegetables completely and come about half way up the meat. Cover with a double layer of foil and then a tightly fitting lid and bake at 300F/150C/Gas 2 for 30 minutes per lb/500 g plus 30 minutes or until tender.

Pressing

Remove when cooked, wrap tightly in foil while still hot and put between two boards with a weight on top, leave overnight.

Serving

It can be eaten hot, but the spice flavour is best appreciated when cold. Serve with Grated Boiled Beetroot mixed with a well flavoured vinegar (I use the Japanese Red Umeboshi Plum Vinegar which has a unique effect on beetroot) and olive oil.

As a sandwich — spiced beef makes excellent sandwiches with a little mustard or chutney.

BEEF cooked in claret

6-8 servings

> We have one great advantage, that makes amends for many inconveniences, that is, wholesome and agreeable drink, I mean French Claret. . . .
>
> Edward Burt (Chief Surveyor to General Wade during the making of roads through the Highlands) Letters from a Gentleman in the North of Scotland (1724-28)

With so much borrowing back and forward between Scotland and France, the use of French claret to cook Scottish beef seems an obvious combination. The cheapest cut of beef can be used with no loss of flavour, in fact the harder working muscles like the leg have more flavour than other less active ones.

To cook the trimmings

5 oz/150 g lean bacon
6-8 very small onions
14 oz/400 g button mushrooms, chopped

Cook the bacon in an enamelled cast-iron casserole or frying pan till lightly brown. Add the onions and cook uncovered for about 10 minutes. Then add the mushrooms, stir, cover and cook gently for another 10 minutes. Keep aside till serving.

To cook the meat

4 tablespoons oil
3 lb/1½ kg stewing steak, cut into 1½″ (4 cm) cubes
5 cloves garlic, crushed
2 tablespoons flour
1 bottle fruity young claret (Burgundy, Côtes-du-Rhône or Beaujolais)
Salt and freshly milled black pepper
1 teaspoon sugar
Bunch of fresh herbs

Pre-heat the oven to 300F/150C/Gas 2.
Heat the oil in a frying pan and brown the pieces of meat. Put into the casserole, add the garlic and sprinkle over flour. Leave uncovered in the oven to continue browning for 15 minutes, stirring from time to time. Add wine, season lightly, add herbs. Cover and simmer for 3 hours or until the meat is tender. Remove from the oven and stir in the trimmings. Heat through for five minutes and serve with chopped parsley and boiled potatoes. Serve with a Burgundy or Beaujolais.

FORFAR BRIDIES

makes 4

These convenient hand-held delicacies were made by itinerant sellers who mostly plied their trade at local fairs and markets. They almost certainly got their name from one such seller, Maggie Bridie of Glamis. Today they are a bakers' speciality, akin to a Cornish pasty which has been laid on its side, and filled with steak. Forfar is an important centre of the beef trade in Angus and the first bridies I bought in Forfar were made by a local butcher who used the very best rump steak for filling — the pastry was crisp and slightly brittle rather than short and was well-flavoured with beef dripping.

Pre-heat the oven to 400F/200C/Gas 6.

To make the pastry

12 oz/400 g plain flour (3 c)
3 oz/100 g margarine ($\frac{3}{4}$ stick)
3 oz/100 g beef dripping
Water to mix
Salt

Rub the fat into the flour, add salt and mix to a stiff dough with cold water. Divide into four and roll out into large ovals. Leave to rest.

To prepare the meat

1 lb/500 g rump or topside
3 oz/75 g beef suet, finely chopped ($\frac{3}{4}$ c)
2 medium onions, finely chopped
Salt and ground black pepper to taste

Beat out the steak with a meat bat or rolling pin and cut up roughly into $\frac{1}{2}''$ (1 cm) pieces. Put the meat into a bowl with the onions and suet, season and divide into four. Cover half of each oval with the meat leaving about $\frac{1}{2}''$ (1 cm) round the edge for sealing. Wet edges, fold over and seal. Crimp edge with fingers, make a hole in the top and bake on a greased baking sheet for about 45 minutes.

TRIPE SUPPERS

6-8 servings

The frequenter of Douglas's, after ascending a few steps, found himself in a pretty large kitchen — a dark fiery Pandemonium, through which numerous ineffable ministers of flame were continually flying about, while beside the door sat the landlady, a large fat woman, in a towering head-dress and large flowered silk gown, who bowed to everyone passing. . . . The House was noted for suppers of tripe, rizzard haddocks, mince collops and hashes which never cost more than sixpence a head.

Robert Chambers
Traditions of Edinburgh, 1868

Even cheaper Tripe Suppers were provided for the poor at 'eating houses' in the industrial towns of the late 19th century. W. Anderson writing in 'The Poor of Edinburgh and their homes' (1867) describes how they were allowed 'as muckle as a man can eat' for a penny, and a plate of potatoes for another penny.

Tripe is a dish of strong character which arouses extremes of feeling in people not necessarily because it might be associated with poverty — you just love it or hate it. This is a simple stew or hot pot of tripe, potatoes and onions which has the advantage of having everything cooked in one pot.

Use a 8 pt oven casserole.

Pre-heat the oven to 275F/140C/Gas 1.

Arrange in layers with seasoning in between — finish with a layer of potato

2 lb/1 kg prepared tripe cut into 2″ (5 cm) squares

2-3 medium onions, finely sliced

2½ lb/1¼ kg potatoes, sliced ¼″ (½ cm) thick

1 marrow bone/or knuckle of veal/or ham bone — place in the base

Seasoning — 3-4 bay leaves; salt; 2 teaspoons dried thyme

(1 tablespoon fresh); 1 heaped tablespoon crushed garlic and salt.

Press down well and pour in water to cover. Bring to the boil. Cover with double layer of foil under a tightly fitting lid and bake for 3-4 hours. Serve with lots of freshly chopped parsley.

VEAL SWEETBREADS AND KIDNEYS

4 servings

On Monday 21st March 1737 the Murrays of Ochtertyre near Crieff had 'sweetbread and kidneys' for supper. Entirely appropriate, since that very day, according to the household accounts, they had 'killd an oxe' and for several days following they ate tripe in a variety of guises, which all goes to show the healthy Scots respect for innards even among the aristocracy. The theory that innards went to servants does not apply at Ochtertyre. Servants fared very well, frequently eating beef and pig as well as 'puddings and hagas'.

If sweetbreads are not available use all kidneys and vice versa.

1 lb/500 g veal sweetbreads (or lamb's)

8 oz/225 g veal kidneys (or lamb's)

4-5 tablespoons unsalted butter

Salt, freshly milled black pepper

For the sauce

2 tablespoons Madeira

¾ pt/450 ml double cream (2 c)

1 teaspoon grated nutmeg

1 teaspoon potato flour diluted in 1 tablespoon cold water (optional)

To prepare both throat and heart sweetbreads

Wash well in running water for a few minutes and then leave them to soak for an hour with a tablespoon of salt. This removes traces of blood. Drain, rinse and put in enough cold water to cover. Add the juice of $\frac{1}{2}$ lemon and a pinch of salt, bring to the boil and simmer until the sweetbreads become firm and white. This will only take a few minutes for lamb's sweetbreads; veal's will take about 10 minutes depending on size. Don't overcook. Drain them, reserving the cooking liquid for stock and refresh under cold running water. Remove the skin and membranes, tubes and hard bits, etc. For a firm texture, they may be pressed between two plates or boards with weights on top, and left overnight.

To make the sauce

Melt the butter in a pan. Slice the sweetbreads in 1″ ($2\frac{1}{2}$ cm) pieces. Skin and slice the kidneys in similar-sized pieces. Toss both in butter and cook quickly for about five minutes. Remove with a slotted spoon and keep hot. Add the madeira to the pan and boil for 2-3 minutes, mixing with the pan juices. Add the cream and nutmeg, and reduce for about ten minutes. Remove from the heat and whisk in the potato flour, put back over heat to thicken. Adjust seasoning and pour very hot over the sweetbreads.

Serving

They can be served plainly on hot buttered toast or fried bread or with plain boiled rice.

Sometimes they are served in small pastry cases or vol-au-vent cases or on a bed of spinach. Lady Clark of Tillipronie serves them with sorrel which sounds good. The sharp piquant sorrel should make an excellent foil for sweetbreads.

Another easy and very effective way of serving is to put them between layers of puff pastry which has been cut into rectangles and already cooked, rather in the style of a Gateau Mille Feuilles, though with only one layer of filling.

For the above quantities use 8 oz/250 g puff pastry. Pre-heat the oven to 350F/180C/Gas 4. Roll out the pastry to $\frac{1}{4}$″ ($\frac{1}{2}$ cm) thick and score lightly in a diamond pattern. With a sharp knife cut 4 rectangles 2 × 3″ (6 cm × 8 cm). Brush with egg and bake for 20 minutes till risen and brown. Split open, remove any doughy bits in the middle and fill with cooked mixture. Replace lid and serve.

Serve with a White Burgundy.

SWEETBREAD PIE

8 servings

Sweetbreads are a natural ingredient for pies and have been used for centuries in all kind of combinations highlighting their interesting flavour and texture. I like the subtle blend of pork, bacon, mushrooms and garlic in this pie which I make frequently and which is originally from Jane Grigson's Good Things, 1971.

Pastry

A unique short crust pastry for all those who complain they are non-successful-pastry-makers. It makes a light crisp crust and it's simple and quick to make — fat and boiling water beaten together (30 seconds); flour stirred in (10 seconds).

It is one of Stella Atterbury's ideas in It's Never Too Late — an original Cookery Book (1963) — the story of how she learnt the hard way how to run a hotel when her husband retired. It is full of salutary stories of what not to do, but also includes some imaginative and inventive ideas for coping in the kitchen — this pastry is one of them and can be made in large quantities and stored for a few weeks.

2 oz/50 g butter/margarine* (½ stick)
2 oz/50 g lard (½ stick)
2 fl oz/50 ml boiling water (¼ c)
6 oz/75 g plain flour, white or wholemeal or a mixture (1½ c)
½ teaspoon salt

Cut the butter/margarine and lard in small pieces into a bowl and pour on the boiling water. Whisk them together till the fat is all melted and mixed through — can also be done in a processor. It should make a thickish creamy mixture but this depends on how well the fat creams. It does not matter if the fat and water are still separated at the end of whisking. Now add the flour and salt and mix in, cover and place in refrigerator till hard — about an hour.

For the filling
   Prepare — 1 lb/500 g veal sweetbreads (see p. 135).

Mince finely together
   ¾ lb/350 g lean pork and/or veal
   ½ lb/250 g hard back pork fat
   2 rashers unsmoked bacon

Add
   2 large eggs; 1 heaped tablespoon flour

Cook together till soft
   4 oz/125 g mushrooms, finely chopped (2 c)
   2 tablespoons onion, finely chopped
   1 clove garlic, crushed

Line a 3 pt/1½ L capacity loaf tin with the pastry, keeping enough aside for the lid.

Lay in ⅓ of the forcemeat and ½ the mushrooms on top. Arrange ½ the sweetbreads on top. Continue — forcemeat/mushrooms/ sweetbread, finishing with a layer of forcemeat. Mound up nicely to support the pastry, cover, decorate and brush with egg. Bake 350F/180C/Gas 4 for 1 hour (protect the lid if necessary). Serve warm or cold.

Note: May be made without pastry but cover with double layer of foil — leave off towards the end of the cooking to brown top. Cool and press under a light weight overnight.

*Use hard fats with low water content.

POTTED HOUGH

4-6 servings

A simple uncomplicated flavour. And a popular item in butchers' shops where it is made in varying sizes and with subtle differences in flavour from shop to shop. To make it at home it should be regarded as the basis for useful stock so add a few extra bones and use left-over jellied stock for soup. Serve for high tea.

1 lb/500 g hough (shin of beef)
Nap bone (put in more to make extra stock)
Blade of mace
3/4 whole cloves
Salt and pepper

Place in a large pan, cover with water and boil for 6 hours. Strain. Leave stock to get cold overnight and then remove the fat. Now chop up the meat very finely, put into a pan and cover with stock; you may not need all of it. It should make a good firm jelly when cold. Bring to the boil and simmer for a few minutes. Leave to cool and then season well. Pour into wetted moulds and serve with very hot toast and salad.

POTTED TONGUE

Potted meats are a very old British tradition. They were popular high tea dishes, served with bread and butter and spicy pickles. Today, they can be served in smaller quantities at the beginning of a meal instead of the ubiquitous 'pâté' which was originally a French pie with pastry and not the soft meat paste that is served today.

Pound together in mortar
Pinch nutmeg, ground ginger, mace, thyme, small garlic clove
Mix together to a smooth paste
Spice mix
8 oz/250 g cooked tongue
4 oz/125 g softened butter (1 stick)

Pack into small ramekins or one large dish. Clarify some butter, strain over tongue and leave to cool. It should make a layer about $\frac{1}{4}$" ($\frac{1}{2}$ cm) thick. Will keep for several weeks in a cool place.

Lamb

Such a display of mutton broth . . . and Roasted jiggets of lamb.

D. M. Moir
Mansie Wauch, 1828

Sheep and goats were the first wild animals gathered together into herds by prehistoric man, who saw the great advantages of having milk and meat 'to hand'. Indigenous in their wild form to parts of the Near East, it was most probably in Iraq, somewhere about 9000 BC, that domestication began and from then on farmers and their herds have moved westwards.

They reached Britain about 4000 BC when sheep and goats became established here as valuable milk, meat and wool producers. In the middle ages the Border hills were well trodden by sheep who helped to keep the English wool trade in business as well as providing milk for cheese. Sheep and goats were also kept by Highlanders for meat, milk, cheese and wool, but in much smaller numbers compared with the Borders. Just a few sheep and goats were kept for domestic use and practically none were exported. The vast army of sheep which came nibbling their way up strath and glen as a result of the Clearances were of value to their breeders principally as meat to satisfy the growing urban markets of the 19th century, making a complete reversal of purpose.

Today for every Scotsman there is a sheep-and-a-half roaming the hills while Englishmen and Welshmen have less than half a sheep apiece and even Ulstermen only run to about two-thirds.

Breeds

While England can name some forty native breeds, Scottish sheep husbandry is based on only three native breeds — Blackface and North and South Country Cheviots with some local variants. Much cross breeding goes on to improve stock and give a good proportion of meat to bone as well as tender well-flavoured flesh.

The **Blackface** is the hardy breed. It is the most numerous in Britain today and can stand up to the worst snowstorms on open hills and still produce lambs in the spring. Compared with other sheep blackface sheep have a fierce wild look which characterises their temperament as tough, courageous and determined animals whose natural instincts keep them foraging for food in the most appalling conditions. Since Scotland has such a vast area of wild hill country, blackface sheep predominate on these high heather clad hills. 'This small hill lamb is perhaps the finest quality in the world, giving a carcase free from superfluous fat and waste. This lightweight carcase satisfies a high demand by the housewife whether it be sold through Smithfield, a High Street butcher, the supermarkets or the continent'. British Sheep (The National Sheep Association 1982).

Other breeds native to Scotland are the **Cheviots** which are named after the Cheviot hills which extend across the borders between Scotland and England. They are also hardy hill sheep but are more often found on upland farms and grass-covered 'white' hills (as opposed to 'black' which are heather covered). They produce a lightweight carcase, low in fat with a high percentage of well-flavoured lean meat. These are one of the oldest breeds in Scotland and are described as **South Country Cheviots** to distinguish them from the breed developed in the mid-18th century and described as the North Country Cheviot. The South Country Cheviot has a history which goes back at least to the 14th Century and since the Church owned muc'i Border lands then they were originally bred for their wool by the monks of the Border Abbeys. To improve the wool quality, Merino sheep were introduced and the wool manufacturing towns of Selkirk, Galashiels, Hawick and Langholm became famous for their durable woollen products made from Cheviot sheep.

A Border sheep farmer named Robson who was involved in crossing the Cheviots with a variety of other breeds besides the Merino sheep was responsible for starting the development of a different variety of Cheviot called the **North Country Cheviot**. It wasn't till late in the century that they were taken north by Sir John Sinclair. He took five hundred to his farm in Caithness and called them 'Cheviots' and many more followed to the big Sutherland hill farms where more crossings particularly with Merinos took place. Today the breed is still found mainly on the colder exposed east side of Scotland from Shetland to the Borders. It is a tough breed which produces a large carcase with a high proportion of lean to fat.

There are many other breeds of sheep to be found in Scotland today, as you will see from a trip round the annual Royal Highland Agricultural Show at Ingliston near Edinburgh. Talking with Scottish sheep breeders who are constantly striving for perfection, it is clear that one of their main aims is satisfying a customer who is becoming more interested in lamb for its flavour, low fat and quality lean meat.

In the Lowlands there are flocks of English Leicesters, Suffolks and, in lesser numbers, some of the Down breeds and a few imported breeds including Texels (from the island of Texel off the north west coast of Holland) that are used for crossing with the native Scottish breeds.

Another native breed is the small **Shetland** sheep which grazes on rough grasslands, heather and seaweed on the Shetland shores. It is one of the smallest British breeds and retains many of the characteristics of wild sheep. They are very hardy and self-reliant, surviving severe gales and winter blizzards. Because it is impossible to be more than three and a half miles from the sea anywhere on the islands, the air, activated by the strong winds, carries salt over all the pastures. This, combined with the heather and seaweed, gives the meat a unique, slightly gamey flavour which has been favourably compared with the much sought-after French Agneau de Pre-Sales, which are the lambs fed on the salty grasses of the Northern Coastal region of France. Like the Shetland lamb, the Pre-Sales lamb is five to nine months old at the time of killing, but because of the poor quality winter grazing, Shetland Lamb is smaller in size. Despite this, the harsh environment has ensured that only the fittest lambs survive, making them well conditioned, hardy and vigorous.

In the past the Shetland breed of sheep was kept mostly for its very fine soft wool which was carded and spun in the crofthouses. This wool was not clipped but 'rooed' — pulled away by hand when the sheep started to lose its coat in summer, the finest wool coming from the neck. It was this neck wool which was used in the famous shawls which were so fine that they could pass through a wedding ring.

Shetland lamb has never become widely known on the greater part of the British mainland, partly due to distance and difficulties of transport. The scarcity of numbers has also been a limiting factor. The lambs are normally born from May onwards and become available from the end of September through October and November. The meat is tender and lean.

Other native breeds which are at present being preserved from extinction by the Rare Breeds Survival Trust are the **Boreray** from the island of Boreray in the St Kilda group. Also the **Soay** sheep from the St Kilda islands and **North Ronaldsay** sheep from the Orkney island where they live entirely on the shore. (A stone dyke round the whole island fences the sheep off the precious arable land which is kept for other livestock, and the sheep feed entirely on seaweed which produces a uniquely flavoured meat and milk with a very high iodine content.)

Availability

Most lambing takes place on hill sheep farms during April, though some low ground farms may start as early as February. A few low ground farms produce early lambs from the end of December. Born and reared indoors, they are available in limited quantities for Easter but because of high production costs, are expensive.

Lamb is at its best and most plentiful from July through to December, with most of the lamb from Scottish hill farms coming on the market from September onwards. Killed before its first birthday it is still lamb but thereafter becomes hogget (year old sheep).

Mutton has a good flavour and was the meat used originally for traditional Scottish dishes based on long, slow, moist cooking. It is difficult to buy now since butchers prefer to deal with the more uniform quality of lamb. Some will admit that people do come in asking for mutton and, of course, it is still theoretically available since not all sheep are killed before they reach their first birthday. You may occasionally see a large mature sheep hanging in a butchers, but it will be destined to end up in pies rather than sold over the counter as mutton. Most Scottish mutton is exported.

A good source of mutton is the Halal butcher who provides for the Muslim communities in Scotland, where the mutton flavour is greatly appreciated.

To BOIL A GIGOT with Turnips

Served with Caper Sauce

Only successful with well matured mutton. Lamb is not robust enough to stand the long slow cooking and will end up anemic and tasteless.

Mountain or wether mutton, from four to five years old, is by far the best. . . . Simmer in an oval-shaped pot that will just hold it, letting the water come very slowly to the boil. Skim carefully. Boil sliced carrots and turnip with the mutton, and the younger and more juicy they are the better they suit this joint. All meat ought to be well done, but a leg of mutton not overdone, to look plump and retain its juices. About two hours slow boiling will dress it.

Garnish with slices of carrot. Pour caper-sauce over the meat, and serve mashed turnip or cauliflower in a separate dish.

Meg Dods
The Cook and Housewives Manual. 1826

ROAST RACK OF LAMB

4-8 servings

The advantage of roasting lamb chops in one piece on the bone is that they have a juicier, fuller flavour, since the bone on one side and the fat on the other prevent the meat juices running out. While a single rack is good for an everyday meal, a pair placed together with a stuffing in the centre (Guard of Honour) makes a splendid presentation for a party. Spring Lamb is best (6-12 months) and the meat should be cooked medium rare for the fullest flavour.

For a single rack buy one with 8 uncut chops and ask the butcher to prepare — he should saw through the backbone but not remove since it protects the meat and can be removed before carving. He may trim the ends of the bones, but this is not essential.

For a double rack ask for two matching racks from the same animal if possible. The top 2-3 inches of the ribs need to be stripped to allow the two sides to interlace. The ends of the bones may be cut in a point using a sharp knife and tapping with a mallet.

1 rack (8 chops) or 2 racks (8 chops each)
Herb and Breadcrumb stuffing for double rack (see p. 129)
Salt and pepper
Oil for basting

For single rack
4 servings

Heat oil in oven and when very hot add meat. Turn meat in the oil and brown in a hot oven. For a medium-rare result cook for about 15 minutes at 450F/230C/Gas 8. This will obviously depend on the thickness of the chops. Allow another 5-10 minutes for well-done. Leave to rest before carving. Follow the line of the rib bones and serve two chops per person. Garnish with mint or watercress and serve with a green salad and Redcurrant or Herb Jelly (see p. 235).

For double rack
8 servings

Place stuffing in the centre, interlace the rib bones, press well together and tie with string. Heat oil in roasting tin. Season meat and brown in a hot oven 450F/230C/Gas 8 for 15 minutes. Lower the heat 350F/180C/Gas 4 and roast for another 20-25 minutes. Baste occasionally. Leave to rest for 10 minutes before carving. Carve by following the rib bones and cutting two chops together Serve with the stuffing in the centre. Creamy Gratin Dauphinois (see p. 262) is a good accompaniment to this with a green vegetable; or it may be garnished with mint and served with a green salad and some Redcurrant jelly for a lighter meal.

GRILLED OR BARBECUED LEG OF LAMB

This is best barbecued over charcoal with some fresh rosemary thrown over the hot coals before and during the cooking. The meat has to be boned out first though your butcher may be willing to do this for you.

To make the marinade

Put the following into a large wide shallow dish:
¼ pt/150 ml dry red wine (2 c)
4 tablespoons olive oil
1 medium onion, finely sliced
1 carrot, thinly sliced
6 parsley stalks
2 bay leaves
A sprig of rosemary
1 clove garlic, crushed
1 teaspoon salt
Freshly ground black pepper

To bone out the meat

Begin by loosening the pelvic bone following the contours of the bone. When you expose the ball and socket joint that connects the pelvic bone to the thigh bone, cut through the tendons joining the bones. Make a straight cut down the length of the thigh bone on the inside of the leg and again following the contours of the bone, loosen the flesh from the bone.

Marinading the lamb

Bat out the meat to a fairly even thickness, place in a dish which it will fit into neatly and add marinade. Leave overnight turning once or twice.

To cook the lamb

Grill or barbecue over a high heat for about 10-15 minutes depending on the degree of pinkness you like. Baste frequently with some of the strained marinade to keep it moist. Make a gravy with some of the strained marinade and the pan juices. Serve with a green salad and baked potatoes.

Note: If your grill pan is not large enough to cope with a whole leg it can be roasted in a very hot oven — 450F/230C/Gas 8 for 30-40 minutes. Turn and baste once or twice during the cooking. Leave to rest 10 minutes in a warm place before serving.

BRAISED LAMB SHOULDER WITH CARROTS AND TURNIPS

6-8 servings

1 lamb shoulder (approx 4-5 lb/2-2$\frac{1}{2}$ kg)
3 tablespoons olive oil
3 large carrots, peeled and sliced
$\frac{1}{2}$ medium turnip, peeled and sliced
2 large onions, finely chopped
$\frac{3}{4}$ pt/450 ml white wine/water or stock (2 c)
Bouquet garni
Pre-heat the oven to 325F/170C/Gas 3.
Heat oil in a large pan and brown meat all over. Place in large casserole just large enough to hold it. Add onions to pan and brown. Add some more oil if necessary, heat through and then add carrots and turnips. Toss in oil for 10-15 minutes.

Remove meat from casserole and place vegetables in base then meat on top. Season well. Add white wine or water to pan and boil up with pan juices. Pour over meat and add enough liquid to come just over half-way up. Cover and cook slowly for about 1$\frac{1}{2}$ hours till the meat is almost tender. To crisp the surface — remove the lid and turn up the oven to 450F/230C/Gas 8 and brown the surface — should take about 15-20 minutes. Remove the meat, the bones should slide out fairly easily. Cut meat in wedges and serve with some of the vegetables. Taste the cooking liquid for seasoning and serve in a sauce boat or pour over meat when serving. Serve with baked potatoes.

LAMB AND KIDNEY PIE

8-10 servings

Tender lamb is marinaded overnight in honey, redcurrant jelly and lemon juice to make a richly flavoured filling for this pie.

$2\frac{1}{2}$ lb/$1\frac{1}{4}$ kg stewing Scotch lamb
$\frac{1}{2}$ lb/250 g lamb's kidney
2 tablespoons flour
$\frac{1}{2}$ pt/300 ml stock or water ($1\frac{1}{4}$ c)
6 oz/175 g cooked gammon (English: ham)
Salt and pepper
$\frac{1}{2}$ lb/250 g puff pastry

For the marinade

2 medium onions, finely sliced
3 tablespoons honey
1 lemon, zest and juice
2 tablespoons redcurrant jelly

Pre-heat the oven to 400F/200C/Gas 6 for the first 20 minutes. Then turn down oven and cook for a further 80 minutes at 325F/170C/Gas 3.

Size of pie dish — $2\frac{1}{2}$ pt ($1\frac{1}{4}$ L)

Cut the lamb into dice and finely slice the kidney. Add to the marinade ingredients and leave overnight. Add flour, gammon, salt, pepper and stock. Mix well and place in pie dish. Cover with pastry and bake. Cover pastry if necessary towards the end of the cooking if it looks as though it is overcooking.

SCOTCH PIES

Scottish Bakers make these pies in large quantities, mostly with mature mutton which butchers don't like selling, since the public complains about its toughness. They are made in special straight-sided moulds usually about 3-3½″ (7.5-8.5 cm) in diameter and are about 1½″ (4 cm) deep. They are easily recognised by the rim of pastry which stands up above the lid making about ½″ (1 cm) space which can be filled with hot gravy, or beans and potatoes. They should not be eaten cold — bakers often sell them hot and they are also sold in Fish and Chip shops but are not usually made at home. Originally tavern food, they are an early form of 'fast food' for working people. In the Candleriggs in Glasgow, there still stands 'Grannie Black's' (now a pub and on a different site from the original). She was a Glasgow character who is said to have made such good mutton pies that their fame spread far and wide. They cost twopence and were known as 'Tuppeny Struggles'.

How to use a whole Sheep or Lamb

These are Lady Clark's notes dated 1893 and are really about how to use up all the bits and pieces which are not actually part of the main meat carcase. It was a comprehensive guide for thrifty Scots, who have a natural dislike of waste and though there are few today who are actually faced with the prospect of dealing with the whole animal in a domestic situation, there are still lots of practical pieces of interest for using cuts which can be bought over the butcher's counter.

'Heads are available, though not on display. Sometimes difficult to get if there is a circus in town since they are favourite food for lions and tigers. I suppose the same holds true if you live near a zoo.

'The blood makes Black puddings, with sieved oatmeal, or groats, or rice. . . . The head, trotters and breast of mutton, with some of the superfluous fat on this last cut off, make, with vegetables, the best broth, and afterwards all the meat is useful in other ways. The sheep's head, whole, is served with feet ('trotters') round as garnish, and with broth as sauce; or cut up in squares in dressed sauce as an entree, vegetables in centre and fried brains as garnish; or can be boiled and turned out of a mould solid.

'The boiled breast of mutton used to boil with Sheep's Head, can afterwards be crumbled, with mixed herbs, and broiled or baked a nice brown, to eat hot. If for upstairs, serve a sharp sauce in a boat with chopped gherkins or capers in it.

'Kidneys can be sliced for breakfast, with bacon, or in an omelet, and the liver sliced and fried and served with bacon and fried potatoes.

'The sheep's heart is hard if roasted; it is better stuffed and braised — but must be eaten at once — it chills so immediately. A sheeps sweetbread is not worth cooking though in the lamb it is excellent. A lamb's head can be served upon a 'fugie', a mince of heart, sweetbread, liver etc. but no kidneys. Make it savoury.

'Much of the rest is used for Haggis. Any bits not otherwise wanted are very welcome additions to the scraps set aside for the keeper's dogs.'

GRILLED FLANK (Breast) OF LAMB with Tomato Sauce

4 servings

Made from well-flavoured lamb this succulent delicacy is moist and tender inside, crisp and crunchy on the outside. It also has the advantage of using up the cheaper flank cut. Flank stuffed and rolled is also good roasted.

To prepare the meat

Use the two pieces of flank (2 lb/1 kg) which have been simmered in some broth till tender or poached on their own till tender with some vegetables. While still warm, remove the bones which should slip easily out of the meat. To make a good flat surface for grilling, put the meat between two boards overnight with a weight on top. The next day, cut each flank into 5-6 triangles or rectangles of an equal size.

Coating the pieces

Mix 4 oz/125 g fresh breadcrumbs (2 c) with salt, pepper and some finely chopped herbs. Dip the meat in beaten egg (2 eggs) or some melted butter and then cover with breadcrumbs, pressing in well. Remove excess crumbs.

Grilling

Place on a buttered baking tray, brush with butter and grill quickly under a hot grill about 5 minutes each side. Baste with more butter if necessary. The purpose is simply to toast the coating and heat through the meat. Overcooking will dry out the meat and make it tough.

Serving

Serve garnished with watercress and with a 'sharp' sauce. A well flavoured Tomato Sauce (see p. 257) is very good with this and can also be used for lamb chops, steaks or with meatballs.

LAMB'S FRY

4-6 servings

Very thin strips of liver, heart, sweetbreads and kidneys are cooked very quickly to preserve flavour and texture — the heart may need a little longer.

Heat 4 tablespoons olive oil in a pan and add 2 lambs' hearts pared free of fat and tough vessels, split in half and cut lengthwise into thin strips. Toss over a high heat for 2-3 minutes reducing the heat if necessary.

Turn up the heat again and add 7 oz/200 g lamb's liver sliced and cut into thin strips, a kidney thinly sliced and about 4 oz/125 g sweetbreads, thinly sliced (see p. 135 for preparation). Sauté for one minute or until the liver and kidney have just changed colour.

Add 1 handful of chopped parsley mixed with 1-2 cloves crushed garlic. Squeeze over some lemon juice and serve straight from serving dish.

HAGGIS

Walk into any butcher's shop in Scotland and ask how many pounds of haggis they make in a week — you will be astonished. And this, for every week of the year; not just at the national festivals of St Andrew's Day and Burns' night when demand often outstrips supply and butchers are frequently sold out by the end of the morning. If the desire for haggis is strong at home, it becomes an obsession for exiled Scots who have vast quantities air-freighted to all parts of the globe for these two nights of the year.

My first haggis-making exploits were as a student when the whole process took the best part of a day to complete. The raw Sheep's Pluck*, while not a pretty sight, didn't worry me at all but the windpipe hanging over the side of the pot which the whole pluck was cooking in, quietly disgorging the blood and other impurities from the lungs into a jar

*A Sheep's Pluck is the part of the animal which has been 'plucked' out of the belly and includes the liver, heart and lungs which are all joined together with the windpipe at one end.

which we had placed on the cooker, did not appeal. It was about ten years before I had another go, when I was working in a hotel which bought whole sheep and as the plucks started filling up the precious deep freeze space, prompted by necessity, I got out my old Haggis recipe in The Glasgow Cookery Book (John Smith, Glasgow, Revised Edition, 1962).

It is a traditional recipe which most butchers will tell you is basically what they work from, though no two of them will produce the same haggis. Variations are secret and have been developed over many years testing the Scottish palate for preferences. Haggis lovers have very definite ideas about the best qualities of haggis and a competition is held each year to find the best butcher's haggis.

Qualities of a good Haggis
The flavour is a matter of taste, with some liking it spicy and 'hot' with plenty of pepper, while others prefer a milder flavour with more herbs than spices. Relative proportions of meat to oatmeal, suet and onions also depend on individual preferences as does the type of offal used. Some butchers will use ox liver because their customers prefer the flavour, while others stick to the traditional sheep's — there are all kinds of permutations which make haggis eating something of an adventure.

More a question of quality, the meat should have no tough gristly bits sometimes found in a badly-made haggis and the texture should be moist and firm, rather than dry and crumbly.

Traditional method
1 sheep's bag and pluck
4 oz/125 g suet, finely chopped (1 c)
4 medium onions, finely chopped
$\frac{1}{2}$ lb/250 g pinhead oatmeal (2 c)
2-4 tablespoons salt
1 level teaspoon freshly ground black pepper
1 level teaspoon dried mixed herbs (2 for fresh)

Preparing the pluck and bag
Wash the bag in cold water, scrape and clean well. Leave overnight in cold water. Wash the pluck and put it in a pan of boiling water. Let the windpipe lie over the side of the pot and have a small jar underneath to catch the drips. Simmer gently till all are tender — this depends on the age of animal but is usually between one and two hours. Place the cooked pluck in a large basin, cover with the liquid which it was boiled in and leave overnight.

Making the Haggis
(The next day)
Toast the oatmeal in the oven till thoroughly dried-out but not browned. Cut off the windpipe, trim away all skin and black parts. Chop or mince the heart and lungs, grate the liver. Add the oatmeal, salt, pepper, herbs and about 1 pt/$\frac{1}{2}$ L (2$\frac{1}{2}$ c) of the liquid the pluck was boiled in. Mix well, fill the bag rather more than half full of the

mixture. Press out the air, sew up and prick with a long needle. Place in boiling water, simmer for 3 hours, pricking again when it swells. The bag may be cut into several pieces to make smaller haggis in which case cook for only 1½-2 hours.

Serve hot with 'tatties' — Creamed Potatoes flavoured with nutmeg (see p. 181); 'neeps' — Mashed Turnip flavoured with allspice (see p. 194) and a good blended whisky.

Other ways of serving

'Haggis meat, by those who cannot admire the natural shape,' says Meg Dods, 'may be poured out of the bag, and *served in a deep dish. No dish heats up better.*' It is also a very practical way of serving haggis to large numbers provided it is well covered to prevent drying out. Knobs of butter dotted over the top surface are a good idea. Slices of haggis can be grilled, fried or wrapped in foil and baked in the oven with a bit of butter on top. The slices can be served as part of a Mixed Grill or for breakfast with bacon and egg. It is very good fried and served simply with fried onions or with an onion sauce lightly flavoured with whisky. I have had a slice of fried haggis served in a roll and described as a 'Haggisburger'. It was served with a whisky-flavoured chutney and was an excellent snack. It can also be used with mince in a Shepherd's Pie.

Provided you are careful about the dominating flavour it can be used as a stuffing. It should not be used with delicately-flavoured meat like chicken unless it is a very mild haggis. Other ingredients can be added to the haggis such as nuts or cooked rice. Mixing in a little tomato sauce (see p. 257) can work well.

An Edinburgh butcher, well-known for his quality haggis, Charles MacSween has recently made a vegetarian haggis with an excellent flavour which is proving popular. It has a variety of vegetables, spices, oatmeal and brown rice.

Perhaps the most unusual idea is that of serving cold haggis. Some years ago I met a chef whose local butcher made such a good haggis that he served a slice of it cold with hot toast as a starter course. It seemed that he used pork fat and meat rather than suet along with a delicate combination of herbs and spices with excellent results.

Variations in other recipes include adding the juice of a lemon or a little 'good vinegar'. Even flavouring with cayenne pepper. Quantities of oatmeal and suet vary a lot with up to 2 lb/1 kg oatmeal and 1 lb/500 g suet to a single pluck. Some are boiled for up to 6 hours. Meg Dods says that, 'A finer haggis may be made by parboiling and skinning sheep's tongues and kidneys, and substituting these minced, for most of the lights, and soaked bread or crisped crumbs for the toasted meal.' For those who can't face a whole pluck she also says that the parboiled minced meat from a sheep's head can be used for haggis.

Origins of Haggis Pudding

Like pies, puddings have always been made with a collection of miscellaneous ingredients; the one under a pie crust, the other boiled in the stomach bag of an animal. The term 'pudding' came from the habit in 15th and 16th centuries of referring to the entrails of animals and men as 'puddings'.

Pudding Lane in London is thought to have derived its name, not from an association with edible puddings, but because 'the butchers of Eastcheap have their scalding-houses for hogs there, and their puddings, with other filth of beasts, are voided down that way to their Dung-boats on the Thames.'

From the 15th century to about the 18th century, recipes for early puddings are closely connected with something called a 'Haggus' or 'Haggas' pudding. The general principle involved the use of the stomach bag with a filling of the cooked entrails plus some other ingredients. 15th-century recipes use the liver and the blood of the sheep, while later recipes in the 17th century, referring to making a 'Haggas Pudding in the Sheep's Paunch' use a wider variety of ingredients — parsley, savoury, thyme, onions, beef, suet, oatmeal, cloves, mace, pepper and salt, sewn up and boiled; served with a hole cut in the top and filled with butter melted with two or three eggs. Another recipe uses a calve's paunch* and the entrails minced together with grated bread, yolks of eggs, cream, spices, dried fruits and herbs, served as a sweet with sugar and almonds: while yet another recipe uses oatmeal steeped and boiled, mixed with spices, raisins, onions and herbs.

Although the derivation is obscure, some etymologists claim that the term may have been transferred from the now obsolete name for a magpie which was 'Haggiss' or 'Haggess'. A medieval comparison may have been drawn between the magpie's habit of collecting and forming an accumulation of varied articles and the same general principle applied instead to ingredients for the pudding. This analogy is carried even further, with the unproven theory that another early word for the magpie may be responsible for the word 'pie' since at one time the magpie was known as a 'maggot-pie' or a 'Margaret-pie' or even simply as a 'pie'.

Whether the habits of the magpie had anything to do with what we know to-day as puddings and pies, the Haggis pudding has a British rather than a Scottish pedigree with the English making Haggis well into the 18th century. The Scots' deeply rooted instincts, bred by centuries of surviving at poverty levels, to use up all the odds and ends of an animal seems to me the best reason why we have continued to make it. The fact that we actually still like to eat it is proof enough of its virtue.

---

*Baxters of Fochabers made one of the largest Haggis, weighing 170 lb, by stuffing the mixture into the interior of two cows' stomachs which had been sewn together.

CHAPTER SIX

FRUIT
& VEGETABLES

& SWEETS, PUDDINGS, SOUPS & OTHER DISHES

She put into the carriage a basket of excellent gooseberries,
and some of the finest apricots I ever saw or tasted, which have
grown out of doors; the season has been unusually favourable
and her husband was fond of cultivating his garden.

Robert Southey — at Inverness
Journal of a Tour in Scotland in 1819

It had always seemed to me that the Scots were at a disadvantage when it
came to growing fruits and vegetables. Not only has Scotland a colder,
wetter climate than the rest of Britain but in the past was deprived of
many important influences which brought new crops and growing
expertise, like the Flemish gardeners who settled in the South of England in the 15th century with their improved stock and new varieties.
Neither had we Romans planting cherries for us, as they did in Kent, nor
kings like Henry VIII, who planted fruit trees around the country. And
yet Scottish gardeners of the 18th and 19th centuries were famous
throughout the world.

It is true that the Cistercian and Benedictine monks who came to
Scotland in the 11th and 12th centuries and settled in the fertile areas of
the Borders, the valleys of Strathmore and the Morayshire coast,
brought with them new crops and horticultural knowledge. The range
and variety of fruits and vegetables grown by them and subsequently in
the gardens of the aristocratic houses of the land were considerable. In
the Ochtertyre House Book of Accomps (1737-1739) such things as
asparagus, spinach, artichokes, French beans and cauliflower crop up
quite frequently in their menus. But the common people who, after all,
make up the bulk of the population, were limited to a narrow range, it
seems. Possibly people in and around the larger towns found supplies of
a wider variety, but the average Scottish peasants of around the 18th
century depended on the limitations of his 'kail-yard' (garden) which
meant kail, possibly cabbages or leeks, some bushes of gooseberries or
blackcurrants, and, by the end of the century, potatoes.

Ever enterprising, Scots made use of wild fruits and berries instead. Blaeberries, Brambles, Wild Raspberries, Rowans, Sloes, Rosehips, Geans and Nettles were all used as well as many wild herbs like the wild Garlic which was used to flavour cheese (see Hramsa p. 246). They made a lot of jams and jellies with these wild fruits and used them in interesting and imaginative ways like the drink which Thomas Pennant was given when he visited Mr Macleod of Arnisdale in 1769. 'I shall never forget the hospitality of the house: before I could utter a denial, three glasses of rum, cordialised with jelly of bilberries, were poured into me by the irresistible hand of good Madam MacLeod.' As one of the most eminent naturalists of the 18th century his observation on the fruits eaten on Jura is interesting — 'Sloes are the only fruits of the island. An acid for punch is made of the berries of the mountain ash (rowan): and a kind of spirit is also distilled from them.'

I can find no reference to any use of the superb fungi which grow so profusely in Scottish woods. Presumably they were viewed with suspicion, as they still are to-day.

Serious horticulture, to provide for growing markets, began in the 18th century and has been developing ever since. Today Scots successfully grow crops in large quantities which turn the disadvantages of the colder, less sunny climate to best use.

Raspberries and peas are probably the most outstanding ones and Scotland is a major producer in Britain. They ripen more slowly here, and as a result develop a better flavour, while the colder weather means less pests and diseases and therefore higher yields. Everyone in Edinburgh in the 18th century knew that the street cry — 'Fine rosy-cheekit Carse o' Gowries — the tap o' the tree' meant apples and pears. Today, instead, it would have to be 'Raspberries and Peas' since these are the two main crops of the area now, with a few others besides. No apples or pears are grown here commercially now, nor in any other part of Scotland today for that matter.

The Scottish Crop Research Institute in the heart of the country at Invergowrie has been for more than thirty years now breeding varieties of all Scottish horticultural crops with a view to increasing yields, producing disease-resistant plants which will fit the special needs of the consumer, while at the same time maintaining quality. Raspberries took on a whole new dimension for me after an afternoon spent among their experimental canes at Invergowrie. The seemingly endless permutations on size, colour, brightness, firmness and flavour; all to be considered in the search for a perfect raspberry.

Summers, when we were sent to 'the berries' had not endeared me to them. I never seemed to pick fast enough or make enough money to make all the agony of the red stained and scratched hands worthwhile. Others did, but then I graduated to a factory in Dundee and the pay was better, though the love-hate relationship with the red berries continued. Peas were canned and frozen there as well, and we sat for endless hours picking out the debris from moving conveyor belts full of blanched peas, which destroyed my enthusiasm for them too.

But new varieties of raspberries have been developed at the Institute by plant breeders with a view to increasing the shelf life of freshly sold ones. They not only cater for the growing popularity of 'Pick-Your-Own' fruit but also satisfy processing needs and have subtle differences of flavour from the Malling Jewel variety which I had been most familiar with. Among the many varieties which I tasted was Glen Clova which has a sharp acid flavour with a real tangy after-taste which might be too sour for some palates. Glen Moy has a more rounded flavour, neither too sharp nor too sweet and the berries were large with a good 'shelf life', particularly necessary for the fresh market. (For pickers' interest it has smooth rather than prickly canes). Another variety which has been developed without prickles is Glen Prosen, which has a good flavour but the berries are slightly smaller than the ideal for fresh markets though they are exceptionally firm.

Tayberries and Tummelberries were another revelation. These are the hybrid crosses between blackberries and raspberries of the same type as the American Loganberry. The Tayberry has a strong personality, a rich sweet aromatic flavour and an exotic deep purple colour. It is a firm berry which cooks well. Tummelberries (not yet available for commercial distribution) are less forceful in flavour, more reminiscent of the raspberry with a sharper acidic tang. In shape they are rounder and redder than the Tayberry. The Tayberry is not widely available throughout Scotland but has received more interest in England where there are several plantations. In Scotland some of the raspberry growers have the Tayberry in small quantities and Pick-Your-Own growers find them enormously popular with customers.

Strawberries are a minor crop in Scotland — only 800 hectares compared with England's 6,250 hectares. The most common variety grown is Cambridge Favourite, although several other varieties have come and gone in the last ten years and others will undoubtedly appear in the future. Strawberry growing in Scotland has migrated from the smallholdings of the Clyde valley to the arable farms of Tayside, Fife and the North East. About half of the Scottish crop is sold fresh, mostly on the English market. Today plums are the principle fruit grown in the Clyde valley.

At the moment Blackcurrants are also mostly grown in England for the juice market, but new, hardier varieties are being developed for growing in Scotland for fresh markets, and these may be more available in the future. American high bush Blueberries have been made available to growers in Scotland by the Research Institute and some growers have taken up the crop. They take a long time to establish but when they do, could remain cropping for fifty years. They are the same genus as our low-grown Blaeberry and therefore like our acid soil. Their flavour is milder though, and quite different.

Mainly due to the demands of the processing industry and supermarkets the Scottish vegetable crop has increased by 30% since 1970. Half of the total vegetables grown is peas. Of the rest which are grown in quantity, beans, turnips, cabbages and carrots come next with lesser amounts

of **brussels sprouts, calabrese, cauliflower** and **leeks. Rhubarb, lettuce** and **tomatoes** are the only other crops which Scotland grows in any quantity though this excludes potatoes which, because they are grown in such large quantities, are regarded as an agricultural crop.

Despite all this increased growing of vegetables it seems that the Scots continue to lag behind as eaters. Their favourites are carrots and turnips (Swedes) — but they eat less than half the national average of green vegetables and only slightly under it for fresh fruits. This possibly gives the wrong impression since there may be great regional variation in the popularity or even availability of fresh green vegetables. It is a well known fact that Highlanders will often not eat them, even if they are readily available, while people in and around the market garden areas of Edinburgh are enthusiastic green vegetable eaters.

When Robert Southey was visiting Aberdeen in 1812, he referred to the lack of vegetables. 'But garden stuff,' he says, 'is of late introduction into Scotland, tho' the Scotch now exceed us as gardeners: Wesley says that when he was first in that country, they had only one sort of flesh-meat even at a nobleman's table, and no vegetables of any kind.'

It might almost seem that the gardeners were so good that they only wanted their gardens to be looked at. Robert Louis Stevenson describes a crusty old gardener who was very reluctant to part with a cabbage lest it spoil the look of things, while a description of the kitchen garden at Blair Castle in the 18th century makes it quite clear that vegetable and herb gardens were elaborate showpieces which visitors made special excursions to admire — 'It was about 1200 feet long. Down its whole length there was a lake containing several islands. On two of them thatched houses had been built as breeding-places for swans and wild ducks. There was a pigeon-house at one corner and a gardener's cottage at another, and at one end there was a semi-circular summer-house with a glass front.' Marjorie Plant, <u>Domestic Life in Scotland in the Eighteenth Century</u> (1952).

Another problem was the fact that gardens were often situated quite a distance from the kitchen, which was inconvenient for a busy cook. Whatever the reasons, it seems that while good use of them was made in combinations of soups and stews, the Scots did not appreciate them as important in their own right.

Scottish Soft Fruits: Raspberries, Strawberries, Blackcurrants, Brambles (Blackberries), Red Currants, Blaeberries

It was quite a pantry: oatcakes, barley scones, flour scones, butter, honey, sweetmeats, cheese, and wine, and spiced whisky, all came out of the deep shelves of this agreeable recess, as did the great key of the dairy; this was often given to one of us to carry to old Mary the cook, with leave to see her skim and whip the fine rich cream, which Mrs Grant would afterwards pour on a whole pot of jam and give us for luncheon. This dish, under the name of 'bainne briste', or broken milk, is a great favourite wherever it has been introduced.

Elizabeth Grant of Rothiemurchus
Memoirs of A Highland Lady 1797-1827

If the jam is lightly set, more in the style of a 'conserve' than a jam, this is an excellent way of combining fruit and cream but ideally the fruit should be fresh. Such jewel-bright colours and lovely shapes need no embellishments save the simple white background of cream. Its bland rich flavour highlights the natural sharpness of all these ready-to-eat fruits when they are ripe and full of fragrant bouquet.

Soft fruits have been linked with cream for centuries. In the 15th century the cream was made from almonds pounded and mixed with water: then the mixture was strained and the liquid used as cream. The recipe for 'Strawberye' which appears in the Harleian MS 279 (1420) also includes a formidable collection of flavourings which they added, with typical medieval passion for spicing — pepper, ginger, cinnamon, galyngale (from the root of the Cypress rush) and vinegar. No quantities are given so we shall never know whether it was just a pinch or more which was added.

Five ways of combining fruit with cream

1. **Fruit + Cream.** The simple fresh fruit, either singly or in a combination with cream, whipped or pouring as a garnish. Soured cream and natural yogurt can also be used in combinations.

2. **Fruit + Cream + Sauce.** Fruit plus cream with the addition of the juice of the berry or another berry for a sauce or a syrup sauce.

3. **Fruit Purée + Cream.** Consistency and texture will depend on the type of fruit and thickness of the cream.

4. **Fruit Purée + Cream — iced.** The answer for strawberries which are the only soft fruit which freezes badly whole.

5. **Fruit + Cream Cheese.** These two are combined in the classic Scottish dish of Cream-Crowdie (Cranachan) though the cheesecake is another way of combining them, as is the French Coeur a la Crème, traditionally served with strawberries.

1. Fruit and Cream

Presentation is one important factor, and the other is using fruit which is fully ripe and in its prime. White or glass dishes are the best foil for these brightly-coloured fruits if to be served simply. Creating a **fruit platter** is another way of letting the fruit speak for itself.

AN ASHET OF FRESH FRUIT

or Fresh Fruit Platter

At the end of meal a huge dish was put on the table, and on it an abstract design of prepared fruit, very bold and Matisse-like. We were each given a fork, to spear little pieces of this and that as we sat back and talked. It seemed to me the best possible way to end a meal with glory and without exhaustion for the cook.

Jane Grigson
Sunday Times Magazine, December 1982

This also makes an excellent centre-piece for a buffet table or is a good way of serving fruit at a simple family meal. Everyone helping themselves, and leftovers used for fruit salad the next day.

Creating colour contrasts and textures is all part of the fun of presentation. It is first a question though, of what is fresh and ripe and secondly what will make the most stunning effect.

Go to the shop or market first and look at the fruits; then start to create the picture.

My own experience of doing this with fresh fruit is that a **whole pineapple** not only provides an interesting green shape with its tufted

top, and a soft yellow colour contrasting with the bright reds and blacks, but it also combines well flavourwise with raspberries and strawberries in particular. The same applies to **melon** of all kinds, and both these fruits can be cut into boat shapes. Leave the tops on the pineapple and cut as for melon, cutting loose the fruit with a sharp knife close to the skin. Then cut the fruit into small bite-sized wedges keeping the boat shape form, and then place on the ashet.

Peaches combine well with soft fruits as do **apricots, nectarines, greengages** and **plums** — they should all be cut into bite-sized pieces. **Apples** and **pears** are a good texture contrast but should be chopped at the last minute to avoid discolouration. The same applies to **bananas,** unless you toss them in lemon juice. **Grapes, cherries** and **gooseberries** are excellent as they are. I wouldn't bother removing stones for this kind of dish unless it was for some sort of formal occasion. **Oranges, tangerines** and **sweet grapefruit** should be segmented either with or without the pith.

The odd exotic fruit which is usually too expensive to use in quantity can be added with great effect. **Mangos, fresh figs, kiwi fruit,** and **passion fruit** are the ones I've used most. Toasted nuts are also a good idea. I like to use **hazelnuts** with raspberries and **almonds** with strawberries. If you need some white colour then strips of **fresh coconut** are excellent.

Assembling the fruits
This should be done in two stages. Work out the ones which you can safely arrange in advance without any drying out or discolouring. Have some rough idea of how the finished platter is going to look and then prepare as much as possible in advance. It is not necessary to spend hours arranging patterns of fruit. Throw it together quickly; like a good watercolour painting it should not be 'over-worked'.

Serve with or without a jug of whipped cream and drink with a chilled sweet white wine or a light fruity Bordeaux.

2. Fruit, Cream and Sauce

'GOURMET' STRAWBERRIES

4 servings

The sauce is a simple purée of the fruit, sharpened with lemon. This is a good summer sweet. The idea comes from Gourmet, an American food magazine.

1 lb/500 g strawberries, washed and hulled
Juice of 1 lemon
Sugar to taste

Take about a quarter of the strawberries and purée in the liquidiser or processor with lemon juice and sugar. Taste for sweetness. Put the strawberries in a bowl and sieve the purée on top. Chill for about half an hour before serving. Serve with or without cream.

Note: this works equally well with raspberries, or could for that matter be used with any other soft fruits. There is lots of scope for experimentation by mixing the combinations rather than serving the fruit with its own fruit purée. I have often used Strawberries with Raspberry Purée and vice versa. Of course the classic one is Peaches with Raspberry Purée (Melba) but a very good combination which is often used is a Red Currant Purée with Strawberries and I have served ripe Blackcurrants and Redcurrants in a Raspberry Purée with great effect.

HOW ESCOFFIER SERVED STRAWBERRIES
at the Carlton Hotel, London

4 servings

Known in classical cuisine as 'Strawberries Romanoff' this dish has had many interpretations but all have depended on Escoffier's original combination of strawberries and oranges.

Soak some large strawberries in orange juice and Curacao. Put them into a silver or glass dish and cover them with Chantilly cream.

Auguste Escoffier
Ma Cuisine. 1934

1 lb/500 g strawberries — sprinkle with sugar overnight
Add $\frac{1}{4}$ pt/150 ml ($\frac{3}{4}$ c) freshly squeezed orange juice
5 tablespoons orange-flavoured liqueur

Leave to macerate for 1 hour
Transfer to serving dish. Whip 12 fl oz/325 ml double cream ($1\frac{1}{2}$ c). Sweeten with 2 tablespoons vanilla sugar — spread over berries and serve.

BRANDIED FRUIT CUP

8-10 servings

This combination of dried fresh fruits allow plenty of scope for variation according to season. It is a cross between a 'compote' and a fruit salad but will keep well for a few days, so is worth making up in quantity.

To prepare the dried fruit

5 oz/150 g dried apricots (1 c)
12 oz/350 g mixed dried fruit (2 c)
Place in a saucepan with water to cover and simmer till tender — cool and cut up into pieces.

Add

1 lb/500 g fresh cherries
1 grapefruit, segmented
4 oz/125 g preserved kumquats
1 lb/500 g figs in syrup
3 bananas, sliced
Strawberries, raspberries or any other soft fruits in season
Juice of 1 lemon
Sugar to taste
Cognac — a few tablespoons
Combine in a large bowl, add the juice of one lemon and sugar and cognac to taste. Leave overnight for flavours to develop and blend together.

Serve slightly chilled with Nutball Biscuits (see p. 226)

RED PEARS WITH RASPBERRIES

Simmer 3 lb/1½ kg raspberries till soft.
Pour into jelly bag and leave overnight to drain off juice
(approx 1½ pts/¾ L).
Put into a pan with 1 stick of cinnamon; 1 lb/500 g sugar (2½ c) and
3 lb/1½ kg peeled halved pears. Simmer very gently till the pears are
just soft. Put into preserving jars. Boil up syrup to reduce a little if
necessary, add some brandy to taste, cool and pour over pears.

RASPBERRY VINEGAR

Fruit vinegars frequently crop up in 18th-century cookery books. Mrs Dalgairns' recipe (1789) uses a pint of vinegar to a quart of rasps. It is left for three days, stirred daily, then strained. A pound of sugar is used to every pint of juice, then it is boiled for ten minutes, cooled and bottled with one glass of brandy added to every quart of vinegar.

It was used mostly as a refreshing drink diluted in cold water though it was also used diluted with warm water for sore throats. In Yorkshire it is served with Yorkshire pudding as a sweet. It can give a lift to any vinaigrette or mayonnaise and a tablespoon can be used most effectively when finishing sauces for meat and game when a sweet-sour flavour is required.

USING WINE AS A SAUCE with soft fruits

The fruit is usually prepared just before serving, piled into a wine glass and the wine poured over when ready to eat. If left for some time the fruit tends to disintegrate and the flavours too lose their identity and crispness.

Choosing the right wine

This is a matter of knowing your wine and not letting either fruit or wine dominate. Too much sugar will obscure the flavour of the wine. There is a tradition in Bordeaux that pouring a fine old claret which has begun to decline over lightly crushed strawberries gives the wine a momentary sparkle of life. A sweet Sauterne is good with raspberries.

MARINATED STRAWBERRIES AND RASPBERRIES with Whipkull

serves 4

Whipkull is a Shetland speciality which was originally eaten with thin crisp, butter shortbread for Yule breakfast (see p. 271). Eggs and sugar are beaten over heat till thick and creamy, then flavoured with rum. This version uses a little cream, which is not traditional.

To marinade the fruit

$\frac{1}{2}$ lb/250 g strawberries
$\frac{1}{2}$ lb/250 g raspberries
1 mango (optional)
4 tablespoons kirsch
Sugar to taste
Slice the strawberries and cut up the mango into small dice. Leave the raspberries whole. Divide between 4 flameproof dishes and sprinkle with kirsch and sugar. Leave in a cool place for a few hours.

To make the sauce

3 egg yolks
3 tablespoons sugar
$1\frac{1}{2}$ tablespoons kirsch
1 teaspoon lemon juice
1 teaspoon grated lemon rind
4 fl oz/125 ml whipped double cream ($\frac{1}{2}$ c)
Beat the eggs and sugar together over hot water till they are thick and creamy, then beat in flavourings and finally fold in the cream. Pour this, divided equally, over the marinated fruit and place under a very hot grill about 2-3″ from the heat. Grill till the tops are golden brown and serve immediately.

3. Fruit Purée and Cream

Straight fruit purée mixed through whipped double cream sounds simple enough, but there are many variations. The degree of puréeing is a matter of taste but it is generally agreed that uniformity leads to boredom, and mashing the fruit, rather than reducing to a fine pulp, gives a more interesting texture. Some of the fruit can even be left whole. Also for the same reasons, the cream need not be thoroughly mixed in, but can create a lovely marbled effect if it is only partially mixed through the fruit.

WHIPPED FRUIT PUDDING

4 servings

To begin with, a thickened fruit syrup is made, and then the crushed fruit and cream or yogurt mixed through. It is a good way of 'stretching' the fruit if in short supply, with no real loss of flavour. It is similar in method to a Russian 'Kissel'.

Maple syrup with strawberries, give this dish a special taste and fragrance. But don't just stick to these flavours — mix and match your favourite fruits and juices.

$\frac{3}{4}$ pt/450 ml orange fruit juice (2 c scant)
1 oz/50 g potato flour or arrowroot (1 tablespoon)
3 tablespoons maple syrup or 2 tablespoons honey
Juice from $\frac{1}{2}$ lemon
$\frac{1}{2}$ lb/250 g raspberries and strawberries
$\frac{1}{4}$ pt/150 ml whipped double cream or natural yogurt or soured cream or any mixture of all three ($\frac{3}{4}$ c)
Pinch of cinnamon and nutmeg

To make the syrup

Heat the juice and then blend the thickening with a little of the hot juice. Return to the pan and bring to the boil to thicken, stirring all the time. Pour into a bowl and whip with a wire whisk or beaters till light and fluffy. Leave to cool.

Finishing the dish

Mash up the fruit roughly, leaving some berries whole and fold in with the cream or equivalent. Chill. Serve with whole berries for garnish and/or chopped toasted nuts.

4. Fruit Purée with Cream — Iced

Ice cream making in Scotland has been dominated by Italians for at least a century. Their 'real' ice cream cafés are a welcome haven for weary shoppers and the cheerful friendly Italian service an added bonus. Recipes are jealously guarded secrets and there is an annual award for the best ice cream by the Association of Ice Cream Makers in Scotland. Needless to say Italians dominate the event.

The classic Scottish way of eating an ice cream cone is with a topping of raspberry syrup. Of uncertain origins, this is known as a **MacCallum** and one theory claims that it was made by a Glasgow 'Taly' for a customer called MacCallum who was also a supporter of Clyde Football Club whose colours, of course, are red and white.

Ice cream became a 'street food' for the ordinary people around the mid-19th century though it had been eaten by the wealthy classes for much longer. According to Henry Mayhew, writing in 'London Labour and the London Poor' (1850), the initial reception was not at all favourable. People who tried it complained that it gave them the 'shivers' and he forecast an uncertain future for the trade.

A RICH ICE CREAM suitable for moulding

Known as a parfait in classical cuisine

This is the simplest way of making ice-cream at home in the absence of any special ice cream-making equipment. Mixtures like this which have a high proportion of egg yolks and cream do not crystallise as they freeze and so it is not necessary to have an ice cream churn: it is not even necessary to stir occasionally while they are freezing — all you need in the way of equipment is three clean bowls. The mixture can be set in a special mould and turned out for serving. To remove from the mould simply run briefly under some hot water to loosen, about half an hour before serving.

Quantities, Flavours
It is better not to make up in very large quantities since some of the delicate flavouring will be lost if kept for any length of time in the deep freeze. I would say about one month maximum. Some flavours are more robust than others. Bear in mind also that the frozen flavour will be less strong than unfrozen so flavour strongly rather than mildly.

Serving
Never serve too cold or too hard. Ice cream should be allowed to soften slightly for about 30 minutes at room temperature which will greatly improve the texture and also the flavour.

3 egg yolks
3 tablespoons icing sugar
2-3 teaspoons lemon juice
$\frac{1}{4}$ pt/150 ml whipping cream, whipped ($\frac{3}{4}$ c)
$\frac{1}{2}$ lb/250 g strawberries or raspberries or any other fresh fruit in season

Put the eggs and sugar over hot water and beat till thick and creamy. Press the fruit through a sieve to make the purée or purée in the liquidiser or food processor. With fruits like strawberries and raspberries you will also have to sieve after liquidising to remove the pips. Add the lemon juice. Mix the egg and sugar with the purée, folding in lightly and then fold in the cream. Taste for flavour and pour into a plastic container or mould and freeze.

ETTRICKSHAWS HOME-MADE ICE CREAM

At Ettrickshaws Country House Hotel in Selkirkshire Peter Slaney makes an even simpler version of this using 1 lb/500 g each of fruit pulp and sugar to every pint of whipped double cream. He simply mixes all together with a 'generous measure of any complementary liqueur' and freezes, then serves with a home-made cinnamon biscuit.

KINLOCH ICED HONEY AND WHISKY CREAMS

This is another simple combination, also based on the parfait method, which has special Scottish flavours and which Claire Macdonald of Macdonald makes at the Kinloch Hotel on the Isle of Skye. It comes from her book Sweet Things (1984).

½ pt/300 ml double cream, whipped (1¼ c)
3-4 tablespoons whisky
3-4 tablespoons heather honey
4 egg yolks

Put the eggs and honey into a bowl and beat over gentle heat till they are thick and creamy. Add the whisky to the cream and fold gently into the egg mixture. Taste for flavour and pour into 8 ramekin dishes or 1 large mould. Freeze, cover when firm with cling film.

CLEAR SHARP FLAVOURED WATER ICE

Known as a Sorbet in classical cuisine

Uncomplicated mixtures of fruit purée and sugar syrup give the kind of clean penetrating flavours which were used in meals of many courses somewhere about the middle to 'refresh the palate'; Queen Victoria particularly liked a rum-flavoured one. For eating styles today, they are possibly better suited at the end of a meal and garnished with some of the fresh fruit they have been made from — though I have also seen on menus recently herb-flavoured ones such as mint and fennel served at the beginning of the meal.

Making the syrup

8 oz/250 g granulated sugar (1¼ c)
½ pt/300 ml water (1¼ c)
Juice of 1 lemon
Juice of 1 orange

Dissolve the sugar in the water, bring to the boil and simmer for about five minutes. Cool and add the orange and lemon juice.

Preparing the fruit

1 lb/500 g raspberries, strawberries or any other soft fruit
Pass through a sieve or purée in the liquidiser or processor and then sieve.

Making the water ice

Mix the purée and syrup together and pour into a plastic container with a lid. The shallower it is, the quicker it will freeze. Put into the deep freeze and remove every half hour or so to stir in the crystals which have formed giving it a beat to prevent large crystals forming. When it is uniformly solid but not too hard, it can be beaten into 1 stiffly beaten egg white to give it more volume and a lighter texture. Beat the egg white in the bowl first, and then gradually add spoonfuls of the water ice. It must not be too hard or it will be difficult to mix in. Re-freeze. Like all ices they should not be kept for too long in the freezer since their flavour will begin to fade after a month or so.

PEACH HIGHLAND CREAM

4 servings

This is only one of the many superb dishes which were created by Chef Paul Rogerson while cooking in several British Transport Hotels in Scotland. His sensitivity for Scottish raw materials, his creative flair and his ability to transfer his enthusiasm to paper when he came to write menus have made an important influence in the development of what he liked to call the 'modern taste of Scotland'.

4 fresh peaches
$\frac{1}{4}$ pt/150 ml water ($\frac{3}{4}$ c)
2-3 tablespoons sugar
2-3 tablespoons whisky
4 tablespoons raspberry sorbet
3 egg yolks

Put the peaches briefly into boiling water to loosen the skins, peel. Put the water, sugar and whisky into a pan and boil up for 5-10 minutes. Poach the peaches very lightly in the syrup — they should be only slightly softened. Remove and leave to cool in the syrup. When cool remove peaches from the syrup, halve them and take out the stones. Fill the centres with raspberry sorbet and put back together again.

To make the sauce beat the egg yolks over hot water till thick. Reduce the syrup to about 3 tablespoons and add to the egg yolks. Beat till fairly thick and half fill four wine goblets. Place the peach on top of the sauce and decorate with some fresh raspberries. Serve slightly chilled with a thin crisp shortbread.

5. Fruit, Cream and Cheese

Fresh fruit with a complementary cheese is, from the cook's point of view, one of the easiest ways of ending a meal. Soft fruits with a soft cheese are ideal.

CREAM-CROWDIE (Cranachan)

Unique Scottish flavours — whisky, heather honey and oatmeal combine with cream and soft fruits in this versatile tradition.

The best way to make and eat this is in the traditional way; mixing your own, to your own taste as you sit round a table with family or friends. The toasted oatmeal doesn't lose its 'bite' when mixed and eaten immediately, though some do prefer it softened, as it is when the mixture is made up some time in advance.

The ritual eating was originally a celebration of 'harvest home' when brambles and blaeberries would most likely have been used. (For origins of Crowdie see p. 245.)

Set on the table the following

A bowl of Cream and Crowdie — 2 parts crowdie to 1 part freshly whipped double cream (this was the traditional mixture but obviously may be varied according to taste with soured cream and natural yogurt used if preferred).

A bowl of pinhead (coarse) oatmeal which has been toasted slowly and gently in the oven. This drives off excess moisture, concentrates, and greatly improves the flavour.

A bowl of fresh soft fruit — either a single fruit, or combination, but must be soft and fresh. Picking fruit is traditionally done by children and they are sent out to collect a bowlful.

Jar of Heather honey to sweeten, though sugar may also be used. Bottle of whisky.

Give each person a bowl and spoon (in old Scots households the bowls would have been wooden and the spoons made of horn). The ingredients are then passed round the table and each person creates their own mixture, lubricating it with a generous tot of whisky.

Other Scottish Cream Sweets

TRIFLE

That most wonderful object of domestic art called trifle . . . with its charming confusion of cream and cake and almonds and jam and jelly and wine and cinnamon and froth.

Oliver W. Holmes
Elsie Venner. 1861

I always think of trifle as something akin to the court jester. The foolish part of the meal, the light, passing triviality which comes at the end, adding that essential element of fun and enjoyment. Highly decorated trifles were the centrepiece of the table in the days when everything was laid out in advance, hot and cold dishes, sweet and savoury, and people ate in a kind of sit-down-buffet style with dishes being passed and removed throughout the meal.

A trifle is a difficult dish to define, since it lends itself to so much improvisation — you make of it what you fancy. Looking back through 18th and 19th-century recipes it seems that while the contents vary enormously, the basic structure remains fairly constant.

There is a **first layer** of sponge and/or biscuits. The sponge is sometimes stuck with flaked almonds or they are strewn on top of it. The biscuits always contain almonds (macaroons or ratafias) and the whole is always thoroughly soaked in some kind of wine or spirit. White wine is popular, also sherry and Madeira. Brandy and rum are the most common spirits.

On top of this there is always a **layer of jam**, most frequently raspberry but also marmalade on one occasion.

The **third layer** is a rich thick custard, thickened with lots of eggs: they thought nothing of adding eight eggs to a pint of milk or cream. The thickness varies, but is usually between one and two inches and it is hardly ever flavoured, the bland richness acting as a foil for the highly flavoured bottom layer.

On top of the custard is the **cream layer** which has several variations. Sometimes it is left plain, only sweetened and with a hint of lemon zest. Or the cream has beaten egg whites added. Mostly, though, it is described as a 'Whipped syllabub' and the variations are endless. Syllabubs developed in the 16th century as a sweet drink made originally by milking the cow on top of some wine. The object was to produce a frothy head to a drink which was drunk from a special syllabub pot. The liquid was drunk from the spout first, then the froth eaten with a spoon. In the 18th century they were served in special syllabub glasses showing the two layers of cream and liquid.

Flavourings which I've come across include

White wine with lemon zest
Port with nutmeg
Brandy, sherry or Madeira, nutmeg and lemon
Nutmeg, beer, cider and currants (farmhouse syllabub)
Rosemary, nutmeg, lemon juice and zest, white wine, and a red fruit
    juice or thin fruit purée
Nutmeg, strong beer and brandy
Nutmeg, lemon juice, rum and brandy

Lemons and nutmeg keep appearing and they are particularly good in cream. The alcohol content is a matter of taste, but sherry and brandy are good combinations and the ones that I use most, though there is something to be said for a good white desert wine which gives a more gentle result. This is better if there is a lot of flavouring in the bottom layer and you want to make a contrast.

You are instructed to make the dish 'high and handsome'. To 'garnish with a few sprigs of light flowers of fine colours. . . or a sprinkling of Harlequin comfits*. This last we think vulgar, but it is in frequent use,' says Meg Dods (1826).

*More commonly known as 'hundreds and thousands'.

TO MAKE A TRIFLE

8 servings

Layer (1), the base + layer (2), jam

> 8 oz/250 g left-over sponge cake
> 4 oz/150 g almond biscuits (see p. 226)
> 1 tablespoon flaked almonds
> 10 fl oz/300 ml wine/brandy/sherry/madeira/port (1¼ c)*
> Put cake in the bottom, crumble biscuits on top, scatter with flaked almonds and soak everything in the alcohol. Cover with a layer of raspberry jam. Leave for at least an hour.

Layer (3), the custard

> ½ pt/300 ml single cream or milk (1¼ c)
> 3 large egg yolks
> 1 tablespoon caster sugar
> 1 teaspoon cornflour
> Vanilla essence
> Put the cream in a pan and heat till almost boiling. Blend together the egg yolks, sugar and cornflour. Pour the hot cream over, stirring well. Strain and return to the pan. Cook very gently stirring all the time till it thickens. This can be done in a double boiler. Leave till almost cold, add a few drops of vanilla essence before pouring over the first layer.

Layer (4), the cream or syllabub

> Use Syllabub recipe on p. 170
> or
> ¾ pt/450 ml whipping cream (2 c) whipped stiffly and flavoured with some lemon zest
> Decorate with fresh flowers or crystallised voilets and toasted almonds

*Whisky may also be used though I prefer not to use it in Trifle. The Scottish sweet liqueurs are good.

For a **CHILDREN'S TRIFLE** omit all the alcohol and use fruit juice instead. Use fancy sweets to decorate on top along with some well-washed flowers which they can eat, such as nasturtiums, rose petals, primroses, violets, mimosa, lilacs, cowslips, fruit or herb flowers. To crystallise them for longer keeping pick the flowers on a dry day, remove all stems and green. Wash and dry thoroughly. Paint each flower with lightly-beaten egg white, then hold with tweezers and dip in caster sugar till thoroughly coated. Place on baking sheet and dry off in a warm airy place. When dry place between sheets of greaseproof paper in an airtight tin.

CALEDONIAN CREAM

4 servings

Mrs Dalgairns (1789) pours her Caledonian cream into a 'shape with holes with thin muslin in', she mixes 1 tablespoon orange marmalade (minced) with 1 glass brandy, sugar to taste and the juice of 1 lemon to 2 pints of cream. This is not perhaps the best method, since some of the brandy and lemon flavour will inevitably be lost in draining, which I have omitted.

The following recipe is simple and quick. Using cream cheese with a bitter Seville marmalade gives a sharp flavour to the cream mixture which goes on top of sweet oranges. Fresh cream may be used instead of the cheese, and with a less bitter marmalade makes a sweeter result.

For the cream

4 oz/125 g cream cheese ($\frac{1}{2}$ c)
4 fl oz/125 ml double cream ($\frac{1}{2}$ c)
1 tablespoon thick bitter Seville Marmalade (see p. 232)
2 tablespoons brandy (or rum)
2 teaspoons lemon juice
Sugar to taste
Blend all together in liquidiser or processor till smooth.

Finishing the dish

Fill four long-stemmed glasses firstly with 4 oranges which have been segmented free of pith, sprinkle with some brandy (about 1 teaspoon each — optional) then pile the cream on top. Serve garnished with a few strands of orange zest which have first been boiled in water for a few minutes to remove some of the bitterness. Serve slightly chilled.

SEVILLE CUSTARD CREAMS

6-8 servings

The sharp and intense Seville orange flavour enlivens these rich custard creams. Sweeter oranges may be used instead with good results, the flavour is less powerful.

2 Seville oranges
4 egg yolks
4 oz/125 g caster sugar ($\frac{1}{2}$ c generous)

1 tablespoon sweet orange juice
1 tablespoon Grand Marnier
½ pt/300 ml double cream (1¼ c)
Pare off the thin zest of the Seville orange — put into boiling water
and boil for a few minutes. Drain and put into a liquidiser or
processor with the sugar, the juice of the Seville oranges, the sweet
orange juice and the liqueur. Purée together then add the eggs and
whisk the mixture till thick and fluffy. Bring the cream to the boil
and pour slowly onto the orange and egg mixture. Whisk until cold.
Serve in glasses with some fresh oranges which have been
segmented free of pith.

BISCUITS AND CREAM

Unbelievably simple to make — layers of biscuits and cream are stuck
together in a log shape and the whole is then covered in cream. Left for a
while, the biscuits soften and the cream absorbs the flavours with
delectable results. I have used it so often to keep eager little cooks busy
that I put it here as a tribute to the mother in whose kitchen I first saw it
being put together, and to all other mothers and the many hours they
spend keeping children happy in the kitchen.

All it takes is a packet of biscuits (home-made ones if you happen to
have them) — 1 × 10 fl oz/300 ml carton of whipping or double cream;
some well-flavoured jam and a little vanilla essence.

To make — whip the cream stiffly and flavour with essence, spread
the biscuits first with jam and then cream. Sandwich them together
standing them on their ends so that you build up a kind of log shape. The
cream should make it all stick together quite easily. Finish by spreading
the cream on top and sides of the log; decorate with some fresh fruit or
grated chocolate and leave to soften for at least 2-3 hours.

I mostly use a thin shortbread biscuit and blackcurrant jam, sometimes raspberry. Ginger snaps are very good on their own without the
jam.

RHUBARB CUSTARD TART

For some inexplicable reason Scots manage to eat 25% more rhubarb
than the English, according to Household Food Consumption (1982).
Maybe it is something to do with the fact that the 18th-century Scots
had a craze for growing rhubarb plantations while regarding it as a cure
for all ills!

In the past it was quite common to pour custard, cream or even butter
through the hole in the centre of a fruit pie halfway through the cooking. When it was a custard mixture it was known as a 'caudle'. This is the
same idea, though there is no top to the pie. The custard is cooked till
nicely brown and risen.

Line a 9″ (22 cm) flan with pastry 12 oz/375 g short pastry
(see p. 136) and fill with neat rows of tightly packed fruit about

$\frac{1}{2}''$ (1 cm) thick. Takes about 1 lb/500 g rhubarb. Bake at
400F/200C/Gas 6 till the fruit is almost soft.

Custard

2 eggs
2 fl oz/50 ml double cream ($\frac{1}{4}$ c)
Sugar to taste
Pour custard over fruit and finish baking. When cool sprinkle with
icing sugar and serve warm or cold.

RHUBARB AND BANANAS

Layers of cooked rhubarb and sliced bananas contrast with each other
both in texture and flavour in this quick-and-easy sweet.
1 lb/500 g rhubarb
1 orange
2-3 tablespoons brown sugar
3 bananas
Pinch of cinnamon
Cut up the rhubarb and place in baking dish, cover with orange
juice and zest and sprinkle over sugar. Bake till just soft. Leave to
cool then arrange in a glass dish with layers of finely sliced bananas
ending with a layer of rhubarb. Sprinkle with some freshly ground
cinnamon and serve.

SYLLABUB

A richly flavoured cream
6-8 servings

Excellent with a crisp buttery shortbread but can also be served with
fresh fruits or used in trifle.
7 oz/200 g caster sugar (1 c)
2 lemons, grated zest and juice
1 cinnamon stick
Place in pan, dissolve sugar and simmer gently for a few minutes to
concentrate flavours.

Add

8 tablespoons dry sherry
8 tablespoons brandy
Warm through and decant into a jug — add 1 pt/600 ml double
cream ($2\frac{1}{2}$ c) and whip. Serve warm with a rich crisp shortbread.

BUTTERSCOTCH SAUCE

A good 'store sauce' — one of its most useful functions is as part of a
sundae.
3 oz/75 g butter ($\frac{3}{4}$ stick)
2 tablespoons syrup
5 oz/150 g moist brown sugar

2 fl oz/50 ml water ($\frac{1}{4}$ c)
1 tablespoon plain flour
$\frac{1}{4}$ pt/125 ml milk ($\frac{3}{4}$ c)
Place the butter, syrup, sugar and water in a pan and stir till the sugar is dissolved, then boil for 3 minutes without stirring. Sieve flour and stir in. Gradually add milk and continue stirring till it thickens. Leave to cool, cover and store. It will keep in a cool place for at least 2-3 weeks.

Some other ways with Scottish Soft Fruits

BLACKCURRANT AND APPLE PUDDING

New England Blueberry Slump
4 servings

A popular American dessert which is a stew of fruits topped with squares of very plain scone dough which nicely absorbs the fruit flavours — Louisa May Alcott named her house Apple Slump. Any variety of fruits in season can be used: a mixture of half blackcurrants and half apple is very good so also are Tayberries. Quick and easy — a 'good fun' pudding for children to make.

1 lb/500 g blackcurrants and apples or other combinations
4 tablespoons sugar
2 tablespoons water
Put into a large frying pan and simmer very gently till heated through and just beginning to run with juice.

To make the scone mix
    5 oz/150 g plain flour (1 c generous)
    1$\frac{1}{2}$ teaspoons baking powder
    1$\frac{1}{2}$ oz/40 g butter
    Milk to mix
Put into a bowl, rub in the butter and add enough milk to make a stiff paste. Roll out the mixture about $\frac{1}{2}$" thick and cut up into 1" (2$\frac{1}{2}$ cm) squares.

Lay on top of fruit, cover and simmer very gently for about 15 minutes. The scone will be well risen on top and soaked in fruit juices underneath. Serve hot with cream.

A RICH STRAWBERRY TART with a lattice top otherwise known as 'windows'

6-8 servings

This is the kind of tart which was a frequent standby in the past when preserves played a much larger part in the business of surviving through the winter. Cooks in inns and taverns could be relied on to produce an interesting variety of quickly-filled tarts using home-made preserves and a pastry shell as a base. The pastry for this tart is richly-flavoured with almonds and spices; the filling is strawberry jam.

For the pastry

4 oz/125 g plain flour (1 c)
4 oz/125 g unblanched ground almonds ($1\frac{1}{2}$ c)
$\frac{1}{2}$ teaspoon ground cinnamon
$\frac{1}{2}$ teaspoon ground cloves
Grated rind of a lemon
5 oz/150 g butter ($1\frac{1}{4}$ sticks)
2 egg yolks or 1 large egg
1 teaspoon lemon juice

Filling

1 lb/500 g strawberry jam (p. 235)

To make the pastry

Mix together flour, almonds, cloves, cinnamon and grated lemon rind. Rub in butter, make a well in the centre and drop in egg and then lemon juice. Work with the tips of your fingers, gradually bringing in the flour mixture till all comes together in a smooth soft ball. Or blend together in processor. Chill 1 hour before rolling out.

To make the tart

Roll out $\frac{3}{4}$ of pastry to fit a greased 9″ (22 cm) flan tin. If the pastry breaks then press in to the flan with fingers making sure that it is an even thickness. (The better the pastry, the more difficult to handle). Fill with strawberry jam, or any other kind of jam. Cut the rest of the dough into strips and arrange in diamond pattern on top. Brush with egg. Bake 350F/180C/Gas 4 for 45 minutes. Serve with cream.

STRAWBERRIES AND SHORTBREAD

4 servings

Gleddoch House stands high with a spectacular view of the Clyde and the hills beyond. Once the home of a Glasgow shipbuilder it is now a hotel and country club. Its chef, Charles Price, cooks with flair, imagination and sensitivity for Scottish produce and traditions. This is a sweet which he prepares 'to order' — it is quickly assembled once you have the items ready.

Basic Shortbread Mix (see p. 207)
Roll out the shortbread into two thin rounds and mark into 6 triangles. Bake till golden and crisp.

To make the sauce

> ¼ pt/150 ml double cream (¾ c)
> 3-4 tablespoons orange juice
> 3-4 tablespoons orange flavoured liqueur
> Beat the cream till thick then add the orange juice and liqueur.
> Taste for flavour.

To prepare the strawberries

> 4 well-shaped, medium-sized strawberries, with stalks left on
> 4 tablespoons sugar
> 4 tablespoons water
> Dissolve the sugar in the water and bring to the boil. Heat till it
> reaches 230F/180C and the mixture begins to look syrupy. To test,
> dip your finger in water and then very quickly into the syrup; the
> thumb should slide smoothly over the fingers but the sugar will
> cling.

Assembling the dish

> Pour a thin layer of the orange cream on the plate. Arrange three
> triangles of shortbread on top. Dip the strawberries into the syrup,
> leave them for a few seconds to lightly warm through. Remove and
> place on shortbread. Serve immediately while the strawberries are
> warm.

HAZELNUT MERINGUE CAKE with fresh raspberries and cream

> The top should be crisp, the centre soft and moist, slightly chewy — the
> flavour heavy with hazelnuts. The two layers of meringue are sand-
> wiched with a thick layer of whipped cream and an equally thick layer of
> raspberries. It should be made up a few hours before eating so that the
> raspberry juice seeps through into the bottom layer of meringue. The
> nuts can be either finely or coarsely ground, the latter giving a crunchier
> texture.
>
> This is a good cook-ahead-and-stop-worrying cake since the
> meringues will keep for several weeks if they are tightly, but carefully,
> wrapped in foil and kept in an airtight tin.

For the meringue

> 8 oz/250 g hazelnuts (1½ c)
> 4 egg whites
> 8 oz/250 g caster sugar (1¼ c)
> Line 2 × 8″ (20 cm) sandwich tins.
> Pre-heat the oven to 350F/180C/Gas 4.
> Toast the hazelnuts in a cool oven for about 10 minutes then cool.
> Grind them till fairly fine. (This is a matter of taste.) Whisk the egg
> whites till well bulked up but not too stiff and then add the sugar a
> tablespoon at a time, beating well. Finally fold in the ground nuts
> and pour into the prepared tins. Bake for 20 minutes till the
> meringue is set but not dried out. Remove from the tins and leave to
> cool.

Assembling the cake

  8 oz/250 g raspberries (2 c)
  8 fl oz/250 ml double cream, stiffly whipped (1 c)
  Spread the cream thickly on one half, cover the other half with
  raspberries and place cream on top of raspberries. Dust thickly with
  icing sugar and leave for an hour at least before serving.

LEMON PUDDING

6-8 servings

  This is the forerunner of the Lemon Meringue Pie. Instead of separating
  the eggs and making a meringue top, whole eggs are added to the filling
  which is rich, sharp and creamy.
  5 eggs
  6 oz/200 g caster sugar (1 c)
  4 oz/100 g butter (1 stick)
  3 lemons, zest and juice
  Pre-heat the oven to 350F/180C/Gas 4.
  8" (20 cm) flan tin

Pastry

  4 oz/125 g flour (1 c)
  2½ oz/65 g butter (⅓ cup)
  1 tablespoon caster sugar
  1 egg yolk
  Sift flour onto board, add sugar, rub in butter and then make a well
  in the centre. Drop in the egg yolk and put the tips of your fingers
  into it and start working in the flour gradually, keeping the mixture
  in one lump until all the flour is worked in. It should be smooth,
  firm but pliable. Or blend together in processor. Roll out to fit tin.

To make filling

  Put the butter into the oven for a few minutes to soften. Put the
  eggs and sugar into a bowl and beat for a few minutes; it is not
  necessary to beat in air so they should not be too frothy. Now beat
  in the softened butter gradually, then the juice and zest of the
  lemons.
  Pour into the pastry and bake in a moderate oven for about
  30 minutes or until the filling is set and lightly brown on top.
  Eat warm or cold with whipped cream.

Potatoes

... We were conducted ... into a room where about twenty Scotch Drovers (i.e. cattle drivers) were regaling themselves with whisky and potatoes.

Robert Chambers
Walks in Edinburgh. 1825

I wonder if the Scottish drovers ever gave a thought to where this staple item of their diet came from. Perhaps they knew that they were discovered in the 'New World' and that the ancient Inca civilisation had built its empire on potatoes.

The Incas cleverly discovered a method of 'freeze-drying' the tubers, which wasn't difficult considering they were growing them in the high and fertile valleys of the Andes whose peaks climb to above 20,000 feet and glitter eternally with ice and snow. The 'preserved' potatoes were stored in warehouses in large enough quantities to see the Incas through the years of famine and allow them to conquer other peoples when they were starving. The 'chuño' or dried potato is still to be found in the markets of Cuzco and Puno. On first appearance they look like little grey pebbles — steeped in water for a few hours they soften and are then boiled and eaten well-flavoured with mountain herbs and perhaps red chillies.

When the Spanish Conquistadors arrived in South America in the 16th century they discovered potatoes and found them very useful as 'ships' stores' and as such they were subsequently brought back to Europe.

Initially a novelty and grown only in formal gardens as a luxury, their importance was first appreciated during the Napoleonic wars when the authorities in Britain, like the Incas, saw their usefulness as a home-grown food source making for much-needed self-sufficiency, and they encouraged everyone to grow them.

There was a gradual, if reluctant, acceptance of the potato in Scotland throughout the earlier part of the 19th century. It was a welcome necessity in areas where there were an impoverished small-holding peasantry, poor communications and lack of monetary resources. Potatoes are a versatile root crop and will flourish in many conditions. As in Ireland, the potato became the staple crop for the mass of the population in certain parts of Scotland. It arrived when these areas were receptive to a saviour from a widespread and increasing deterioration, cultural, social and economic, in the life of the people. Conditions in Ireland were worse.

Writing in the <u>Economic History of the Hebrides and Highlands</u> (1808), J. Walker says — 'Typical of the suspicion with which new methods were viewed was the attitude to the introduction of potatoes: in 1743 the Chief Clanranald brought a small quantity for the first time to South Uist, but the farmers suffered imprisonment before they would submit to planting them. When autumn came they brought the obnoxious roots to the Chief's door, protesting that he might force them to plant them, but not to eat them. Hunger was, however, a more effectual argument and within twenty years many Highlanders were subsisting on potatoes for nine months of the year.'

The association with the Irish whom they did not much like, and poverty which they wanted to avoid, is claimed to be the main reason why the southern English adopted the potato much later than the Scots, Irish, Welsh and northern English. But they also had wheat bread and a greater variety of other foods.

Regional differences in climate and custom in Scotland also meant that some parts depended on the potato more than others. In the Highlands and Islands, coinciding with the period of the Clearances, and a rapid growth of population in towns, it became an important staple item of diet. Its advantage was that it grew underground and was therefore less susceptible to the vagaries of weather than oats and barley. Also it produced more food per acre and, provided it didn't get diseased, it was generally considered a better proposition than the traditional cereal crops. It also combined well with the other staples in these parts — milk and fish. Elizabeth Edmondston writing in <u>Sketches and Tales of The Shetland Isles</u> (1856) says that — 'Fish with oat bread or potatoes . . . without any accompaniment at all, forms the three daily meals of the Shetland cottager.'

Lowlanders had other alternatives and though potatoes were widely grown, they were partly used for feeding horses, cows, poultry and pigs and, according to A. Fenton in <u>Scottish Country Life</u> (1976), they made up only 'one third of the food of the common people'.

Potatoes still have a special place in the diet of the peoples who inhabit the high Andes. The varieties they eat, though, show little resemblance to those we eat in Britain today and were you to sit down in a Peruvian home to a dish of potatoes you might almost believe it was a different species, the colours and flavours are so different. Likewise their treatment is different and they are often eaten in pride of place at the beginning of a meal so that their flavour may be more fully appreciated. If not flavoured with herbs or chillies, olive oil and lemon, they are eaten with the cheeses which conquering Spaniards introduced.

Over the years, tastes and fashions in potatoes in Britain generally have changed as their function in our diet has altered. Too much used as a cheap and sometimes boring adjunct to meat, they are not regarded as important in their own right. This was not always so, as the 16th-century herbalist John Gerard points out: potatoes he says are 'meat for pleasure, being either tosted in the embers, or boiled and eaten with oil, vinegar and pepper, or dressed any other way by the hand of someone cunning in cookerie'.

Growing potatoes for 'seed' is a major agricultural business in Scotland with much of these potatoes exported to England and further afield. The fact that in England a moister, waxier potato (e.g. Arran Pilot, Majestic) is preferred to the drier mealier one (e.g. King Edward, Golden Wonder) which Scots prefer has meant that Scotland has grown the waxy ones for export and the 'ware' potatoes (i.e. the left-over larger ones which are not suitable for 'seed') have often found their way into the Scottish market despite Scottish preferences.

While tastes may change, there has in the past been this distinct preference for the dry mealy potato, which requires care if it is being boiled since it will break up and disintegrate into 'potato soup' if cooked too fast. Many bake well. Slow gentle simmering or steaming is necessary whereas the advantage of firm waxy varieties is that they can be quickly boiled at a high temperature without any disintegration.

In the development of potato varieties, change is also taking place all the time, as new varieties are bred and introduced and old ones taken off the market. At Dornock Farm in Perthshire, Donald MacLean, Chairman of the National Vegetable Society, has built up a special collection of potato varieties. Writing in the Scots Magazine in October 1978 he says — 'This autumn I will be harvesting small amounts of over 200 varieties and disposing of them all over the UK to appreciative gourmets and enthusiasts, thus in small measure, keeping alive my kind of dodos and dinosaurs'. At present, there are some eighty varieties which are grown in Scotland but only about thirty are available in any quantity (100-1000 tons). Of these there are perhaps only a handful which are commonly known and appreciated, so look out for differing potato varieties on sale, and ask, if the names are not displayed.

Buying

All sacks of potatoes sold to the market must bear the variety name — it is not yet legally binding for the shopkeeper to display the name of the variety, but if asked he must be able to tell what it is. Many shopkeepers do display name tags (provided free) but some big stores still do not. Only by constantly being asked will they realise that the variety is important to the cook who needs to select the right variety for specific cooking uses.

The following information comes from Potato Varieties — a Fact sheet on Special Properties (UK) Compiled by Donald MacLean.

COMMONEST GROWN (In acres 1975-1985)
Earlies — Estima; Maris Bard; Home Guard; Pentland Javelin; Arran Comet; Ulster Sceptre; Wilja. Maincrops — Desirée; King Edward; Maris Piper; Pentland Crown; Pentland Dell; Pentland Hawk; Pentland Sauire; Record; Cara; Romano.

GOING OUT OF PRODUCTION (Scarcer Now)
Earlies — Arran Pilot; Catriona; Craigs Alliance; Maris Anchor; Red Craigs Royal; Sharpes Express; Ulster Chieftain; Ulster Classic. Maincrops — Arran Banner; Arran Consul; Croft; Dr McIntosh; Dunbar Standard; Majestic; Pentland Ivory; Red King Edward; Redskin.

YELLOW FLESHED
Aura; Bintje; Ukama; Colomo; Duke of York; Record; Spunta. Paler Yellow — Catriona; Desirée; Estima; Foxton; Golden Wonder; Jersey Royal; Manna; Pink Fir Apple; Vanessa; Wilja.

LIABLE TO AFTER-COOKING DISCOLOURATION (Blackening)
Arran Comet; Home Guard; Pentland Dell; Pentland Hawk; Pentland Ivory; Pentland Javelin; Ulster Chieftain; Wilja.

LIABLE TO AFTER-COOKING DISINTEGRATION (Loss of Shape)
Edzell Blue; Golden Wonder; Home Guard; Kerr's Pink; Pentland Dell; Record; Sharpes Express; Wilja.

SUITABLE FOR FRYING — CHIPS
Arran Victory; Desirée; Dunbar Standard; Estima; Golden Wonder; Kerr's Pinks; Pentland Dell; Record; Red Craigs Royal; Redskin.

FOR JACKET BAKING
Golden Wonder (best); King Edward; Desirée; Pentland Dell; Maris Piper; Pentland Squire.

FOR POTATO SALAD (Remains firm when diced cold)
Good — Aura; Eigenheimer; Etoile du Nord (Red Star); Fir Apple; Jersey Royal. Fair — Red Craigs Royal; Maris Peer; Coloured Flesh; Purple Congo; Red Cardinal.

EATING QUALITY
Waxy and/or Moist — Arran Comet; Arran Pilot; Bintje; Colomo; Craigs Alliance; Desirée; Dr McIntosh; Estima; Home Guard; Irish Peace; Jersey Royal; Majestic; Maris Bard; Maris Peer; Pentland Crown; Pentland Hawk; Pentland Javelin; Royal Kidney; Foremost; Ulster Sceptre; Vanessa; Wilja.
Floury and/or Dry — Arran Consul; Arran Victory; Catriona; Di Vernon; Duke of York; Dunbar Rover; Dunbar Standard; Edzell Blue; Epicure; Golden Wonder; Kerr's Pink; King Edward; Maris Piper; Record; Red Craigs Royal.

SHAPE AND COLOUR
White — Arran Comrade; Blanka; Colomo; Corine; Croft; Dr McIntosh; Dunbar Standard; Estima; Home Guard; Kingston; Manna; Maris Peer; Pentland Dell; Pentland Ivory; Pentland Javelin; Pentland Squire; Provost; Ukama; Ulster Sceptre.

Coloured — Cara; Catriona; Desirée; Diana; Di Vernon; Drayton; Foxton; Liro; Red Cara; Red Craigs Royal; King Edward; Romano; Ulster Classic; Vanessa.

Irregular or deep-eyed — Arran Banner; Edzell Blue; Epicure; Kerr's Pink; Majestic; Redskin.

The maincrop varieties which have been most widely grown in recent years are Desirée and Maris Piper. Pentland Crown, which is also widely grown is now declining but Pentland Squire is increasing in the area grown. King Edward is still quite extensively grown and is regarded as a quality potato with a good cooking quality. The main variety which is grown for crisping is Record. With the introduction of Desirée, Scots have become more used to eating yellow-fleshed potatoes again. Early this century, varieties such as Champion (1876), an old floury Scottish variety which was popularly eaten with salt herring in 'Tatties and Herring', was yellow-fleshed. About 1975 there was a peak in popularity for white-fleshed potatoes like Majestic, which has now been displaced by more yellow varieties of continental origin such as the Dutch Desirée. The Scottish Plant Breeding Institute at Pentlandfield near Edinburgh has produced most of the top dozen varieties including all the Pentland types.

Although the characteristics of a variety ought to remain the same wherever planted, flavour is greatly affected by soil, manuring, climate and cooking.

Storing

Keep in a cool, dark place: warmth makes them sprout, damp encourages storage diseases, and light turns them an unhealthy green. Polythene bags induce problems since they can't breathe properly and condensation accumulates in the bag.

MEALY POTATOES

Farm carts used to trundle through the streets in the 19th century selling 'Mealy tatties', the potatoes very simply boiled in salted water. 'Mealieness' refers to the texture and only floury varieties will do. They must be well 'dried off' after cooking. First boil the potatoes in their skins and when cooked, drain well. For really well-dried Scottish potatoes then go to an open door and, holding the handle of the pot in one hand and the lid in the other, lift one side of the lid up and down quickly, sending out billows of steam; this way the heat is kept in and the moisture driven out. It should only take a few minutes.

After this treatment, place a folded cloth on top of the potatoes and cover with the lid to keep warm. Alternatively leave the lid off, if just about to serve, though they will discolour if exposed to the air too long. Put under a very gentle heat for a few minutes before serving. In the days of the kitchen range these dried out potatoes would sit in the corner quietly continuing to steam with the cloth absorbing the moisture till they were required.

STOVIES

I feel sure, though I have no proof, that this Scottish method of cooking potatoes was influenced by early and close ties with France, since the concept of slicing the potatoes thinly and cooking slowly is exactly how the French cook their classic Gratin Dauphinois (see p. 262).

There is some confusion about the origin of the word 'stovie' and it has been claimed by F. Marian McNeill (The Scots Kitchen, 1929) that it comes from the French verb 'étuvier' to stew. But it seems that 'to stove' is a genuine Scottish and North of England verb which comes from the use of the word 'stove' to define 'a closed box or vessel of earthenware, porcelain, or (now more usually) of metal, portable or fixed to contain burning fuel' (OED). It was originally applied to the idea of 'sweating'. Gervase Markham in 1631 talks about letting a bird 'stove and sweate (sic) till evening' while later recipes show that it becomes more associated with stewing, but remaining almost a cross between sweating and stewing since often, as in stovies, very little water is used.

This is a basic method which may take on all kinds of variations depending on taste, and what you happen to have available — it is beautifully versatile.

To make Stovies

4-6 servings

Melt about 2 oz/50 g fat in a heavy pan with a tight-fitting lid. The type of fat depends on taste and availability but good dripping from meat or bacon obviously gives a better flavour as does butter but there is no reason why oil, though not traditional, should not be used.

Slice very finely 3 medium onions and when the fat is hot add to the pan. Reduce the heat and cook gently while preparing the potatoes. Peel and slice about $\frac{1}{4}$" (1 cm) thick 2 lb/1 kg potatoes. Some people slice some thin some thick so that the thin ones reduce to a mush while the thick ones stay whole when cooked. Add to the pan and stir well coating all sides with fat. I begin the cooking by sweating them for about 10 minutes with the lid on the pan, stirring when necessary to prevent sticking. The heat must be at its lowest possible. After 10 minutes a little water or stock or gravy from the roast may be added. If you like stovies fairly dry, add only about 2-3 tablespoons, while if you like them wet add more. Cover again with the lid and cook till potatoes are soft. Add cooked meat or fish at this point and only just heat through. Taste for seasoning and add spices if you wish. Nutmeg was a favourite with potatoes but allspice was also used. A hearty grinding of black pepper is certainly a good idea. Some people like stovies with brown bits through them and for this you must reduce much of the cooking liquid and fry the potatoes for a little, mixing in the browned bits something in the style of American 'Hashed Browns'. Before serving sprinkle with a handful of finely chopped parsley or chives. Chervil is also very good with potatoes.

STOVIES AND MUSHROOMS

4-6 servings

Using the stovie method, potatoes are layered with mushrooms and then baked slowly in the oven.

2 lb/1 kg potatoes, peeled and finely sliced
1 tablespoon oil
4 tablespoons softened butter
1 lb/500 g mushrooms, sliced
More butter for top — about 4 tablespoons softened

Pre-heat the oven to 350F/180C/Gas 4.

Melt the oil and butter in an oven dish. Dry the potatoes and add. Toss over a high heat to seal them. Remove half from the pan and spread in the bottom of the dish. Cover with the mushrooms and add some more butter, then spread on the remainder of the potatoes. Sprinkle the top with more butter.

Cook in a moderate oven for about 30 minutes. Towards the end of the cooking time sprinkle a little more butter over. If necessary cover with a buttered greaseproof paper. The top should be golden and the potatoes soft.

CHAPPIT TATTIES with spring onion

4-6 servings

With much interchange between Ireland and Scotland it is not surprising that the Scots like and make this dish, much loved also in Ireland, where it is known as Champ. A simple peasant dish most common in the North of Ireland where it makes potatoes into a main meal dish.

Florence Irwin in <u>The Cookin' Woman</u> (1949) describes how it was cooked and served in an Irish farmhouse — butter was a luxury to most and by no means an everyday ingredient.

'Two stones or more of potatoes were peeled and boiled for the dinner. Then the man of the house was summoned when all was ready, and while he pounded this enormous potful of potatoes with a sturdy wooden beetle (potato masher) his wife added the potful of milk and nettles, or scallions, or chives or parsley, and he beetled till it was smooth as butter and not a lump anywhere. Everyone got a large bowlful, made a hole in the centre, and into this put a large lump of butter. Then the champ was eaten from the outside with a spoon or fork, dipping it into the melting butter in the centre. All was washed down with new milk or freshly churned buttermilk.'

2 lb/1 kg mealy potatoes — cooked, steamed dry and mashed
$\frac{1}{2}$ **pt/300 ml hot milk (1$\frac{1}{4}$ c)**
4 oz/125 g butter (1 stick)
Pepper and salt

With either

Nettles — 1 cup, chopped or minced nettle tops or
Chives — $\frac{1}{2}$ cup chopped chives or
Spring Onions — 6, finely chopped or
Parsley — 2 large tablespoons chopped parsley or
Peas — 1 cup fresh peas
There are three methods — either the greens are cooked in milk till
soft and then added to the potatoes or they are added to the heated
milk just before serving rather than cooked or they are simply added
to the potatoes raw.

Whatever method is preferred, the mixture must be thoroughly
beaten over heat till smooth. Serve very hot in hot plates with butter
'Irish style', if you like.

OATMEALED POTATOES

4-6 servings

This is best with new potatoes. Boil or steam 2 lb/1 kg potatoes and
while they are cooking toast 2 tablespoons pinhead oatmeal slowly in
the oven. Drain the potatoes, toss in 1 tablespoon butter and then coat
with the toasted oatmeal. Sprinkle with chopped parsley, chives or
chervil and serve.

DRIPPING POTATOES

This is antiquarian in origin but may have some practical significance
today. They are, of course, roast potatoes, but if you use a rack to roast or
have a spit, then they are easily the best flavoured, potatoes absorbing as
they do all the dripping flavour from the meat. In the days when all roasts
were cooked on a spit, cooking things under the roasting joint was a well
developed art to which Yorkshire pudding owes its existence. This is
how they are described in The Cookery Book of Lady Clark of Tillypronie
(1909):

'Wash the potatoes and peel them very thin; boil them 10 minutes
with a little salt, and then put them in a Yorkshire-pudding tin under the
joint which is roasting before an open fire, to catch the gravy; when
enough moistened, put them into the oven, still in the tin, turn the potatoes often, and baste them with a little dripping, till crisp and brown.
Serve very hot, but not round the joint, or they will become sodden.
Potatoes done in this way are mealy inside and crisp on the outside.'

POTATO SCONES

Traditionally eaten for high tea or fried with bacon for breakfast. Someone recently likened this to Italian Gnocchi and there seems no reason why it should not be adapted (see p. 258).

½ lb/250 kg mashed potatoes — slightly warm
1 oz melted butter (¼ stick)
2 oz/50 g flour (½ c)
Salt

Add the butter and salt to the potatoes and work in as much flour as the mixture will take without becoming dry.

Roll out very thinly, cut into rounds and quarters — prick with a fork and cook on a hot girdle about 3 minutes on each side. Wrap in a towel till required.

POTATO SOUP

4-6 servings

A hearty soup which makes a main meal dish with crusty bread and cheese. Potatoes combine well with all the onion family and are also good with many herbs. As an alternative to the ubiquitous parsley, chervil (much liked by Indians and available fresh in many of their own shops) adds a new dimension to potatoes.

1 medium onion or leek, finely chopped
3 stalks celery, finely chopped
3 medium-sized potatoes peeled and diced
2 oz/50 g butter (½ stick) or
2 tablespoons oil
Salt and pepper
Fresh chervil for garnish

Chop the vegetables into roughly even sized pieces. Begin by melting the butter and sautéing the onion till yellow and soft. Then add the other vegetables and continue sautéing with the lid on over a low heat for 5-10 minutes.

Add

3 cups water or stock and season with salt and pepper and bay leaf. Cook till vegetables are tender.

Serving

When ready to serve add 1 cup milk and 1-2 tablespoons butter. Garnish with parsley, chives, chervil or dill.

POTATOES AND HARD BOILED EGGS

4-6 servings

Edward Burt, travelling in the Highlands in the early 18th century was thankful for a 'hard egg' on one occasion when he couldn't face the 'roasted hens' which he says were 'very poor, the skins much broken with plucking; black with smoke and greased with bad butter.' Lady Grisell Baillie notes that 60 dozen eggs were used in one month. They were eaten frequently for supper with peas, with spinach, with mush-rooms but most often with potatoes and sometimes ham.

This dish has the the the merit of being easy and quick to make while using left-over potatoes. The idea of finishing the dish with a sharp butter sauce comes from Richard Olney's Simple French Cooking, (1974).

2 lb/1 kg cooked potatoes
4 hard boiled eggs
For the sauce
2 tablespoons finely chopped shallots
4 oz/125 g butter
Handful of chopped parsely
Salt and pepper
2-3 tablespoons wine vinegar
Layer the potatoes and eggs in a heated earthenware gratin dish. Cook shallots in butter till soft and yellow, and add salt and pepper and wine vinegar. Pour the contents evenly over the potatoes and eggs and serve hot.

Leeks

Thought to have been introduced to Britain by the Romans — the Scots have made good use of them in soups and stews and in particular in the classic combination with chicken, Cock-a-Leekie. Musselburgh developed a reputation for particularly fine leeks and leek seed from this area is considered unusually good by horticulturalists. Their reputation as a vegetable in their own right rather than a useful addition to soups and stews has developed recently and is reflected in the fact that while in the past Scots liked a long leaf and short 'blanch', i.e. white, there is more of a demand now for 'long blanched' leeks, which were always more popular in England. The potential of young tender ones with light sharp flavours is fully realised when served sautéed with butter or raw with vinaigrette.

Buying

Very large leeks have a coarser flavour than young thin ones. They can be useful in richly flavoured soups and stews but for serving on their own as a vegetable or for salads use the young tender ones. The season lasts from August to May and near the end of the crop they often start to 'shoot', i.e. start forming the flower head which makes a hard woody stalk in the centre and which has annoyingly to be thrown away. Open up the leaves at the top to check that this is not forming.

Preparing

Most of the grit is usually in the top half of the leeks, so if you want to use the bottom white half whole then it is usually quite safe to cut off and just wash the outer leaves. Trim off root and any wilted green leaves. All of the green ought to be useable unless the leeks are mature, in which case the tops will be too coarse and should be removed. If using the whole leek slit from the base to the tips to half, then make another slit to quarter which then opens up the leeks for easy washing. Leave to soak for a few minutes, if they are very earthy, to loosen the soil.

COCK-A-LEEKIE

8-10 servings

Essential elements of this classic Scottish soup are chicken, leeks and a good beef stock. Prunes add interest to the flavour and colour contrast of the finished soup, but their addition or omission continues to arouse heated debate. Meg Dods infers that the prunes were only added when the leeks were old and bitter, but since people are so divided on the subject my solution is to cook them separately in some of the stock then stone them and serve them in a separate dish with the soup, thus keeping everybody happy. Raisins were also used in the past and prune-haters may accept these more readily.

Many of the early recipes talk about serving the whole chicken in the soup tureen when, presumably, they must have then jointed it at table since there are references to whole joints being served in the broth. (In Peru all soup served today still comes in this style, with an island of large chunks of vegetables and meat in the centre of the plate.) The chicken would have been removed to an ashet and carved as the soup was ladled into plates. Grisell Baillie describes her Cock-a-Leekie as 'Chicken soup with chickens in it' which nicely describes the Scots' liking for soup/stews or 'Mouthful' soups, as Meg Dods calls them, 'with plenty in them'.

The system was to sup the broth first then eat the joint with a knife and fork. Scottish soup plates are large and wide for this purpose. Some other more refined recipes use only slices from the breast in serving.

6 pts/3 L water
2 lb/1 kg knuckle of veal, hough (shin) bone or piece of boiling beef
1 boiling fowl or chicken
Bundle of fresh herbs
2 lb/1 kg leeks
2 medium onions, finely chopped
Salt and pepper

To make the stock

Put the bones/beef in a pan with the cold water and herbs and bring to the boil, skim, turn down the heat, cover and simmer for about 1 hour. Now add the chicken and simmer gently till the chicken is just tender. This will depend on the age of the bird. Strain and leave to cool. Remove any excess fat. Cut up the chicken into small or large pieces for returning to the broth when ready.

Finishing the broth

Melt the fat in a large pan and add the onions. Cook till soft and yellow. Meanwhile clean the leeks and chop finely. Add to the onions, stir well, cover and leave to sweat for about five minutes stirring occasionally. The leeks should be really soft now. Add the strained stock and the chicken meat and bring to the boil. Simmer for a few minutes to heat everything through. Taste for seasoning and serve.

LEEKS braised in claret

4 servings

I make this dish at the same time as Cock-a-Leekie, so that the white ends of the leeks, instead of going into the soup, are served as a vegetable. (You must add about 2 medium onions to the soup to compensate for their loss.) The acid of the wine firms the leeks and gives a good flavour.

1 lb/500 g white of leek, cut into 2″ (5 cm) lengths
2 tablespoons butter or oil
Bundle of fresh herbs
1 clove garlic, crushed
1 tablespoon flour
$\frac{1}{2}$ pt/250 g claret (1 c) or stock with 1 tablespoon wine vinegar
Handful of freshly chopped parsley

Trim the base of the leeks and cut off the white ends into even-sized pieces. Melt the butter in a wide-based pan and add the leeks. Sprinkle with salt and add herbs. Toss the leeks over a gentle heat for about five minutes. Add garlic and sprinkle over the flour. Continue cooking for a few minutes turning the leeks in the pan then add the wine to almost cover. Cover the pan with a lid and simmer very gently till the leeks are tender. Keep shaking to prevent the leeks sticking. Garnish with parsley and serve.

SAUTEED CHICKEN AND LEEKS with Skirlie

4 servings

The chicken and leeks combination seems to me worth developing and this simple method of cooking preserves the natural flavour of both. Skirlie (see p. 32) is a good accompaniment to all birds.

Chicken joints, ready prepared, may be used for this dish or you can joint a whole chicken yourself. This has the advantage of giving you the backbone and the giblets for stock as well as the added satisfaction of making your own neat joints. There are various ways of jointing a chicken for different purposes. It can be cut off the bone into quarters (2 legs, 2 single breasts), into five pieces (2 legs, 2 wings, 1 breast), or into 7 pieces if it is large enough (divide the legs into two giving 4 legs, the 2 wings, 1 breast). The following method is for the larger chicken giving 7 pieces.

To joint a chicken

Begin by **cutting off the leg** at the ball and socket joint. First locate the joint with your fingers and then cut through the connecting skin and flesh. Bend the leg back away from the body until the ball is visible and cut round the sinew to remove the ball from the socket, then cut through the rest of the flesh. Repeat on the other leg. Separate thighs from drumsticks at the joint.

Next **remove the wings** — with the chicken on its side hold onto the wing, pull back and find the ball and socket joint with your knife. Cut through to loosen socket joint only. Cut along through about half of the breast so that this part of the white meat is still attached to the wing. Then holding the chicken firmly, pull the wing piece out. Repeat with the other side.

To **separate the breasts** sit the chicken on end with the neck on the board and, holding onto the back, cut through the entire length of the bird with a heavy sharp knife; this means cutting through the ribs and straight down to the wing joint. Bend the back and then cut through the bones at the shoulder to sever the breast from the carcass. The back may be used for stock. You will now have 7 joints.

1 × 3 lb/1½ kg chicken
3 oz/75 g butter (¾ stick) or 4 fl oz oil
Salt, freshly ground black pepper
¼ pt/150 ml water, stock or dry white wine (¾ c)
3 leeks + 1 oz/50 g butter (¼ stick)
Handful chopped parsley

Cooking the chicken

Melt the butter/oil in a large heavy pan which has a tight-fitting lid. When hot, add the chicken pieces and brown over a medium heat turning as they brown. Lower the heat, sprinkle the chicken with

salt and pepper, cover the pan and simmer gently for 5-8 minutes.
Turn the pieces and add half of the liquid. Cover and cook for
another 10 minutes till the chicken is cooked.

Finishing the dish

Remove the chicken pieces to the serving dish and keep warm. Add
the rest of the liquid to the pan and turn up the heat. Stir the juices
with a wooden spoon, scraping the browned bits from the bottom of
the pan. Boil until reduced by half and a good consistency. Taste for
seasoning. Pour over the chicken; sprinkle with parsley and serve
with leeks and Skirlie (see p. 32).

Cooking the leeks

Melt butter in a pan and add leeks, toss over a gentle heat till they
are soft — it will only take a few minutes. Season and serve
immediately.

LEEK SALAD

A dish for small slender young leeks which have a delicate flavour. They
may also be added to other raw salads with great effect. Allow about two
leeks per person depending on size.

Dressing

4-5 tablespoons oil
1 tablespoon vinegar/lemon juice
Freshly ground sea salt and black pepper
Pinch of sugar
Handful of chopped parsley
Put the dressing ingredients into a screw-top jar and shake well.
Taste for seasoning. Clean leeks in the usual way and then chop into
1" slices. Put in salad bowl and toss in the dressing. Good with
cooked ham, spiced beef, mutton ham or pickled tongue.

LEEK AND BACON PIE

4-6 servings

This pie 'emerged' one day from a collection of odd things which had
accumulated in the fridge. It is an excellent one-meal-in-a-dish pie
which simplifies serving beautifully. Cooked vegetables are arranged in
a pie dish with a bacon and leek sauce and the top is finished with a crisp
crumbs and cheese. It could just as easily be made in a shallow gratin
dish or with a range of other ingredients. The green leeks and the differing reds of carrot and sweet potato are attractive.

To make the sauce

2 oz/50 g butter ($\frac{1}{2}$ stick)
$\frac{1}{2}$ lb/250 g chopped bacon
2 oz/50 g flour ($\frac{1}{2}$ c)
1 pt/250 ml chicken/vegetable stock ($2\frac{1}{2}$ c)
2 finely chopped leeks
Melt half the butter in a pan and add the bacon. Cook for a few
minutes and then add the rest of the butter. Stir in the flour, cook

for a few minutes, then add chicken or vegetable stock. Simmer till thickened then add finely chopped leeks.

To assemble the dish

3 medium potatoes — cooked
1 large sweet potato — cooked
4-5 medium carrots — cooked

Peel and mash the sweet potato, spread in base of gratin dish, cover with a layer of carrots and then sliced potatoes. Pour over leek and bacon mixture. Cover with a mixture of grated cheese and breadcrumbs and grill till crisp and brown on top, or brown in the oven.

LEEK TART

6-8 servings

A thick layer of buttered leeks is encased between two layers of light flaky pastry — a good slice to go with ham and pickles. Some cooked ham could be mixed with the leeks or a layer of grated cheese spread on top of the leeks and the dish served as a main course with a green salad.

1 lb/500 g leeks, chopped finely
3 oz/75 g butter ($\frac{3}{4}$ stick)
1 lb/500 g puff pastry
2 tablespoons double cream
Salt and pepper
Pre-heat the oven to 400F/200C/Gas 6.

Melt the butter, add the leeks and stew gently without browning till the leeks have just softened, add the cream, season and leave to cool.

Cut the pastry in half and roll out two rectangles 12″ × 10″ (30 × 25 cm) $\frac{1}{8}$″ ($\frac{1}{4}$ cm) thick. Halve along the widest edges to make four rectangles or leave in two pieces if you wish. Place the bottom half on the baking sheet. Place the mixture in the centre, spread out to about 1″ ($2\frac{1}{2}$ cm) from the edge, wet edges and press the other round on top. Seal well round the edge, flute, brush with egg yolk and score a trellis design on top. Bake for 20 minutes till risen and brown. Serve hot, but may also be cooked in advance and reheated.

Carrots

The Dutch are credited with developing the bright orange carrot which we use today, although earlier ones were purple and came from the East. Their principal use in Scotland has been in broths and stews, though their sweetness was much appreciated by 19th-century cooks who made delicious sweet souffle-type puddings with them. Their sweet, moist qualities also made them useful additions to a Clootie Dumpling, while

Americans have celebrated them for the same reasons by popularising the Carrot Cake.

Buying

Young spring carrots are sold in bunches, usually with foliage attached. They should be about the thickness of a man's thumb. Maincrop varieties are sold trimmed and loose and should be tender with no woody core.

CARROT OR TURNIP SOUP

6-8 servings

The Scots have a reputation as skilled soup makers. A tradition not confined to traditional classic varieties but a constantly developing feature of Scottish eating as Scots today refine and develop in new and original ways.

This is only one of a fascinating collection of ideas for soups from Mollie Katzen, who cooked in the Mosewood Restaurant in Ithaca, New York. All her soups have a feeling of adventure to them, which makes them a challenge constantly to refine and improve.

2 lb/1 kg carrots or turnips (Swedes)
1½ pt/850 ml water or stock (3¾ c)
1½ teaspoons salt

Cooking the vegetables

Put in a pan, bring to the boil, cover and simmer for 12-15 minutes. Leave to cool to room temperature.

Cooking the onions and nuts

2 medium onions, finely chopped
1-2 small cloves garlic, crushed
2 oz/50 g whole cashews or almonds (½ cup)
3-4 tablespoons butter or oil

Sauté in butter with a little salt till the onions are soft and yellow.

Finishing the soup

Purée everything together in a blender till smooth. Return the purée to a pan and whisk in **ONE** of the following:

1 cup milk
1 cup yogurt or buttermilk plus a little honey
½ pt/300 ml double cream (1¼ c)
¼ pt/150 ml sour cream (¾ c)

Heat very slowly.

Seasoning combinations to choose from

1. 2 pinches nutmeg; ½ teaspoon dried mint; dash of cinnamon (this is good with carrots — the Turks and Persians combine carrots with rice in a sweet cinnamon flavoured pilau which they eat with lamb).
2. ½-1 teaspoon each — thyme, marjoram, basil.
3. 1 teaspoon fresh-grated ginger root, sautéed in butter plus a dash of sherry added just before serving (this is best with the turnip

version. Bashed Neeps in Scotland are traditionally flavoured with ginger).

Garnish with grated apple or toasted nuts or yogurt or sour cream.

CARROT CAKE which may be used as a pudding

Carrots have been used as the basis for puddings for many centuries, not principally for their carrot flavour, but for the moist sweetness which they impart. This is Mrs MacIver's recipe (1773) which has something of the 'Genoese sponge' concept about it. It is rich, moist and full of subtle flavour — also expensive by today's standards though eggs in the 18th century were so cheap and plentiful that — 'Beat 10 eggs . . .' was commonplace.

Boil some good carrots and when they are well cleaned weigh ½ lb beat very fine in mortar, mix 2-3 spoons of sweet cream along with them. Beat 10 eggs, keep out ½ of the whites with ½ lb sugar. Mix all well together and season it with beat cinnamon or grated orange as it makes it eat like an orange pudding. Mix 8 oz of oiled butter in it just when you are about putting into the oven.

Carrot cakes today are popular and vary in type and contents from really dark spicy fruit cakes to much lighter sponges. None of them, strangely, seem to use cooked carrots.

Here are two different types which I make frequently. The icings are interchangeable.

A RICH MOIST CARROT CAKE

8-10 portions

This is Thelma MacBeth's Carrot Cake which she makes along with other superb Scottish baking specialities for the Wood'n Spoon Restaurant in Kingussie. It is best made in a loaf tin though it can also be made round. The icing may be omitted and the cake served instead as a pudding with an Orange Sauce.

8 oz/250 g wholemeal flour (2 c)
8 oz/250 g brown sugar (2 c)
4 teaspoons baking powder
2 teaspoons cinnamon
1 teaspoon salt
½ cup oil or melted butter
4 eggs, beaten
½ cup chopped walnuts
14 oz/400 g grated carrot (3 c)
(Grated zest of 1 orange — my addition)
Pre-heat the oven to 350F/180C/Gas 4.
2 × 1 lb/500 g loaf tins or 1 × 2 lb/1 kg loaf tin or 9″ (22 cm) round cake tin

Sift the dry ingredients together then add walnuts and carrots. Mix well. Add oil/butter and then mix in the eggs. Pour into tins and bake for about 1 hour.

Icing
$\frac{1}{2}$ lb/250 g icing sugar (2 c)
3 oz/75 g cream cheese ($\frac{1}{2}$ c scant)
1 teaspoon vanilla essence
3 oz/75 g butter ($\frac{3}{4}$ c)
Beat together till fluffy. Ice top and sides of cake.

Orange sauce
Put 3 tablespoons Brandy Marmalade (see p.233) in the liquidiser or processor with 4 tablespoons of water and purée till the orange chips are fine. Put into a pan and reduce till a thin syrupy consistency.

A LIGHT SPONGY CARROT CAKE

6-8 servings

Two spices, cinnamon and nutmeg, blend to give a delicate aroma and taste to this cake which comes from The Cranks Recipe Book by David and Kay Canter and Daphne Swann (1982).
6 oz/175 g grated carrot ($1\frac{1}{4}$ c)
2 eggs
4 oz/125 g raw brown sugar (1 c)
3 fl oz/75 ml oil ($\frac{1}{3}$ c)
4 oz/125 g 80% wholemeal self-raising flour (1 c)
1 teaspoon ground cinnamon
$\frac{1}{2}$ teaspoon ground nutmeg
2 oz/50 g desiccated coconut ($\frac{3}{4}$ c)
2 oz/50 g raisins ($\frac{1}{2}$ c)
Pre-heat the oven to 375F/190C/Gas 5.
7″ (18 cm) square cake tin — greased and lined
Grate carrots or reduce finely in a processor.
Beat the eggs and sugar till thick and creamy. Whisk in the oil slowly and then add the other ingredients. Mix lightly and pour into the tin. Bake for about 20-25 minutes until firm and golden brown. Cool and ice.

For the orange icing
Beat together till soft — $1\frac{1}{2}$ oz/40 g butter or margarine and 3 oz/75 g raw pale brown sugar ($\frac{1}{2}$ c). Add the grated zest of 1 orange and spread over the cake. Decorate the top with 1 oz/25 g chopped walnuts.

GLAZED CARROTS

4 servings

Because of their natural sweetness, carrots are ideal for this method of cooking vegetables. The slow cooking with butter and sugar gives them an attractive syrupy coating. Turnips, parsnips and beetroot are also good cooked in the same way. Beetroots should be cooked till soft first.
1 lb/500 g carrots
1 oz/25 g butter ($\frac{1}{4}$ stick)
1 tablespoon brown sugar

Salt
Cold water
1 teaspoon lemon juice
Slice larger, older carrots into even sized pieces and leave new
carrots whole. Put into the pan with butter, sugar, salt and enough
water to come half way up the carrots. Cover and simmer till the
carrots are almost cooked — this will depend on age and also
whether you like vegetables well cooked or with a 'bite' left in them.
There should not be too much liquid left now. Remove the lid and
boil hard to evaporate, gently shaking the pan to prevent the
vegetables from sticking. Take the pan off the heat and finish with a
knob of butter, shaking the pan well to coat all the carrots. Taste for
seasoning and sprinkle with freshly chopped parsley and a few drops
of lemon juice before serving.

Scottish Turnips

Our club (The Cleikum) put a little powdered gineger (sic) to
their mashed turnips, which were studiously chosen of the yellow, sweet, juicy sort, for which Scotland is celebrated. . . .

Meg Dods
The Cook and Housewives Manual, 1826

Rutabaga, a variety of Brassica campestris, otherwise known as Swedish
turnip since it came from Sweden to Scotland in 1781/2, for some reason was not, as in England, called Swede but plain turnip or 'neeps' in
Scotland. This is a much larger variety of turnip than the one the
Romans are credited with introducing to Britain, which is not only
smaller but has a white flesh (Brassica Kapa) compared with the yellow/
orange of the Swede. It is obviously the yellow variety which Meg Dods
was referring to and it is this one which accompanies Haggis and mixes
so well with Orkney Clapshot. It had its main effect on Lowland Scotland
while the potato was grown instead in the Highlands.

First grown as a garden crop, it was the white variety which the
Romans had introduced which was made famous by men like 'Turnip
Townshend' — the second Viscount Townshend (1674-1738) who pio-
neered the use of turnips on his Norfolk estates as winter feed for cattle,
allowing them to survive through to the following summer and revolutionising our food supplies.

Buying/Preparing

They are available all year round. Smaller ones have less of a woody outer layer, all of which must be removed before cooking, and they also have a milder flavour.

MASHED TURNIP

Often described with Haggis as Bashed Neeps

1 lb/500 g turnip
Cold water to cover
Salt and white pepper
2 tablespoons butter
1 teaspoon grated ginger root or ground ginger to taste
Handful of chopped chives for garnish

Remove the hard woody outer skin of the turnip. It is essential that all is removed since it will not soften with cooking and bits left in are unpleasant. Put into a pan with water and boil till soft. Drain, dry off in the pan over a gentle heat for a few minutes, stirring to drive off excess moisture. Add the butter and grated ginger root. Stir for another few minutes then mash thoroughly with a fork or potato masher. Beat well till smooth. Taste for seasoning and serve. Garnish with a handful of chopped chives.

Variation

To make **Orkney Clapshot** which is often served with Haggis, mix the above mixture with Creamed Potatoes — beat well till smooth. This mixture can be put in a pie or gratin dish, thickly covered with grated cheddar cheese and baked in the oven till browned under the grill.

Kale

The old fashioned easy way of asking a friend to dinner was to ask him if he would take his kale with the family.

Dean Ramsay
Reminiscences of Scottish Life and Character. 1858

Ramsay did not mean that they were necessarily going to eat kale for dinner. It was just that the Scots ate so much of it that the name was transferred to mean the meal itself, whether the vegetable was being served or not. They called it 'Kail' while the northern English referred to it as 'Cale', both names coming from its generic name 'Borecole', a form of Brassica introduced by the Dutch with the original name of 'Boerenckool'.

The reason why kale was such a success in Scotland was its resistance to frost (in fact it improves slightly in flavour after a slight frost) and it also has the advantage of providing a good source of green vegetable throughout the winter.

Buying/Preparing

Limited supplies are available commercially from November through to May though the younger it is, the better from a texture point of view. Young kale is excellent in a salad finely chopped. The thicker coarse woody stems should be removed.

BUTTERED KALE

Fresh young kale tops can be treated for most purposes as for spinach though kale has a stronger, slightly more bitter taste. Most of the recipes in early cookery books recommend boiling the kale first, but I have never found this necessary with the kale which I've bought or been given from gardens. It might well apply if the kale is old and tough at the end of the winter.

Lady Clark of Tillypronie adds a tablespoon of cream to kale as well as two tablespoons of stock before serving. This is then reduced to a 'proper consistency' and eaten with 'brown meat'. She also refers to another recipe which has no butter, stock or pepper. The Scots, she says 'add a dust of oatmeal, or eat kale with a spoon and a piece of oatcake with it'.

1 lb/500 g kale tops
2 oz/50 g butter ($\frac{1}{2}$ stick)
Salt and pepper
1 tablespoon toasted pinhead oatmeal

Wash the kale well, drain and chop finely. Melt the butter in a pan with a good heavy base and a tight-fitting lid. Add the kale and stir for a few minutes. Cover with the lid and leave for 3-4 minutes. Then give a stir and cover again. Leave for another 2-3 minutes and then give another stir. It should have reduced in bulk and be soft and buttery. Season well and serve. Sprinkle the toasted oatmeal on top.

KALE AND CROWDIE PIE

6-8 servings

The pale green filling mixture for this flan is topped with some soured cream then dusted with paprika. Swirled with a fork it makes a colourful pattern on top and is also a good blend of flavours. The filling may also be used for stuffing pancakes.

Filling

1 lb/500 g crowdie cheese (2 c)
3 beaten eggs
$\frac{1}{2}$ lb/250 g chopped kale or spinach

1 small onion, finely chopped
1 tablespoon butter
3 tablespoons flour
$\frac{1}{2}$ teaspoon grated nutmeg
8 fl oz/250 ml soured cream (1 c)
Salt and freshly ground black pepper
Paprika for dusting top
9″ flan shell baked blind (p. 73)
Pre-heat the oven to 375F/190C/Gas 5.
Melt the butter in a pan and sauté the kale till soft as in the last recipe (p. 195). Season with salt and black pepper. Mix with eggs, flour, cheese and nutmeg. Spread into the base of flan shell. Cover with the soured cream, dust the top with paprika and swirl a design on top. Bake for 40-45 minutes.

GREEN KALE SOUP WITH BACON

For the stock
1 lb/500 g unsmoked ham*
3 medium potatoes
4 medium carrots
3 pts/1$\frac{1}{2}$ L water
Put into a pan, cover and cook till meat is tender then remove.
To make up the soup
8 oz/250 g kale or spinach
2 leeks
Remove the coarse stalks from the kale, wash and chop finely. Trim and clean the leeks, chop finely. Mash the potatoes and carrots or liquidise. Add the leeks and kale and bring to the boil then simmer till tender. Chop up the meat and add to the soup or serve separately. Taste for seasoning.

Cabbage

The people of the Orkney and Shetland Isles share with Scandinavians an extensive use of cabbage in their diet in preference to other vegetables. Combined with fish it was a staple item of diet which it never became in any other part of the country. They even pickled cabbage in barrels for winter use in a similar style to Sauerkraut. The chopped cabbage was packed into wooden barrels with layers of animal fat, oatmeal,

*The use of the term Ham in Scotland loosely refers to any kind of bacon and not merely the cured leg joint and cooked meat from it which is the usual English interpretation of the word. In Scotland this is usually called **Cooked Ham** or **Gammon**.

salt and spices. Weighted down it was used as required to make broth. The rest of Scotland used fresh cabbage in soups and stews and with mashed potatoes for Rumbledethumps.

Today it is an important vegetable crop with almost all of it sold in a fresh state, compared with peas and beans, over 90% of the crop of which is processed.

Varieties

White, red and green varieties are available while the leaves can be either smooth or crinkly. **Spring cabbages** are a bright green with a lightly formed heart and a pointed or conical shape. **Summer** and **Autumn** cabbages are more mature, heavier and should be firm and solid. **Winter cabbages** have very firm hearts and can be divided into four types — Red Cabbage; Dutch White Cabbage which are very round and dense, often stored for long periods before reaching the customer; January King and Savoy are the crinkled leaf type which come to market straight from the field; Celtic and other autumn hybrid varieties are also sold fresh from the field.

RUMBLEDETHUMPS

4 servings

The unusual name for this dish comes from the meaning for 'mixed together' — *rumbled*, and 'bashed together' — *thumped*. Scots eat it as a main course meatless dish, though it can also be served as a vegetable with meat.

1 lb/500 g cooked potatoes
1 lb/500 g cooked cabbage
2 oz/50 g butter ($\frac{1}{2}$ stick)
1 medium onion, finely chopped
2 oz/50 g grated Scottish cheddar ($\frac{1}{2}$ c)
Chopped chives

Melt the butter in a large pan and add the onion. Cook gently for 5 minutes without browning. Add potatoes, chives and cabbage and mix together. Season well and put into pie dish. Cover with cheese and brown under the grill or in the oven.

Peas

The Victorians had a real obsession about the indigestibility of vegetables and thought it necessary to boil them for hours to make them edible. Even fresh young peas received this treatment with boiling times of up to three-quarters of an hour! It makes it impossible to view their vegetable recipes with much enthusiasm since the real flavour of the fresh vegetables would have been destroyed. Today, the myth of cooking vegetables 'to death' has been blown and a whole new approach has been developed which depends on gentle handling and light cooking to preserve the natural flavour and crisp texture of the vegetable. Many of these ideas are based on cooking only the very youngest of vegetables which you could argue is not practical from a grower's point of view. However, peas must be picked and eaten young as anyone knows who has left picking too late and got only woody, tasteless specimens. Pea growers will tell you that a crop comes to ripeness within a matter of hours and must be picked and processed immediately.

BUTTERED PEAS WITH MINT

Toss 1 lb/500 g of fresh young peas in 1 tablespoon melted butter and 1 tablespoon stock or water keeping them moving all the time. Finish with chopped mint, a pinch of sugar and salt and pepper to taste.

PUREE OF GREEN PEAS baked in a mould

4 servings

1 lb/500 g cooked peas (as for buttered)
2 fl oz/50 ml double cream ($\frac{1}{4}$ c)
1 egg
Salt and white pepper
Grated nutmeg
Pre-heat the oven to 350F/180C/Gas 4.
Prepare the mould(s) — brush well with melted butter. Purée the Buttered Peas with cream and egg. Taste for seasoning and add a little grated nutmeg. Pour into mould(s) and place in a tray of water coming half-way up the moulds. Place in the oven and poach for 20-25 minutes.
Note: Purées of other vegetables may be used either singly or in combinations making colour and flavour contrasts, with alternating layers of different vegetables.

Sprouting Broccoli Calabrese

A vegetable of the future rather than the past, it has only been grown in Scotland commercially for about fifteen years, but producers are researching new varieties and growing methods in expectation of growing public demand, probably taking a cue from America where its value rose five-fold in the ten years from 1971-81 — its cultivated area during that period doubling in size. To a large extent broccoli has replaced kale as a vegetable in Scotland. It is of Italian origin, the name coming from 'brocco' meaning 'shoot'. Various types are grown, purple, green and white sprouting broccoli and Cape Broccoli. There is also a variety known as Calabrese which is the name of the region in Italy where it has been grown since the Middle Ages.

Buying

Calabrese is available from mid-June through to November or December while Sprouting Broccoli is available from March to May. Cape Broccoli is available in March and April though it can start earlier and finish later. It should have a good green colour. Avoid anything faintly yellowing and choose heads which are tightly packed and firm looking. It may be necessary to peel off the outer layer of the stalk if it is woody. To test try crunching a bit before you decide. The thicker the stalk usually the woodier.

CREAMY BROCCOLI SALAD

4 servings

This excellent salad comes from Mollie Katzen's second book The Enchanted Broccoli Forest . . . and other timeless delicacies (1982) and is written in the same spirit of adventure as her previous Mosewood Cookbook.

1 lb/½ kg fresh broccoli
1 lemon, juice of
2 fl oz/75 ml mayonnaise (¼ c)
2 fl oz/75 ml yogurt or sour cream or a combination (¼ c)
¼ teaspoon salt
¼ teaspoon crushed tarragon
2 finely chopped shallots
Lots of freshly ground black pepper

To prepare the broccoli

Cut off the bottom few inches of the broccoli stalks and discard if they look tough and woody (crunch a bit off the end if you are not sure), otherwise keep for Stir-fried Vegetables (see p. 277).
Young broccoli should have a tender outer skin on the stalks but older specimens may need to have their tough outer skin peeled off with a potato peeler. Divide the broccoli up into manageable-sized spears. Steam till just tender and bright green. Drain.

Finishing the dish

Combine the lemon juice with mayonnaise, yogurt or sour cream, tarragon and shallots and season well with salt and pepper. Toss the broccoli in this till well mixed. Cover and chill.

Mixed Vegetable Dishes

HOTCH POTCH

Spring Vegetable Soup
8-10 servings

> That's Hotch-Potch — and that's cocky-leeky — the twa best soups in natur. Broon soup's moss-water — and white soup's like scauded* milk wi' worms in't. But see, sirs, hoo the ladle stauns o'itsel in the potch. . . .
>
> Christopher North
> Noctes Ambrosianae, 1822-1835

North's enthusiasm for Hotch Potch led him into another eulogy when he describes it as 'an emblem o' the haill vegetable and animal creation'. Its virtue lies in the freshness and variety of the young spring vegetables and the universal liking in Scotland for a soup which has as much in it as possible.

*Scalded

For the stock

>2 lb/1 kg neck of lamb
>6 pt/3 L water
>1 onion stuck with a few cloves
>Bay leaf
>Bundle of fresh herbs

Added vegetables

>4 oz/125 g fresh green peas
>4 oz/125 g fresh broad beans
>3 oz/75 g spring onions, finely chopped
>$\frac{1}{4}$ medium turnip, diced
>2-3 young carrots, diced
>$\frac{1}{2}$ medium cauliflower broken into sprigs
>$\frac{1}{2}$ lettuce, finely chopped
>Salt and pepper
>Chopped chives for garnish

Making the stock

>Put the lamb into cold water and bring to the boil, skim. Add onion stuck with cloves and bay leaf and bundle of fresh herbs and simmer till the meat is tender. Strain, leave to cool, remove excess fat and take the meat off the bone. Chop it up finely.

To finish the soup

>Melt butter in pan and add cauliflower, carrots and turnip. Toss for about five minutes, cover and sweat for five minutes without colouring. Now add peas, beans and spring onions. Toss for a few minutes. Add the strained stock, bring to the boil and simmer very gently till the vegetables are just tender. They will loose their fresh flavour if overcooked. Finally, just before serving, taste for seasoning and add meat, lettuce and chives.

SUMMER VEGETABLE SOUP

>Yellow sweet-corn, red carrots and a variety of greens combine to make this potato-based soup full of both flavour and colour.

>2 large potatoes
>2 cups water
>1 cup fresh green peas
>Kernels from 2 ears of sweetcorn

>Cook the potatoes in water till soft then add peas and sweetcorn.

Sauté in 3 tablespoons butter or oil

>2 medium onions finely chopped
>1 cup diced broccoli
>2 medium carrots, diced
>2 small courgettes, diced
>1 green pepper, diced

>When all are tender and still a good bright colour, add to the potato purée.

Finishing the soup

>2 pt/1 L milk
>1½ teaspoons salt
>¼ teaspoon black pepper
>1 tablespoon fresh thyme
>¼ teaspoon grated nutmeg
>Add to the vegetables and heat through without cooking — serve
>immediately.

LENTIL SOUP

This basic lentil soup is finished with tomatoes, lemon juice, vinegar and molasses which sharpen up the flavour considerably. On the other hand, these flavours may be omitted for a more traditional version. Both are good with grated mature cheddar on top.

Simmer covered for 3-4 hours

>8 oz/250 g red lentils (3 c)
>3½ pt/1¾ L water or stock (or use a ham bone with water)
>2 teaspoons salt

Sauté in 2 oz/50 g butter (½ stick) for 10 minutes

>1 medium onion, finely chopped
>2-3 stalks celery or fennel, finely chopped
>2 medium carrots, finely chopped
>3-4 sliced potatoes
>¼ of a medium turnip, sliced
>Add to the lentil stock and simmer till all are just tender.

Finishing the soup — optional

>3-4 chopped tomatoes
>2 tablespoons lemon juice
>1 tablespoon wine vinegar
>1½ tablespoons molasses
>Black pepper
>Optional — thyme, oregano or basil
>Add to the soup about 30 minutes before serving — taste for
>seasoning and adjust consistency if necessary.

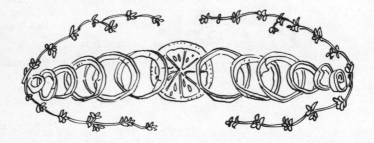

Chapter Seven

SUGAR & SPICE

& Baking, Scottish Sweeties & Preserves

Besides such homely sweets as gundy, glessie, cheugh jeans and black man, there were bottles of 'boilings' (Scotch Mixtures) that glittered like rubies, emeralds, topazes and all the jewels of the Orient, and tasted of all the fruits of the orchard and spices of the Indies.

F. Marian McNeill
The Scots Kitchen, 1929

With such temptations, it is not surprising that Scots have a sweet tooth. Too much sweetie boiling to while away the long winter nights in the days before television — and Scots still continue to have a high sugar consumption compared with the rest of the country.

A glance at the official figures in Household Food Consumption for 1982 (HMSO, 1984) shows that they are above the national average in nearly all things sweet (cakes are an exception) while a national food survey taken over a six year period shows that they buy 16% more biscuits than the rest of Britain and 50% more chocolate ones. (Mintel, Market Intelligence, 1983). Bearing out the Food Consumption figures, a special report on Cakes and Pastries (Retail Business 301, 1983) shows that Scots also buy less of these than the rest of Britain. The huge difference in popularity may have something to do with the fact that the oven came late to Scotland and Scots were more used to crisp hard things which could be baked on their girdles.

Sugar is of fairly recent origins. Before the 18th century honey was the sweetener used by rich and poor, though the rich also had access to expensive sugar loaves. These were made by cutting sugar cane from Arabia, pressing it to extract the syrup, then boiling to evaporate most of the moisture and finally pouring into long conical moulds to harden. A loaf could weigh anything from 3 to 14 pounds and the sugar was chipped off, when required, with pincers. Around the middle of the 17th century, Britain started acquiring sugar cane producing countries in the New World, and they started shipping it back to Europe in ever increasing quantities. The rich indulged in sugar fantasies, which decorated their tables, but the poor didn't see much of it and honey continued to be both sweetener and flavouring for them until sugar became cheaper, which was not until the 19th century.

The Scots, in particular, were enthusiastic bee keepers and their practice of taking the bees to the heather in the summer produced an important supply of very specially flavoured honey. But sugar was gaining hold and getting cheaper all the time as imports increased. The world's first sugar beet factory was built in Silesia in 1801/2, which led the way for an enormous increase in consumption by the mass of the population. The tea drinking habit was spreading and sugar, its inseparable companion, came, by the end of the 19th century, into the possession of the very poorest housewife. It fulfilled a need for a hot cheap stimulating drink which, if nothing else, took away the pangs of hunger.

Yet when sugar was first carried to the west from India by the warriors of Islam in the 8th century it was regarded as a spice. It was valued first as a medicine for curing coughs, colds and consumption. The spice trade from the East has a rich and fascinating history with Arabs monopolising it throughout. The idea of cinnamon, travelling a dangerous four thousand five hundred miles on the open sea from Malaya to Madagascar, then up the East coast of Africa to the Red Sea before it even reached the Arab merchant, who then travelled with it through Europe, gives the spice which we use today a whole new meaning.

The full flood of the spice trade did not come till the 1st century AD but it was ten centuries later before the British really developed a serious taste for them. Crusaders came back to Britain from the 'holy wars' in the 11th, 12th and 13th centuries with supplies of spices, dates, figs, almonds, sherberts and sweetmeats. They told tales of the exotic civilisations where these delicacies were eaten, and they kindled a liking for them among the people, to the extent that spices eventually became a necessity for those who had never left the country.

Spices transformed simple British tastes by adding interest and variety in flavour, as well as colour. They were good at inducing flagging appetites when the rich were trying to eat too much and also they did a good job on tainted meats and fish by conveniently camouflaging any rotten taste. Perhaps this was not one of their most pleasant uses, but it must have been responsible for the habit of adding spices to the salting procedure of meat, giving the finished meat a more interesting flavour and providing us with a 'spiced meat' tradition (see p. 131). Sugar and spices have found their way into all aspects of food preparation now. Cinnamon is still even used as a medicine in a Beechams powder.

It does seem that tastes and palates change from one century to the next. The Romans liked to sprinkle a layer of pepper over their sweet custards while medieval cooks were obsessed with the colour of food, constantly masking everything with a red dye called saunders or with yellow saffron. But despite fickle changes of fashion some foods have shown an amazing ability to survive. The marzipan which we put on top

of cakes comes from the Arab sweetmeat tradition. They continue to eat some of the stickiest, sickliest sweets I have ever tasted. Gingerbread is another survivor, likewise mincemeat, plum puddings and Scottish Black Bun. Except for gingerbread, which we would normally eat at any time of the year, the others are still all associated with a festival. When sugar and spices were much rarer commodities than they are today bakers were only allowed to use them for special festivals and we still tend to keep these traditional sweet spicy foods for high days and holidays.

Buying and Storing

Spices are perishable.

Buy from a shop which has a good turnover. Preferably grind your own, but at any rate, use them shortly after purchase while the flavours are at their best. Keep tightly closed and store in a cool place out of light.

Honey from a single type of blossom is the most expensive but has the best flavour. Highly blended honeys have nondescript flavours and some may contain amounts of ordinary sugar. These often taste sickly sweet whereas pure honey is not over sweet but has a particular bitter sweet tang. Scottish heather honey comes from bees which have been taken to the heather clad hills during the summer months which gives the honey its distinctive flavour and colour.

Honey does not deteriorate if stored for 1-2 years in a cool dark place away from strong smells. Consistencies vary through very runny to completely set. Stand in warm water not hotter than 50C to melt set honey without spoiling flavour or food value. It contains various extra ingredients,* not found in refined sugar and some of them will be destroyed if the honey is heated above 50C.

*Traces of minerals, iron, calcium, magnesium, phosphorous plus small quantities of the vitamins C, B, B2, B5, B6, nicotinic acid and other residues including enzymes, gums, resins and trace elements.

Scottish Baking

If every Frenchwoman is born with a wooden spoon in her hand, every Scotswoman is born with a rolling-pin under her arm. There may be a divergence of opinion as to her skill in cooking, but it is certain that she has developed a remarkable technique in baking — not only in bannocks, scones and oatcakes, but also in the finer manipulations of wheat — in cakes, pastry and shortbread.

F. Marian McNeill
The Scots Kitchen, 1929

Shortbread

'Six, four, two,' the teacher said, 'six ounces of flour, four of butter and two of sugar.' This was my first lesson in making shortbread and the numbers are indelibly printed on my mind whenever I think of it. I also remember the method she taught us — it was very simple. First, the butter was put on a board and the sugar on top. The flour was sifted into one corner. With our hands, we kneaded the sugar into the butter and then gradually started adding the flour, and the dough grew satisfyingly in size. We learnt to judge the consistency. Pliable without being too soft, firm but not too crumbly and we stopped adding the flour when the right consistency was reached, or added more if needed.

Feeling the 'life' of a dough is something which bakers will tell you only an experienced hand can judge. No recipe is a foolproof guide, especially when using things like flour and butter which both have varying degrees of absorbency depending on their moisture content. This delicate balance between the right and wrong consistency so affects the finished result that I'm glad we were encouraged to get our hands into things at an age when habits are formed.

Origin of Shortbread

'Short' has been used for at least five centuries to describe anything which is crisp and easily crumbled. In medieval times they ate 'short-paste' in Lent. Later the word was prefixed to both cake and bread which goes back to the confusion which arose when they called a piece of a 'loaf' a 'cake of bread'. By the early 19th century the Scots were commonly referring to it as 'bread' rather than 'cake' though it would have been more logical to have kept continuity with the oat 'cake' and the pan 'cake'. However, many parts of England and also Americans used 'cake' and so perhaps the Scots felt they just wanted to be different.

By deviating from the rest of Britain the Scots have produced a more distinctive item with no confusion about its definition as a crisp crumbly buttery biscuit. In England and America the short 'cake' continues to apply to a cross between a scone and a biscuit — sometimes a rich tea cake or a cake of pastry served with fruit.

Flour

A soft white flour with a low gluten content is best. If a strong flour is used the dough will be tough and the baked shortbread hard. A soft fine wholemeal may be used in a mixture with white but it does have a stronger flavour and the butter flavour may not come through so well. Some use a little rice flour for a crunchier result while others claim that a little cornflour improves the shortbread. A little of both is also used.

Butter

This is the main flavouring and shortening agent which gives distinction to shortbread — the finished result will be judged by the quality of the butter used. It should have a low water content.

Sugar

Caster sugar gives the best result though some icing sugar may be used for a finer result. Brown sugars tend to dominate flavourwise and spoil the natural flavour of the butter.

6 oz/175 g plain flour ($1\frac{1}{2}$ c)
4 oz/125 g butter (1 stick)
2 oz/50 g sugar ($\frac{1}{3}$ c)
Pre-heat the oven to 300F/150C/Gas 2.
Greased baking tray

Kneading the dough

Put the sugar and butter on the board and knead together. Sift the flour into a corner and start working in gradually till the dough is still soft and pliable and not too firm. Add more flour if you think it can take it without the dough breaking up.

Shaping the dough

Roll out into a **round** or cut into **fingers** or **fancy shapes**. The thickness is a matter of taste but thicker will take longer to bake. The above quantity may be pressed into a swiss roll tin (7" × 11" — 17 cm × 27 cm) and then cut into fingers. (Makes 20 biscuits.) If using a special **shortbread mould**, flour it well then knock out excess flour and press in the dough. Level off with a rolling pin and knock out the round. It can also be rolled into a **cylinder shape** in either granulated sugar or demerara sugar and then put in the refrigerator before slicing into round biscuits.

Before baking, shortbread of all shapes or sizes should be pricked all over with a fork (docked) to let the steam escape evenly and avoid it distorting the shape.

Baking

Shortbread should be baked slowly to develop the rich butter taste. It should be evenly baked to a light golden colour throughout the whole biscuit. If the temperature is too low it will have an undesirable greyish colour inside while if it is too high then it will have a 'bone' in the centre. Place in the bottom half of the oven: thick shortbread can take up to an hour. About five minutes before it is ready, remove from the oven and dust lightly with caster sugar. The sugar will stick to the hot surface much better if done at this stage, though it is not essential that they should be dusted with sugar at all.

RICH SHORTBREAD

Shapes

Oval and oblong shapes are described in early recipes with some variations. Mrs MacIver (1773) shaped hers into an oval then cut through the middle and plaited it at the ends. Some other ovals are cut in two 'the narrow way, so as to have two cakes somewhat the shape of a Saxon arch'. — Meg Dods (1826). Others are divided into squares or oblongs but all seem to agree that the thickness should be one inch.

Use of melted butter

Mrs MacIver uses three pounds of boiling butter to four pounds flour as well as 'a mutchkin of good yest'. Most early methods use melted butter and this seems to have been used well into the 20th century. Which makes a mockery of all those recipes which warn you about putting your warm hands into the shortbread in case you 'oil' it. Janet Murray in <u>Traditional Recipes from Scotland</u> (BBC, 1964) refers to a listener who was reminded of this method when she gave a recipe for a rich shortbread strongly flavoured with caraway and using melted butter.

Rich Shortbread for festive occasions and as a present

A thick round of shortbread with ground or chopped almonds added to the mixture as well as caraway seeds was decorated on top with crystallised lemon and orange peel and sometimes caraway comfits. This was so thick that recipes advise putting a band of paper round the outside as well as sitting it on several layers of paper while baking so that it does not brown too quickly round the edges and on the base. This special shortbread was baked for New Year celebrations and in the North East it was known as a **Pitcaithly Bannock**. Even in the 1820s Scots were sending it as a present from Scotland. Meg Dods put in more almonds and butter to make a very rich Scotch Shortbread 'for sending as a holiday present to England'.

RICH SHORTBREAD

Pitcaithly Bannock

This thick golden round of festive shortbread is traditionally flavoured with almonds, caraway and crystallised orange and lemon peel, which decorates the top. I prefer to flavour only with almonds and press about eight whole blanched ones onto the top surface before baking in the same style as a Dundee cake.

Make up double quantity of the basic mix and add

2 oz/50 g blanched almonds, finely chopped
1 tablespoon caraway seeds
Shape into a large round

Decorate the top with either

1 oz candied orange or lemon peel
or
8 blanched almonds
Bake as for basic mix.

Scones

> We lay upon the bare top of a rock like scones upon a girdle.
>
> Robert Louis Stevenson
> Kidnapped, 1886

Scones belong to the British family of small tea cakes though their Scottish pedigree goes back at least to the 18th century when Robert Burns rightly describes them as 'souple (soft) scones, the wale (choicest) of food'. How they got their name is difficult to say. The OED suggests that the word may be a shortened version of the German 'schonbrot' meaning fine bread, while Chambers Scots Dictionary suggests that the word is from the Gaelic 'sgonn', a shapeless mass. There is no confusion, though, about its pronunciation, at least in Scotland, where it is universally spoken of as a 'skawn' as in gone. The English pronounce them in some regions as the Scots do, while others pronounce the word to rhyme with own.

When to eat

They should **not** be limited to teatime. Savoury ones make excellent accompaniments to soups; they are also good at the end of a meal with cheese. They are so incredibly quick and easy to make, five minutes mixing and ten minutes or so baking, that it is not impossible to make them for breakfast or perhaps for the meal which crosses boundaries between breakfast and lunch, and which the Americans call brunch.

The secret of a good scone

The dough should be as wet as you can handle. The mixing should be done quickly and lightly. There should be the minimum of handling and they should be baked until they are just risen and dried out.

Ingredients

Scots traditionally make scones with buttermilk and bicarbonate of soda — known as Soda Scones. There is a subtle difference in the result which is softer, lighter, moister and with a sharper flavour than scones made with fresh milk and baking powder. If buttermilk is not available then sour milk may be used or fresh milk can be soured by adding about 2 teaspoons of lemon juice.

Mixing and Shaping

'Deftly mixed' is probably as good a description as any of the technique which depends on light quick handling for a perfect result. The flour should be well sifted and the buttermilk poured into a well in the centre. Don't add the liquid drop by drop. Stir with a wooden spoon, gradually bringing in the flour; if you get the mixture dry and 'ragged' looking the scones will not be light. The mixing should be done with as little 'working' as possible and it should be a soft elastic consistency, sticky unless well floured. It should not be handled more than is necessary and for this reason it is not rolled out but lifted in well-floured hands and placed on either girdle or baking tray. Then it is well floured on top and lightly pressed down into a rough round shape (a bannock) for the girdle $\frac{1}{2}$" ($1\frac{1}{2}$ cm) and for the oven $1\frac{1}{4}$" ($3\frac{1}{2}$ cm) and only at this point is it divided into scones. Chambers is right, they are a 'shapeless mass'. If liked, they may be separate or touching; if the latter they will take longer to cook but can be broken after baking.

Baking

All scones may be baked either on a girdle in the traditional way or in the oven. There will be differences in shape and texture. Those baked on the girdle will have smooth flat top and bottom surfaces while the oven ones will be rough on top. The oven ones are more likely to be drier while girdle scones will be moister.

The **girdle baking technique** allows more control over the baking since you can watch them as they cook and learn to judge when they should be turned and, more importantly, when they are ready. The girdle should not be too hot to begin with or the scones will brown too quickly. Cook slowly till risen and till there is a white skin on top. This usually takes about five or six minutes. The heat should have penetrated to the top and the centre well set before turning. Increase the heat if necessary till brown underneath then turn and brown on the other side. It should take about 15 minutes altogether. Open up a little at the edge to check they are quite dry. Wrap in a towel to keep them soft. It is more difficult to judge when they are in the oven but they will take a shorter time than you imagine. Overcooked, they lose their softness and lightness.

Types of Scones

SODA SCONES made with buttermilk

The Irish, who have perfected the art of making these scones, call them bread, which they are, reserving the scone term for the sweet variety. No additional flavouring should be added to soda scones.

Try baking them, as the Irish do, in a pot. Orginally the iron pot was buried in the burning peats to make a 'pot oven' but a heavy based enamel, or other similar pot, which will go in the oven will do just as well. I use a chicken brick with good results since the steam which develops inside prevents a crust forming too quickly, allowing full 'oven spring' which enables the loaf to swell to its maximum size before the top sets. Buttermilk scones (bread) made in this way are much lighter and better risen. It is not necessary to remove the lid half way through as some recipes tell you; it browns well with the lid on. The Chinese steamed bread and the French loaf also make use of this practice.

8 oz/250 g plain flour (2 c)
1 teaspoon bicarbonate of soda
1 teaspoon cream of tartar
½ teaspoon salt
8 fl oz/250 ml buttermilk (1 c)
Moderately hot girdle
Pre-heat the oven to 450F/230C/Gas 8.
7" (18 cm) round pot or chicken brick
Sift the flour, baking powder and salt into a bowl, make a well in the centre and add the buttermilk. Mix till soft elastic consistency, flour and place on baking tray or girdle or in pot or brick. Cook till risen and dry. Wrap in towel when cooked. Serve warm.

SWEET MILK SCONES — BASIC DOUGH

makes 8 scones

These scones can be made either sweet or savoury and can have all kinds of things added to them, even fruits or vegetables. Like shortbread, absorbency of the flour will dictate the exact amount of liquid required for the right consistency, so add more if necessary. Wholemeal flour will absorb more than white.

8 oz/250 g plain flour (2 c)

Raising agent either

1. 1 teaspoon bicarbonate of soda
   2 teaspoons cream of tartar
2. or 3 teaspoons baking powder
3. or use self-raising flour

With

2 oz/50 g butter (½ stick) — this can be varied according to taste or even oil used instead

5 fl oz/150 ml fresh milk ($\frac{3}{4}$ c)
Salt to taste
Pre-heat the oven to 450F/230C/Gas 8.
Bake one third from the top
or
Heat girdle till moderately hot
Sift all the dry ingredients into a bowl and rub in the butter. This
can be done in the processor but the mixing should be done by hand
so it seems hardly worth it unless you are in a desperate hurry to get
them into the oven. Pour the milk into the centre and mix to a soft
elastic dough, slightly stiffer and more manageable than for soda
scones. Knead lightly on a floured surface till smooth and press out
with your hands or roll out. Cut into shapes, flour or brush with egg
on top and bake. Wrap in towel when ready to keep soft and warm.
Serve warm.

SULTANA SCONES

Use an 80% wholemeal self-raising flour. Add 1 tablespoon raw
brown sugar and 3 oz/75 g sultanas ($\frac{1}{2}$ c).

TREACLE SCONES with walnuts or pecans

Mix 2 tablespoons treacle or molasses to the milk before mixing;
2 oz/50 g chopped walnuts or pecans ($\frac{1}{2}$ c).

HONEY SCONES with orange and lemon

Substitute fresh orange juice for 2 fl oz/50 ml of the sweet milk ($\frac{1}{4}$
cup). Add 2 tablespoons honey and the grated zest of a lemon and 1
tablespoon chopped walnuts.

JAM SCONES

Make up the basic dough and divide into two. Roll out both pieces
to $\frac{1}{2}$" (1 cm) thick rounds or rectangles. Brush round the edges of
one with egg or milk and spread 2 tablespoons jam to 1" (2 cm) of
the edge. Put on other piece of dough, press down lightly round the
edges, brush with egg and mark on top into squares.

CREAM SCONES

The cream adds flavour and may be either fresh or sour. Substitute 6
fl oz/150 ml ($\frac{3}{4}$ c) for the sweet milk and add 2 eggs. The sour cream
gives a sharper more interesting flavour.

FRESH FRUIT SCONES

Use soft fruits — raspberries are very good, add about 4 oz/125 g to the basic mix. Add sugar to taste. Serve with fresh cream. For an Apple or Rhubarb Scone: Add to the basic mix 1 egg; another 2 oz (50 g) butter; 3 tablespoons sugar and 1 lb/500 g peeled, cored and roughly chopped cooking apple or chopped rhubarb. Spread in a greased baking tin 11″ × 7″ (27 cm × 17 cm). Sprinkle with a layer of granulated sugar and bake.

HERB SCONES for serving with cheese

Add 1 teaspoon dried herbs, 2 teaspoons fresh to the basic mix.

CHEESE SCONES for serving with soup

Add 5 oz/150 g grated Scottish cheddar cheese (1 c generous) and a large pinch of cayenne pepper sifted in with the flour. Season well with salt. Brush with egg and sprinkle cheese on top.

ONION SCONES

Melt 2 tablespoons bacon fat in a pan, add 1 small onion, finely chopped and cook till soft but not browned. Leave to cool. Add most of it to the dough but keep back some to put on top after brushing with egg. For **Cheese and Onion Scones** add the onion mix to the cheese scones and put both onion and cheese on top. For **Cheese and Onion with Herbs** combine last three variations. Chives are particularly good.

SCOTTISH PANCAKES AND CRUMPETS

The word 'cake' was originally applied to a small regularly shaped item which was eaten as bread and known as a 'kaak of bread' (see origins of oatcake p. 22). The sweetening part came later, as did the change in size to the large sweetened and flavoured items we call cakes today. The Scottish 'pan-cake' is a throw-back to the original meaning, as is the Yorkshire 'tea-cake'.

In the late 17th century there emerged another type of cake — the crumpet. This got its name 'crompid cake' from the fact that it curled up or bent into a curve when baked, the verb 'to crump or crimp' meaning to curl. The original crumpet was baked very thinly and cooked on a girdle, which is why it curled. English crumpets are quite different affairs now. The Scottish crumpet is still thin, but not baked hard enough any more so that it will curl naturally, though they are usually rolled up into a curl when eaten.

The same mixture can be used for both pancakes and crumpets; the difference is in the consistency, with crumpets mixed to a much thinner consistency.

8 oz/250 g plain flour (2 c)

Raising agent either

1. 1 teaspoon bicarbonate of soda
   2 teaspoons cream of tarter
   with fresh milk
2. or 1 teaspoon bicarbonate of soda
   1 teaspoon cream of tarter
   with buttermilk
3. or 3 teaspoons baking powder
   with fresh milk
4. or use self-raising flour and fresh milk

With

1 tablespoon syrup, honey or sugar
1 large egg
8 fl oz/250 ml liquid (1 c) for pancakes
12 fl oz/375 ml liquid (1½ c) for crumpets
Pre-heat the girdle till moderately hot and grease very lightly.

Mixing the ingredients

Sift the dry ingredients into a bowl. Mix the honey and egg with the milk and pour into a well in the centre of the flour. Mix till smooth but <u>do not beat</u>.

Size

Drop spoonfuls onto the heated greased girdle. Pancakes should spread up to about 3″ (7 cm) while crumpets are much larger, about double the size of pancakes.

Firing

Turn when the heat has penetrated to the top surface and it's beginning to bubble. They should be lightly brown underneath and should only take 1-2 minutes on each side.

Wrap in a towel immediately they are cooked and serve warm.

Scottish Cookies

I want a plain ham-and-egg tea . . . and some cookies and cakes.

R.M. Williamson in <u>Scotland</u>. Readings etc.
Edited. T.W. Paterson. 1929

A **Cookie** is a plain, round, yeasted, sweet bun. It is very light in texture with a dark golden shiny top. Split, filled with whipped cream and dusted on top with icing sugar, it is known as a **Cream Cookie**: with an iced top only it is known as an **Iced Cookie**. These three types are the most common ones available in bakers' shops in Scotland. Spice and fruit may also be added, with the appropriate descriptive epithet.

The name was probably adopted from the Dutch 'koekje' which was actually the diminutive of 'koek' — cake. Confusingly, Americans use the word to mean a 'biscuit'. A 'cookie shine' is the Scottish equivalent of the English 'bun fight'. 'From the frequent appearance of these (cookies) at tea-parties the latter are irreverently spoken of as cookie shines.'

PLAIN COOKIES

makes 25-30

> 1½ lb/750 g strong plain flour (6 c)
> ½ pt/250 ml milk (1¼ c)
> 1 oz/50 g fresh yeast (2 pkg or cakes)
> (2 teaspoons dried)
> 1 teaspoon salt
> 4 tablespoons sugar
> 4 oz/125 g butter, softened (1 stick)
> 2 large eggs
> Pre-heat the oven to 425F/220C/Gas 7.
> 2 large greased baking trays

Mixing and Kneading the dough

> Begin by warming both the milk and flour separately to blood heat. Yeast will work much more efficiently if everything is warm. Blend the fresh yeast with a little of the milk or dissolve the dried yeast in some and leave until it begins to froth up.
>
> Make a well in the centre of the flour and add most of the milk, yeast, salt, butter and eggs. (Keep back some of the egg for glazing.) Bring together with your hands till it is a soft, sticky dough, adding more milk if necessary. If it is too wet, add more flour. So many recipes tell you to knead the dough for so many minutes that it is confusing and really what you must do is knead it until it is the right consistency, and the time it takes to reach this stage varies. It should be transformed during the kneading process from a soft sticky mess to a smooth, silky rounded ball which comes away from your fingers easily. If the gluten content of the flour is poor, achieving this result is impossible. Always use a strong flour.

Rising

> Cover the bowl with a wet towel (dough likes a damp steamy atmosphere for rising) and leave in a warm place till it has almost doubled in size.

Knocking Back and Shaping the dough

> Knock all the air out of the dough, give it another knead to re-distribute the yeast and shape the dough into 25-30 small round buns about 2″ (5 cm) in diameter.

Proving

> This is aptly described — to prove that the yeast is still working. Place in a warm place again, cover with a film of very lightly greased cling film and leave till they have doubled in size. Brush with an egg and milk glaze and bake for 10-15 minutes.

Cookie Variations

CREAM COOKIES

Split when cold and fill with whipped cream. Dust on top with icing sugar.

ICED COOKIES

Make up a fairly stiff water icing, colour and coat the top of the cookie.

CURRANT COOKIES

Add 4 oz/125 g currants (1 c scant) to the dough.

SPICE COOKIES

Immediately spices are ground they start to lose their aroma. With bought spice it is impossible to know how old and therefore how potent it is, and I have often been disappointed with a result when I thought I'd put in enough spice but the flavour just didn't come through. I found the answer in Elizabeth David's English Bread and Yeast Cookery (1977). 'The remedy,' she says, 'is to blend and grind one's own mixture, in sufficient quantity to last for just a few weeks.'

Blend together in a coffee grinder

$\frac{1}{2}$ oz/15 g nutmeg (about 4 small, 3 large)

$\frac{1}{2}$ oz/15 g allspice (3 teaspoons)

$\frac{1}{4}$ oz/7 g cinnamon bark (6"/15 cm stick)

$\frac{1}{4}$ oz/7 g whole cloves (2 teaspoons scant)

$\frac{1}{4}$ oz/7 g dried ginger root (about 2"/5 cm piece)

Grind till fine. They will not be quite as fine as the commercial variety but this does not matter for baking. Store in an airtight jar, label with the date, keep in a cool place and use within the month. Use 2 teaspoons of this mixture for spicing the cookies.

A SPECIAL YEAST CAKE

for those who don't like Rich Fruit Cakes

This is a lovely rich yeast cake with a delicious sticky top. Good for New Year as a contrast to Black Bun. It will disappear quickly which is just as well since it does not keep, though it does make good toast if there are leftovers. The recipe was given to me by Neil Reiley, a retired Glasgow grocer, who bakes for a hobby in a remote Highland glen, firing his bread in a traditional peat-burning stove. The nearest baker is fifty miles away so it's a question of do-it-yourself or suffer the unpleasant prospect of a life of tasteless manufactured bread.

Many more people are taking up bread-making as a serious hobby in these remote areas and more and more hotels are realising the advantages of freshly-baked bread and rolls as a positive attraction for customers. It is not that bread-making is very time consuming, mostly it gets on with it on its own, and the time spent attending to it is really quite short. It also fills the house with lovely yeasty aromas while the results gladden the palate with satisfying results.

This is a kind of upside-down-cake, since the sticky topping is put in the bottom of the tin and the dough shaped into round balls, placed on top, and then the whole thing is turned out with the sticky top up.

Enriched White Bread Dough

Use dough for Cookies (see p. 215) and follow the basic method for making the dough. When ready for shaping make up the following:

Sticky top

1 oz/25 g butter ($\frac{1}{4}$ stick)
1 oz/25 g brown sugar
1 tablespoon golden syrup
3 tablespoons currants
Pre-heat the oven to 425F/220C/Gas 7.
Grease and line a 7" cake tin (25 cm)
Melt butter, sugar and syrup together and bring to the boil. Remove from the heat and pour into the base of the tin.

Sprinkle over half the currants.

Shape the dough into about 20-30 small balls. Arrange balls in the tin in loose layers sprinkling with rest of the currants. Cover with oiled cling film and leave to rise in a warm place. Bake for $\frac{3}{4}$-1 hour.

WHITE FLOURY BAPS

He grew, the great Macguldroch grew,
On butter'd baps and ale.

R. Couper
Poems. 1804

Lady Clark of Tillypronie (1909) says that — '"Baps" are mixed very slack — water, flour, salt, yeast. (Neither butter, eggs, nor milk.) They are well dusted with flour, and eaten fresh as soon as baked.' The etymology of the word is unknown but it seems clear that they were always breakfast rolls made from a very plain bread dough and the shapes and sizes varied greatly from one part of the country to another, possibly even from one household to another. 'Are ye for your burial baps round or square?' says Mrs Lion in Reminiscences of Scottish Life and Character by Dean Ramsay (1870).

Whatever size or shape they are distinguished by their fresh, soft, white, floury qualities. Most bakers today make them round and call them white or floury morning rolls. The thick floury coating prevents an early crust forming (see p. 211) and allows them to rise well.
Makes about 10 'man-sized' baps.

1 lb/500 g strong white flour (5 cups)
2 oz/50 g lard (¼ cup)
2 teaspoons salt
1 oz/25 g fresh yeast, 2 teaspoons dried (2 pkg/cake)
1 teaspoon sugar
½ pt/250 ml water and milk, warmed (1¼ c scant)
Pre-heat the oven to 425F/220C/Gas 7.
Greased baking tray

Making the dough

Sift the flour into a bowl, add salt and put to warm. Meanwhile cream yeast and sugar together and then mix with the milk and water. Rub the lard into the flour, add the liquid and knead together till smooth and pliable. Leave to rise till doubled in size — about an hour. Knock back, knead and then shape into baps.

Size

The size of oval baps is usually about 4″ (10 cm) long by about 3″ (7 cm) wide at this stage before rising. Round ones are about 4″ (10 cm) diameter. Once shaped, they are brushed with milk, dusted with flour and set in a warm place to prove. When they have risen, dust again lightly with flour and bake for 15 minutes. Dust again lightly with flour, cool and eat warm.

GINGERBREAD

An had I but one penny in the whole world,
Thou shouldst have it to buy gingerbread.

William Shakespeare
Love's Labour's Lost

Gingerbread began its life as enormously popular 'fun' biscuits sold at annual fairs. The gingerbread booth was a colourful affair with ornamental gingerbread in the form of 'crowns, kings and queens, cocks, etc., dazzlingly resplendent with pseudo gold leaf' and brightly decorated with coloured satin ribbons.

It wasn't the kind of soft gingerbread we make today, but a much harder biscuit and therefore more easily shaped. In fact the mixture was not even cooked. Honey was mixed with grated bread, according to a recipe of 1430, till the mixture was stiff, then it was flavoured with cinnamon and pepper, coloured with red and yellow, shaped, stuck with cloves and allowed to dry out. Novel shapes included the inevitable gingerbread men as well as letters and numbers which were used to teach children to read and count.

Robbie Salmond was an eccentric itinerant gingerbread seller, according to J.H. Jamieson in his article on 'Street Traders and their Cries' in the Book of the Old Edinburgh Club (1909). At the Hallow Fair in Edinburgh he was to be found 'encouraging' his customers by occasionally tossing his gingerbread into the crowd and calling 'Bullock's blood and sawdust — Feed the ravens, Feed the ravens.'

Another Edinburgh reference to gingerbread appears in Robert Chambers' Traditions of Edinburgh (1868) when he refers to the shop and 'tavern' run by Mrs Flockhart in the Potterrow. Her nickname was 'Lucky Fykie'* and, in the space of a square of about fifteen feet each way, she had a shop selling a variety of miscellaneous items; a living area; a tiny closet (side room); and adjoining this a small room described as a 'hotel'. 'Each forenoon was this place . . . put into the neatest order; at the same time three bottles, severally containing brandy, rum, and whisky, were placed on a bunker-seat in the window of the 'hotel', flanked by a few glasses and a salver of gingerbread biscuits. About noon any one watching the place from an opposite window would have observed an elderly gentleman entering the humble shop, where he saluted the lady with a 'Hoo d'ye do, mem?' and then passed into the side space to indulge himself with a glass from one or other of the bottles. After him came another, who went through the same ceremonial; after him another again; and so on. Strange to say, these were men of importance in society — some of them lawyers in good employment, some bankers, and so forth. . . . On special occasions Lucky could furnish forth a *soss* — that is, stew — which the votary might partake of upon a clean napkin in the closet, a place which only admitted of one chair being placed in it.'

DARK GINGERBREAD

If someone ever falls heir to my cookery books they will find among them a 1966 edition of Philip Harben's The Grammar of Cookery. It will open automatically at page 151, and apart from the tell-tale signs of food-stained pages, they will find the words 'very, very good' underlined beside this recipe.

'Do not judge this remarkable gingerbread by normal cake standards,' he says, 'it will probably sink in the middle as it cools, and will eat "heavy".'

I have doubled the quantity.

6 oz/125 g plain or self-raising flour (1½ c)
2 teaspoons bicarbonate of soda
½ teaspoon mixed spice (see spice mix p. 216)
2 teaspoons ground ginger
4 oz/125 g butter (1 stick)
4 oz/125 g brown sugar (1 c generous)
6 tablespoons black treacle
2 large eggs, beaten
2 tablespoons raisins
About 4 fl oz/125 ml milk (½ c)

*Lucky — guidwife
Fykie — neat and clean

7″ (18 cm) round greased tin
Pre-heat the oven to 350F/180C/ Gas 4.

Mixing the dough

Sift the dry ingredients together. Cream together the butter and
sugar in a large saucepan which will hold the finished mixture.
When light, add the treacle and warm very slightly. Beat in the egg
and then sift in the dry ingredients. Mix all together and add milk to
make a fairly thin consistency. Bake for about 1 hour till springy
when touched.

LIGHT GINGERBREAD or Gingerbread Scone

Pre-heat the oven to 375F/190C/Gas 5.
Grease and/or line tin 10″ × 9″ (25 × 22 cm)

Melt together in a pan

2 oz/50 g brown sugar ($\frac{1}{2}$ c)
4 oz/125 g treacle ($\frac{1}{4}$ c generous)
2 oz/50 g butter ($\frac{1}{2}$ stick)

Add

3 teaspoons ground ginger
1 teaspoon cinnamon
1 teaspoon mixed spice
1 teaspoon baking soda
8 oz/250 g flour (2 c)
Mix with 1 large egg and enough milk to make a soft dropping
consistency. Bake till risen and firm on top.

GINGER BISCUITS or Parlies

Suitable for making into gingerbread men and other fancy shapes.
Mrs Flockhart's 'Parlies' are described as large and square.

1 lb/500 g plain flour (4 c)
4 oz/125 g butter or margarine (1 stick)
4 oz/125 g soft brown sugar ($\frac{3}{4}$ c)
1 teaspoon ground ginger
4 oz/125 g black treacle or molasses ($\frac{1}{4}$ c)
Pre-heat the oven to 325F/170C/Gas 3.
Greased baking tray
Combine all the ingredients in a bowl and knead together until
evenly coloured. Roll out onto a floured board, cut into the required
shapes and bake for approximately 20 minutes.

BLACK BUN

Also known as 'Rich Bun' or a 'Scotch Christmas Bun' or just as 'Scotch
Bun', it originated in bakers' shops in the days when they were only
allowed to make cakes for special holidays. A lump of the bread dough
was set aside and fruit and spices worked in. Selkirk Bannocks origin-

ated in this way but the Rich Bun was, as it infers, a much richer and spicier affair. In fact so rich that if you have ever made one you will realise why the bakers had to wrap it up — it would never stay together on its own, so they sensibly enclosed it in a thin casing of plain bread dough. Somewhere between then and now, the bread part was abandoned and the rich mixture encased in plain short crust pastry. I find the original version using the bread dough for both filling and casing simpler and more satisfying to make. The result is a lighter more interesting bun with a more open, moist texture while the outside crust hardens to a nice short-pastry-like crispness.

For the dough

> 2 lb/1 kg strong plain white flour (8 c)
> $\frac{3}{4}$ lb/350 g butter (3 sticks)
> 1 oz/25 g fresh yeast ($\frac{1}{2}$ oz/15 g dried or 2 pkg)
> $\frac{3}{4}$ pt/450 ml warm water (2 c scant)
> $\frac{1}{2}$ teaspoon salt

Cream the yeast and add water. Sieve the flour and salt and rub in the butter. Mix in the yeast mixture and knead to a smooth pliable dough adding more warm water if necessary. Cover and set to rise in a warm place till doubled in size.

Fruit and Spice Mix

Many permutations exist and it is worthwhile experimenting with flavours. No alcohol seems to have been used in the past, but it is a good idea to soak the fruit in rum or brandy. With rum I use more cinnamon; with brandy more allspice. Freshly ground spices will have a better flavour.

> 1$\frac{1}{2}$ lb/$\frac{3}{4}$ kg stoned raisins
> 1$\frac{1}{2}$ lb/$\frac{3}{4}$ kg currants
> 4 oz/125 g flaked almonds (1 c)
> 8 oz/250 g mixed peel (2 c)
> 2 teaspoons ground cloves
> 1 oz/25 g ground cinnamon
> $\frac{1}{2}$ oz/15 g ground ginger
> 2-3 tablespoons rum
> 1 egg yolk plus 1 teaspoon water for glaze

Pre-heat the oven to 350F/180C/Gas 4.
Line a 12″ round cake tin with greaseproof paper.
Divide dough into $\frac{1}{3}$ and $\frac{2}{3}$ pieces. Mix fruit spices well together and then sprinkle rum or brandy over fruit; mix thoroughly through. Now work fruit and spices into larger piece of dough. This is done most easily on a flat surface rather than in a bowl since you really have to knead the fruit in; not difficult, since the fruit sticks easily to the dough.

When well mixed in, roll out the smaller piece to a large round a few inches larger than the bun. Place the bun in the centre and bring up the sides to meet in the centre at the top. Bring all the edges together and mould evenly round the bun.

Turn over on join and put into lined cake tin. Leave to prove in a warm place for 30 minutes. Prick all over with a long skewer right through to the bottom of the bun, brush with glaze and bake for about 2 hours.

SELKIRK BANNOCK

This rich yeasted bannock is shaped like a round cob loaf, generously filled with sultanas and raisins, and sold in bakers' shops in the Borders in small and large sizes. When Queen Victoria was visiting Sir Walter Scott's grand-daughter at Abbotsford she is said to have refused all else to eat with her tea save a slice of the Bannock.

2 lb/1 kg strong plain flour
1 oz/50 g fresh yeast (2 teaspoons dried or 2 pkg)
4 oz/125 g butter (1 stick)
4 oz/125 g lard
$\frac{3}{4}$ pt/450 ml milk (2 c scant)
8 oz/250 g sugar ($1\frac{1}{4}$ c)
1 lb/500 g sultanas or raisins or a mixture of the two
1 teaspoon salt
1 egg yolk plus 1 teaspoon water for glazing
Pre-heat the oven to 425F/220C/Gas 7: bake 15-20 minutes.
Reduce to 375F/190C/Gas 5: bake 20-30 minutes.

To make the dough

Sift the flour into a bowl and put in a warm place till it is slightly warmed. Meanwhile either cream the fresh yeast, or reconstitute the dried yeast with a little of the measured milk. Melt the butter and lard and add to the milk; add the sugar and stir to dissolve. Leave to cool till just lukewarm. Make a well in the centre of the flour and add the milk and yeast. Mix to a fairly soft but not sticky dough. Add more milk or flour as necessary. Knead till smooth and silky and till it comes away easily from your hands. Return to bowl, cover with a damp cloth and leave to rise till double in size.

Knocking down/Adding fruit

Turn out the dough onto a floured surface and knead in the fruit. Shape into four small or two large buns. Place on a greased baking tray, cover with some lightly oiled cling film, and leave in a warm place till they have doubled in size. Brush with egg glaze and put in a hot oven for 15-20 minutes then reduce the heat and bake for another 20-30 minutes. Test by sounding one with your knuckles on the base; it should sound hollow. (Large ones will take longer.)

DUNDEE CAKE

Whole almonds, laid all over the surface of this cake before it goes into the oven, are gently roasted to a golden brown during the baking to give this cake its distinctive appearance. Their lovely nutty crunch contrasts with a moist well-flavoured light fruit cake making this a very popular Scottish fruit cake.

8 oz/250 g butter (2 sticks)
8 oz/250 g caster sugar (1¼ c)
5 eggs
10 oz/300 g self-raising flour (2½ c)
3 oz/75 g ground almonds (1 c)
4 oz/125 g currants (¾ c)
4 oz/125 g sultanas (¾ c)
4 oz/125 g raisins (¾ c)
2 oz/50 g mixed peel (¼ c)
Zest of orange
1-2 tablespoons sweet sherry
Milk to mix
2 oz/50 g whole blanched almonds for the top (½ c)
Pre-heat the oven to 350F/180C/Gas 4.
7″ (18 cm) round cake tin, lined

Put the butter and sugar into a bowl and warm slightly. Break all the eggs into a bowl and beat together; warm them slightly till lukewarm. Have eggs, sugar and butter all at the same temperature — they will mix and cream more easily and the mixture will be less likely to curdle. Beat the sugar and butter first till light and creamy, then beat in the eggs gradually. Add some flour if necessary to prevent curdling. Add the fruit, peel, orange zest and sherry and finally sift in the flour and salt. Mix with enough milk to make a soft dropping consistency and turn into lined tin. Level the top and cover with whole almonds. Bake till lightly browned on top and until a skewer inserted into the centre of the cake comes out cleanly. About 1-1½ hours.

'A CAKE WITH APPLES IN IT'

This was made in the autumn to use up excess fruit, and is often mentioned in Grisell Baillie's Household Book (1692-1733). The apples can be put on top, on the bottom or mixed through. Here are two versions, top and bottom. They are mixed through in an Apple Scone (see p. 213).

WITH APPLES AT THE BOTTOM

A light spongy cake. The cinnamon-coated apples, which are put on top, sink during the baking, ending up at the bottom but leaving a hint of cinnamon throughout the cake. The base has a crisp layer of Buttered Oats which contrasts nicely with the moist cinnamon apples and the light spongy texture of the cake.
Pre-heat the oven to 350F/180C/Gas 4.

Preparing the tin

Grease and line the base of a 10″ (25 cm) round cake tin and sprinkle with 4 tablespoons Buttered Oats (see p. 39) or just use plain toasted rolled oats.

Making the cake

> 4 eggs
> 7 oz/200 g soft brown sugar (1 c)
> 6 oz/175 g plain flour (1½ c)
> 1 teaspoon baking powder
> 8 oz/250 g melted butter (2 sticks)
> Beat the eggs and sugar till thick and pale and then add the sifted
> flour, baking powder. Pour the butter in gradually, mix through,
> then pour into the tin.

To finish

> Toss 3 eating apples (peeled, cored and sliced) in 1 tablespoon of
> soft brown sugar and 2 teaspoons freshly ground cinnamon. Drop
> gently on top of batter and bake for 45 minutes or until springy on
> top.

WITH APPLES ON TOP

> This is a much stiffer mixture which holds the apples up on top of the
> cake. The apples are cut so that they fan open during cooking giving a
> pleasing effect on top. It is really only what we know as an Eve's Pudding
> with the apples on top in a decorative form instead of underneath.
> 4-5 well-flavoured eating apples
> 6 oz/175 g butter or margarine (1½ sticks)
> 7 oz/200 g sugar (1 c)
> 7 oz/200 g plain soft flour (1¾ c)
> 3 large eggs
> 1 teaspoon baking powder
> 1 tablespoon melted butter for brushing
> Pre-heat the oven to 350F/180C/Gas 4.
> 9-10″ cake tin, greased and lined (23-25 cm)

Preparing the apples

> Peel and cut in half. Scoop out the core then turn onto cut side and
> make about 4-5 incisions, almost, but not quite, through the apple,
> cutting from north to south pole rather than round the equator.

Making the sponge and Finishing

> Cream butter and sugar till light and fluffy. Beat in the eggs and
> then fold in sifted flour and baking powder. The mixture should be
> soft and loose, but not runny; add some warm water if too stiff. Pour
> into the tin, level top and press in apples. Brush liberally with the
> melted butter, especially on the slits in the apples and bake for
> ¾-1 hour. Serve warm as a pudding, then use later as a cake.
> It will keep for a few days.

VARIATIONS

Prune Cake

Soak 7 oz/200 g prunes for about an hour in $\frac{1}{4}$ pt/150 ml boiling
water ($\frac{3}{4}$ c). Remove stones and halve them. Put in a pan, with the
liquid they have been soaked in, the grated zest of 1 lemon and
$\frac{1}{4}$ pt/150 ml red wine ($\frac{3}{4}$ c). Stew with the lid off till all the liquid has
evaporated. Leave to cool. Put the prunes evenly on top of the cake,
then bake.

Almond Cake

Bake the cake first, remove from tin, cool, and finish with the
following mixture:
3 oz/75 g butter ($\frac{3}{4}$ stick)
3 oz/75 g demerara sugar ($\frac{1}{2}$ c scant)
2 oz/50 g chopped almonds ($\frac{1}{2}$ c)
1 tablespoon plain flour
2 teaspoons single cream
Place together in a pan, bring to the boil, cool slightly and pour over
cake.

Biscuits

To eat with sweets and puddings or serve with tea

... The drop biscuits and almond biscuits that so often
appeared heaped high between dishes of jelly, cream and
syllabub on the dinner-table, at dessert, might also be offered
at tea.

Marion Lochhead
The Scots Household in the Eighteenth Century, 1948

DROP BISCUITS

These light crisp little biscuits are baked till still creamy yellow in the
centre but with a light golden brown edging — they can be flavoured
with either vanilla or almond and may be shaped into fingers or small
rounds.
3 oz/75 g icing sugar ($\frac{3}{4}$ c)
2 oz/50 g softened butter ($\frac{1}{2}$ stick)
2 egg whites
3 oz/75 g plain flour
Pre-heat the oven to 425F/220C/Gas 7.
Cream together the butter and sugar. Break up the whites till they
foam slightly and then add to the mixture gradually, beating well.
Add essence and then finally sift and fold in the flour. Do not beat.
The consistency should be smooth and loose. Add more egg whites if

it is too stiff and more flour if too runny. May be shaped with a
piping bag for a more formal biscuit but otherwise drop in spoonfuls
onto a well greased baking tray and bake for 6-8 minutes till the
edges are lightly browned and the centres still creamy yellow.

ALMOND BISCUITS

The crunchy texture is dominated by flaked almonds. The biscuits can
be bent while warm into a slightly curled shape which adds to their
charm.

Add to the basic mix for Drop biscuits

2 oz/50 g flaked almonds
A few drops of almond essence
Drop in spoonfuls onto greased tray and sprinkle on top with a few
flaked almonds. Bake as for basic mix.

Shaping (optional)
Roll the biscuit round a wine bottle to give a curled effect.

BROKEN BISCUIT CAKE

In the days when grocers had large tins of loose biscuits which you
bought by the pound (now you buy broken biscuits in packets) they sold
bags of broken ones cheaply and this was a popular way of using them.
It is a quick-and-easy, no cooking cake. Good for a children's cooking
session — it keeps well if allowed to.

Melt together

1 lb/500 g good plain chocolate
1 lb/500 g butter or firm margarine (4 sticks)

Add

1 lb/500 g broken biscuits
½ lb/250 g chopped mixed toasted nuts (4 c)
1 teaspoon vanilla essence
Pour into a baking tin 10 × 15″ (25 × 37 cm) lined with
greaseproof paper, level on top and leave to set. Cut in fingers, it
should be about a finger thick. It can also be poured into a lined loaf
tin 1 × 2 lb/1 kg or 2 × 1 lb/½ kg and left overnight to set (may be
pressed with a weight to give a firmer texture), then cut in thin
slices.

NUTBALL BISCUITS

These plump little walnut-flavoured balls, almost more of a confection
than a biscuit, are rolled in icing sugar with delicious results.

Mix together in a large bowl

½ lb/250 g plain flour (2 c)
4 oz/125 g granulated sugar (½ c generous)
½ teaspoon salt
½ lb/250 g butter (2 sticks)
2 teaspoons vanilla essence

$\frac{1}{2}$ lb/250 g finely chopped walnuts (2 c)
Form into a smooth firm paste and roll into small balls the size of a
walnut. Place on greased baking sheet about 1" (2$\frac{1}{2}$ cm) apart.
Bake 350F/180C/Gas 4 for 15 minutes. They should not brown.
Roll in icing sugar when almost cool.

Sweeties

The ecstasy of acquiring a 'Sugar hert' a handful of 'Curly
Murlies' or a bottle of 'Treacle Ale' and a slab of 'Gingerbread' is
impossible to describe.

G.M. Martin
Dundee Worthies, 1934

Sugar hearts were, as you would imagine, fondant shapes but the Curly
Murlies were a more specialised Angus delicacy. They are described by
Martin as 'mixed sweets of various shapes and sizes of the texture of pan-
drops although the curly murlie proper had a rather knarled exterior.
They were formed on a seed or other foundation such as a carvie, clove or
almond. The nucleus of the Curlie Murlie proper was probably aniseed.
It was about the size of a large pea. These sweets were popular on feed-
ing-market days when Jock was expected to give Jenny her "market" in
the form of a pockie of market sweeties or Curlie Murlies.' (Murl means a
crumb or fragment and pockie a paper bag.)

BASIC SUGAR BOILING PROCESS

1 lb/500 g granulated sugar (2$\frac{1}{4}$ c)
$\frac{1}{2}$ pt/300 ml water (1$\frac{1}{4}$ c)
Pinch of cream of tartar to prevent granulation
Dissolve the sugar over a low heat in the liquid stirring with a
wooden spoon until no particles of sugar are left. To test — examine
the back of the spoon for any sugar crystals. Brush the sides of the
pan with water to remove any crystals.
    When all is dissolved, bring gradually to the boil and simmer
gently till required stage is reached.
Stages in Sugar Boiling
Smooth/Transparent Icing (230F/108C) for crystallising purposes.
The mixture begins to look syrupy. To test, dip finger in water and
then very quickly into the syrup, the thumb will slide smoothly over
the fingers, but the sugar will cling.
Soft ball (240F/115C) for fondants, fudges and tablets. To test, drop
a little syrup into cold water and leave for a few minutes. Pick up

between the finger and thumb when it should roll into a small soft ball.

Firm or hard ball (250F/121C) for caramels, marshmallows, nougat and soft toffee. Test as above when the syrup should roll into a hard ball.

Small crack (280F/138C) for toffees and rock. Test as above, when the thread of syrup should break lightly.

Hard crack (310F/154C) for hard toffees and rock. Test as above, when the thread of syrup should break sharply.

Caramel (345F/174C upwards). When the syrup begins to turn a darker brown colour, caramel stage is reached. If allowed to become too dark, the taste will be bitter.

TABLET

Slightly harder than fudge, but not chewey like toffee, tablet has a slight 'bite' to it. It can be varied with all kinds of colourings and flavourings.

1 lb/500 g granulated sugar (2 cups)
2 oz/50 g unsalted butter ($\frac{1}{2}$ stick)
3 tablespoons condensed milk
$\frac{1}{4}$ pt/150 ml water ($\frac{3}{4}$ c generous)

Follow the basic sugar boiling process till **soft ball** stage is reached. Remove from the heat, place the pan on a cool surface and beat till it just begins to 'grain', but before it begins to thicken. Pour into a greased tin and mark just before setting.

Flavourings and colourings

Orange — Add $\frac{1}{4}$ pt/150 ml fresh orange juice instead of water and before pouring mix in the orange zest. The orange flavour changes during the process to make a superbly flavoured tablet.

Vanilla and Walnut — mix in 2-3 drops of vanilla essence and 2 oz/50 g finely chopped walnuts ($\frac{1}{2}$ c) when the sugar is removed from the heat.

Coffee and Walnut — Add $\frac{3}{4}$ oz/20 g instant coffee powder and 2 oz/50 g finely chopped walnuts before pouring.

Coconut — Add 2 oz/50 g dessicated coconut (1 c scant) before pouring.

Cinnamon — Add 1 teaspoon cinnamon oil or $\frac{1}{2}$ oz/15 g ground cinnamon before pouring.

Ginger — Add 2 oz/50 g chopped preserved ginger before pouring.

Peppermint — Add 2-3 drops of peppermint oil before pouring.

Fruit and Nut — Add 2 oz/50 g finely chopped nuts ($\frac{1}{2}$ c) and 2 oz/50 g seedless raisins ($\frac{1}{2}$ c generous) before pouring.

BARLEY SUGAR

1 lb/500 g granulated sugar ($1\frac{1}{4}$ c)
1 oz/25 g unsalted butter ($\frac{1}{4}$ stick)

For the barley water

>1 oz/25 g barley
>1 pt/600 ml water (2½ c)
>½ oz/15 g liquorice stick

To make the barley water

>Put the barley in a pan with the water and liquorice stick.
>Bring to the boil and simmer till the liquorice is dissolved. Remove
>from the heat and leave to settle. Pour off about ½ pt/300 ml of the
>water (1¼ c).

To make the barley sugar

>Put the sugar, barley water and butter into a pan and follow the
>basic sugar boiling process till **hard crack**. Leave to cool slightly in
>the pan then pour onto an oiled slab or formica top and cool,
>working it with a sugar spatula. When almost setting cut into strips
>with scissors and twist each strip as it is cut. Store in an airtight jar.

BLACK MAN or Treacle Candy

>1 lb/500 g brown sugar (3 c generous)
>5 oz/150 g treacle (½ c)
>1 teaspoon cream of tartar
>½ pt/300 ml water (1¼ c)
>Peppermint, almond or lemon essence

>Follow the basic sugar boiling process to **small crack**. Remove from
>the heat and add the essence. Pour into greased tins and when cool
>enough to handle, remove from the tin and pull the mixture with
>your hands. (Commercial sweet makers used to hang the sugar on a
>hook and let it fall naturally turning it up again and again till it was
>almost setting.) Shape into desired lengths with scissors before it
>gets too hard.

BUTTERSCOTCH

>1 lb/500 g brown sugar (3 c generous)
>4 oz/125 g unsalted butter (1 stick)
>½ pt/300 ml milk (1¼ c)

>Follow the basic sugar boiling process to **small crack**. Remove from
>the heat and pour the mixture into well-greased tins. Mark just
>before setting.

GLESSIE

>But the glessy! Who that ever tasted it can forget the stick of
>sheeny, golden rock, which stretched while you were eating it
>to gossamer threads of silver glistening like cobwebs in the
>sun.

Scots Magazine, 1925

$\frac{1}{2}$ lb/250 g soft brown sugar ($1\frac{3}{4}$ c)
1 oz/25 g unsalted butter ($\frac{1}{4}$ stick)
1 tablespoon water
1 teaspoon cream of tarter
$1\frac{1}{2}$ lb/750 g golden syrup

Put the sugar into a pan with the water and butter and dissolve. Boil for a few minutes and then add the syrup. Follow the basic sugar boiling process till **hard crack**. Pour out very thinly into well-greased tins and chop up when cold.

GUNDY

1 lb/500 g demerara sugar (3 c generous)
1 tablespoon golden syrup or black treacle
2 oz/50 g unsalted butter ($\frac{1}{2}$ stick)
$\frac{1}{2}$ pt/300 ml water ($1\frac{1}{4}$ c)
Aniseed or cinnamon flavouring

Follow the basic sugar boiling process to **hard crack**. Remove from the heat and pour into well-greased tins and mark just before setting.

MEALIE CANDY

1 lb/500 g granulated sugar ($2\frac{1}{2}$ c)
$\frac{1}{4}$ lb/125 g treacle ($\frac{1}{4}$ c)
$\frac{1}{2}$ pt/300 ml water ($1\frac{1}{4}$ c)
2 oz/50 g coarse oatmeal, toasted ($\frac{1}{2}$ c)
1 tablespoon crystallised ginger, finely chopped

Follow the basic sugar boiling process to **soft ball** and beat as for tablet (see p. 228) till just graining, then add oatmeal and ginger.

Traditional Scottish Sweeties Past and Present

Almond Cake is really a rich buttery toffee mixture which is poured into a tin which has a thick layer of flaked almonds on the base. A commercial version of this is made in Orkney.

Barley Sugar — see recipe p. 228.

Berwick Cockles were originally home-made and peppermint flavoured, white with pink strips and shaped like the cockle shells which used to be fished up near Tweedmouth harbour. Can now be bought in tins.

Bon-Bons are made with strips of candied lemon or orange peel which are dipped into barley sugar.

Black Man — see recipe p. 229.
Black Striped Balls are black and white striped balls of hard toffee with a strong peppermint flavour.

Butterscotch — see recipe p. 229.
Cheugh Jeans are a very chewy (cheugh) toffee which was made in dif-

ferent flavours — clove, cinnamon, peppermint, ginger or chocolate.

Coltart's Candy (pronounced Coolter) has been made famous by the song which he sang travelling round the country and selling his candy. The candy was aniseed flavoured but the recipe and the custom seem to have been lost when he died, greatly lamented, in 1890.

Claggum or Clack is made with treacle and water, boiled till soft ball stage and then pulled into long sticks of rock.

Curly Andra is a white coral-like sweet with a coriander seed in the centre. The name comes from the Scots' corruption of coriander which is 'curryander'.

Curlie Murlies — see p. 227; also known as Curly Doddies.

Edinburgh Rock, not the customary solid stick with letters down the centre, but a light pastel-coloured sugary confection, delicately flavoured. It was discovered by accident when Alexander Fergusson, popularly known as Sweetie Sandy, came across a piece of confectionery which he had overlooked and left lying for several months. He became one of Edinburgh's most successful confectioners in the 19th century and the rock is now exported all over the world.

Glessie — see recipe p. 229.

Gundy — see recipe p. 230.

Hawick Balls are a cinnamon flavoured hard toffee with a subtle hint of mint. They were originally home-made but became so popular that they are now available in tins.

Helensburgh Toffee is more of a fudge than a toffee and has a rich creamy flavour.

Jeddart Snails are dark brown toffees, mildly peppermint-flavoured. The name and shape were given to them by a French prisoner-of-war from Napoleon's army who made them for a Jedburgh baker.

Lettered Rock — long sticks of hard rock with a strong peppermint flavour, bright pink on the outside, white in the middle with red letters down the middle of the appropriate town.

Mealie Candy — see recipe p. 230.

Moffat Toffee is a hard toffee, amber and gold striped with a sherbert tang. It is now made commercially by a local Moffat family who have been making toffee for generations. One of its early names was Moffat Whirlies.

Oddfellows — a soft lozenge, made in delicate colours and with lovely flavours of cinnamon, clove and rose geranium. Made commercially by confectioners in Wishaw.

Pan Drops, otherwise known as Mint Imperials.

Soor Plooms originated in Peebles and Galashiels where they were made to celebrate an incident in local history when a band of English marauders were surprised and overcome while eating unripe plums. They are round bright green balls with an acid astringent tang.

Starrie Rock is available from a small shop in the Roods in Kirriemuir. It was made originally by a stone mason who was blinded in 1833. The sticks are short and thin, slightly chewy, and with an undefinable flavour which is still a well kept secret.

Sugar-ally is liquorice. Mixed with water in a lemonade bottle it is drunk by children and known as Sugar-ally-Water.

Sugar-bools are small round sugar plums like marbles.

Sugar-hearts are pink, heart shaped fondants.

Preserves

For fifteen shillings a quarter Mrs MacIver taught cookery, preserving and pickling. In her earlier . . . days she sold preserved cherries and raspberries, and also 'plumb-cake'.

Alexander Law
Education in Edinburgh in the 18th Century, 1965

Marmalade

To his delight Henry VIII was given a 'box of Marmalade' as a present in 1524. It was a box of preserved quinces, however, which so pleased the greedy Henry, and not a jam made with oranges which we associate with the word today. The name came from the quince-growing countries of Spain and Portugal where they are called 'Marmelos' and the preserve known as 'Marmelada'. The name somehow became associated with any kind of preserved fruit, and cookery books talk of a 'Marmelade of Cherries or Plums or Apricots' etc. The first mention of oranges or lemons is by the noted epicure, scholar and traveller Sir Kenelm Digby (1603-1665). He had travelled widely in Italy and Spain and developed there a taste for the preserve. His cookery book was published posthumously in 1669.

About a century later a young Dundee grocer and his mother decided to build the first marmalade factory in 1797 after many generations had tested out the popularity of the preserve, making it on a small scale in their back shop with sweetie-boiling pans. At the port of Dundee many strange and exotic things were landed and among them were the bitter Seville oranges, which no one wanted, but which the Keillers bought up, and first made into marmalade about 1700. As a centre of the fruit growing and preserving industry, Dundee was the natural home for marmalade and the Keiller enterprise grew and flourished till the name became synonymous with good marmalade.

Making Marmalade

My own preference is for a thick, bitter marmalade made with Seville oranges, and a lemon added for sharpness. It is necessary to use all the bitter white pith if this is the kind of marmalade you like. Except for the pips, the entire orange is used. The pips, however, along with the white inner skin are the only source of pectin (gelling material) in oranges and so the pips and sometimes all of the white skin is put in a bag and boiled with the rest of the oranges and sugar.

2 lb/1 kg Seville oranges
2 lb/500 g sugar (3 c)
2 lemons

Preparing the fruit

Wash the oranges well and then put in preserving pan. Pour over boiling water, leave for a few minutes and then take out oranges. Peel the fruit as for eating. (The scalding makes this easier.) Put the whole peeled orange and the skin back into the pan, making sure that the fruit is well covered and simmer till the skins are tender, adding more water when necessary. It should take between one and two hours.

When soft, remove the skins and cut into thin chips. There is no alternative to doing this by hand but the skins are soft and not difficult to cut.

Put the remainder of the pulp through a sieve. It goes through easily and you can decide at this point whether you want to put all the bitter pith through or keep some back — entirely a matter of how bitter a marmalade you like. Put the remaining pips and any pulp into a muslin bag and tie up.

Finishing the marmalade

Measure the strained liquid and add **1 lb/500 g preserving sugar (2½ c) for every 1 pt/250 ml of liquid (2½ c),** put into the pan with the chips and add the zest and juice of the lemons.

Bring to the boil and simmer till set. Test by putting a teaspoonful on a chilled saucer and placing in the deep freeze compartment for a few minutes to chill and give you a quick result. The surface should set and crinkle when pushed with the finger. Do not boil too vigorously while the test is being made otherwise setting point may be missed.

Remove from the heat, skim with a slotted spoon, and leave for ten minutes to cool before potting — this prevents the chips sinking. Pour into clean hot jars.

Adding other flavours

Spirits or liqueurs can be added to marmalade at this point before it is set. Leave a space at the top of the jar and add a tablespoonful to a 1 lb/500 g pot size. Stir well, cover and seal. Whisky and brandy are good but for a flavour that really seems to heighten the sharp Seville orange flavour I find rum best. Orange flavoured liqueurs, Drambuie and Glayva are also good but sweeten the marmalade.

FORTINGALL MARMALADE

During the time I was the lessee of the Fortingall Hotel, about thirty-four years, we always made our own Orange Marmalade, rising at the end to a quarter of a ton every spring.

William Heptinstall
Gourmet Recipes From a Highland Hotel, 1967

This is a sweeter marmalade and not so thick as the previous recipe.

3¾ lb/1 kg 425 g Seville oranges
Juice of 4 lemons
9 pts/4½ L water
9 lb/4½ kg preserving sugar

The day before

Halve the oranges and squeeze out the juice. Soak the pips in 1 pint/500 ml water (2½ c). Shred the orange caps by hand or in food processor and soak them in the remainder of the water.

Making the marmalade

Put the shredded peel with the water on to boil and when soft (1-2 hours) add the sugar, orange and lemon juice and the water in which the pips have been soaking. Boil to 218F/105C; test for a set. Pot, seal and cover.

RASPBERRY OR TAYBERRY JAM

The full fresh raspberry flavour is preserved in this non-cooked jam which is thickened with liquid pectin then deep frozen. It can be stored in the refrigerator for several weeks.

3½ lb/1.6 kg fruit
4 lb/1.8 kg caster sugar (5 c)
4 tablespoons lemon juice
8 fl oz/250 ml liquid pectin (1 c)

Put the fruit into a bowl with the sugar and lemon juice and stir till the sugar is dissolved. Add the pectin and mix in well. Ladle into small plastic containers. Cover with lids and put into the freezing compartment if you want to store for some time. Otherwise it can be kept in the refrigerator for several months but will not keep for more than about two weeks at room temperature.

STRAWBERRY JAM

makes 5 lb

Strawberries lack both pectin and acid so both have to be added to make the jam set. To keep the berries whole, it is necessary to use small fruit rather than large. The freezing method may be used for strawberries but I find it less successful.

3 lb/1½ kg strawberries
3 lb/1½ kg granulated sugar (2½ c)
8 fl oz/250 ml liquid pectin (1 c)
Juice of 1 lemon

Put the fruit and lemon juice into a preserving pan and add the sugar. Heat gently till all the sugar is dissolved. Add the pectin and bring to the boil. Boil rapidly till setting point is reached (see p. 233 for test). Remove from the heat, skim with a slotted spoon and leave to cool for a few minutes before potting. Stir before pouring into hot jars, cover and seal.

ROWAN JELLY

An indispensable accompaniment with its sharp astringent tang to roasts of venison and game birds.

2 lb/1 kg slightly under-ripe berries
2 lb/1 kg unpeeled cooking apples

Chop apples roughly and remove stalks from berries. Put into pan with just enough water to cover and bring to the boil. Simmer the fruit till soft and put into preserving bag or muslin to drip overnight. Measure the juice and add 1 lb/500 g of sugar (2½ c) to every 1 pt/600 ml liquid (2½ c). Put into the pan and bring to the boil, simmer till set (see p. 233) for test. Pot, seal and cover.

HERB JELLY

This apple-based jelly is particularly good made with mint — the flavour of herbs comes through strongly if you tie them in muslin, though they may also be finely chopped and added at the end of the cooking time. Place 3 lb/1½ kg coarsely chopped cooking apples in a pan. Just cover with water and cook till soft and pulpy. Pour into jelly bag and drip overnight without squeezing.

Measure juice and weigh out 1 lb/500 g sugar to each 1 pt/500 ml juice. Stir over a low heat till the sugar is dissolved. Tie 4 oz/125 g fresh herbs in a muslin bag and add to the pan. Bring to the boil and simmer till set. Remove from the heat and allow to stand for about 5 minutes. Add some chopped fresh herbs for decoration or place one or two whole leaves in the pots. Pot, cover and seal.

LEMON AND HONEY JELLY

The flavour is reminiscent of a Hot Toddy without the whisky. It is particularly good with ham or some of the stronger game meats. Very quick and easy to make.

3 tablespoons freshly squeezed lemon juice
1 tablespoon lemon zest
1 lb/500 g honey
3 fl oz/75 ml liquid pectin ($\frac{1}{2}$ c scant)

Put the honey, lemon juice and zest into a pan and heat through to dissolve the honey. Add the pectin and continue boiling for 1 minute. Remove from the heat, pot and cover.

SPICED DAMSONS

I never make enough of this to supply the demand. The full rich flavour and deep crimson colour enliven any plate of cold meats. They are also superb with roasts of game.

1 pt/500 ml full-bodied red wine ($2\frac{1}{2}$ c)
2 lb/1 kg ripe damsons
2 × 4″ (10 cm) sticks cinnamon
5 oz/150 g sugar ($\frac{3}{4}$ c)

Dissolve sugar in wine, add cinnamon and bring to the boil for 1 minute. Add damsons and simmer for 2-3 minutes or until they are just soft. Pack into jars and pour over syrup.

MINCEMEAT

From all accounts in early cookery books, large quantities were made and always included some kind of cooked beef. James Beard recreates the original mincemeat in his recipe in <u>Delights and Prejudices</u> (1964), using both freshly-cooked tongue and boiled beef. It was late into the 19th century before the meat was being abandoned from recipes — sometimes it was added when the mince pies were being made rather than in the original mix. Some meat does add an extra dimension to the texture and flavour and with such a high spice and alcoholic level there is no danger of it spoiling. Well-covered it was often kept from one year to the next. Works equally well without meat.

Combine together

In a large earthenware crock or large pot with a lid which is not in constant use (it is easier to have the mixture in one large container to begin with. The fruit takes some time to absorb the liquid and more may have to be added while it is maturing. Once thoroughly matured it can be potted).

1 lb/500 g cooked beef (boiled or roast) or cooked fresh tongue,
minced or finely chopped (optional)
$\frac{3}{4}$ lb/350 g beef suet, finely chopped (3 c)
1 lb/500 g seedless raisins ($1\frac{3}{4}$ c)

1 lb/500 g sultanas (1¾ c)
1 lb/500 g currants (1¾ c)
8 oz/250 g mixed peel (2 c)
½ lb/250 g moist brown sugar (1½ c)
½ lb/250 g strawberry jam
1 dessertspoon salt
1 dessertspoon each — ground cinnamon; allspice; mace
1 ground nutmeg
½ teaspoon grated cloves
Juice and rind of 4 lemons
1 bottle sherry or sweet white wine
½ bottle brandy
Cover well and keep checking once a week, add more sherry/wine/brandy if necessary. Pot, cover and seal after 1-2 months.
Note: Sometimes apples were added to the basic mix but usually they appeared when the mince pies were made either mixed through the mincemeat, or arranged in layers in the pie, or simply placed on top of a mincemeat base. A spoonful of sherry or claret was often added through the hole in the top as they went into the oven. They were served with 'burnt' brandy poured over as they were sent to the table, rather as we flame a Christmas pudding.

TO MAKE A MINCEMEAT TART

Make up 12 oz/375 g short crust pastry (p. 73) and line a 10″ × 1½″ (25 cm × 3½ cm) flan tin. Bake blind. Fill first with a layer of stewed apples then with mincemeat and cover the top thickly with flaked almonds. Bake in a moderate oven till the almonds are nicely toasted. Finish with some thinnish water-icing laced in thin threads over the almonds. Serve warm or cold

APPLE CHUTNEY

The taste and aroma of this chutney depend on a subtle blending of spices, cinnamon, cloves and ginger, cooked in orange juice and cider vinegar.
1½ lb/750 g cooking apples, coarsely chopped
1 tablespoon chopped ginger root
4 fl oz/125 ml orange juice (½ c)
1 teaspoon ground cinnamon
1 teaspoon ground cloves
1 teaspoon salt
8 fl oz/250 ml honey — to taste (1 c)
8 fl oz/250 ml cider vinegar (1 c)
Bring to the boil and simmer uncovered, stirring occasionally for about 45-50 minutes. Cool and store.

RAISIN CHUTNEY

Plump raisins cooked slowly in tomatoes blended with cinnamon and cloves make this outstandingly good chutney which combines well with a variety of cold meats and game as well as mature hard cheeses.

2 oz/50 g butter ($\frac{1}{2}$ stick)
1 lb/500 g seedless raisins ($2\frac{1}{2}$ c)
2 × 200 g tin chopped tomatoes
$\frac{1}{2}$ pt/300 ml water ($1\frac{1}{4}$ c)
4 whole cloves
2 sticks cinnamon bark
2 teaspoons salt
Ground black pepper to taste

Melt the butter in a large wide pan and add the raisins. Sauté the raisins for a few minutes then add all the other ingredients. Cook uncovered for about 1 hour, stirring occasionally, till very thick.

Add

5 oz/150 g brown sugar (1 c)
5 tablespoons cider or wine vinegar

Mix through, simmer for a few minutes. Taste for flavour. Remove cinnamon, pot, cover and seal.

MRS BEETON'S PLUM CHUTNEY

A highly spiced chutney which ought to be stored for at least six months to allow the flavours to mature. After two years the flavours grow and mellow with unique results.

Put into pan and cook for $\frac{1}{2}$ hour

3 lb/1$\frac{1}{2}$ kg stoned plums
2 medium onions, chopped
2 medium apples, chopped
4 tablespoons each — ground ginger, cinnamon, allspice
1$\frac{1}{2}$ tablespoons salt
1 pt/500 ml vinegar ($2\frac{1}{2}$ c)

Add

$\frac{3}{4}$ lb/375 g sugar ($1\frac{3}{4}$ c)

Boil to the consistency of thick jam. Pot, cover and seal.

To make a STORE MUSTARD

This recipe makes a lovely creamy mustard, rich and glossy with a faint sweetness which also keeps very well. Other commercial mustards are equally good. There are an interesting variety of flavours mostly with whole mustard seeds which are produced by Arran Mustard Company. Their Islay mustard is a lovely smooth-tasting blend with an oatmeal base, excellent with both fried and grilled herring.

1 × 4 oz/125 g tin mustard
Same volume of double cream and caster sugar
(8 fl oz/250 ml double cream — 9 oz/250 g caster sugar)

2 eggs
$\frac{1}{2}$ teaspoon potato flour
1 tablespoon acetic acid
Empty contents of the tin into a pan. Then fill up the tin with sugar, empty into pan and then finally fill with cream and add to pan. Add the eggs, mix in the potato flour and cook gently till it thickens. This can be done in a double boiler. When cold stir in acetic acid and pour into pots. Cover and seal.

PICKLE VINEGAR

The outstanding flavour of this vinegar is entirely dependent on the many spices and flavourings together with a long slow maturing in the summer sun.
7 pts/$3\frac{1}{2}$ L white wine vinegar
5 oz/150 g black mustard seeds
2 oz/50 g fresh ginger root
3 oz/75 g whole allspice
$\frac{1}{2}$ oz/15 g cloves
2 oz/50 g black peppercorns
$\frac{1}{2}$ oz/15 g celery seeds
$1\frac{1}{2}$ lb/750 g brown sugar
$1\frac{3}{4}$ oz/40 g grated horseradish
1 head garlic
$1\frac{1}{2}$ sliced lemons
Combine all the ingredients in a large glass jar and leave in the sun all summer or at least four months. Strain and pour over parboiled or raw fruits and vegetables or use in salad dressings.

PRESERVED VEGETABLES

A supply of these is useful for quick meals with cold meats and cheese. Served with bread and butter they make excellent fast food.
1 pt/$\frac{1}{2}$ L white wine vinegar or pickle vinegar (see above)
3 tablespoons olive oil
1 teaspoon salt
2 tablespoons sugar
Put together in a pan and bring to the boil, simmer for a few minutes.

Add

In total about 2-3 lb/1-$1\frac{1}{2}$ kg vegetables. Begin with the hardest ones and cut them all into pieces of about the same size. Carrots, celery, fennel, small onions, cauliflower florets, brussel sprouts, green beans, mushrooms, seeded sweet peppers*, chillie peppers. Nuts (walnuts, hazelnuts or almonds) can also be added.
    Keep the vegetables crunchy, leave to cool then pot, cover and seal. Will keep for 3 months.
*Add sweet peppers just before removing from the heat — do not boil them.

PRESERVED FRUIT

This old-fashioned method of preserving ripe fruit while it was cheap and plentiful takes on new dimensions when flavoured with whisky, brandy, rum or any other spirit or liqueur for that matter. Anton Mosimann, Executive Chef at the Dorchester Hotel in London, is to be seen on the front cover of his book Cuisine à la Carte (1981) beside jars of preserved fruits which his kitchen brigade have prepared, and which he serves as a speciality of the house straight from the preserving jars.

Preparation of the fruit

Pears — peel carefully without removing the stalks, halve and remove the core with a Parisienne cutter or a small vegetable knife. Place in water and lemon juice till required. **Cherries, Plums and Apricots** — remove stalks, wash and stone or leave whole. **Gooseberries** — top, tail and wash. **Peaches** — blanch in hot water, plunge into cold water then peel, stone or leave whole.

Syrup for preserving fruit — general proportions

8 oz/250 g sugar ($1\frac{1}{4}$ c)
1 pt/600 ml water ($2\frac{1}{2}$ c)
1-2 tablespoons lemon juice
2-3 tablespoons spirit or liqueur

Dissolve the sugar in the water, bring to the boil and boil for 1 minute, add lemon juice and flavouring.

Bottling the fruit

Place the fruit carefully in bottling jars. Pour over the syrup to within 1″ ($2\frac{1}{2}$ cm) of the top. Place the rubber ring on the glass lid and place the lid on the jar. Put on the screw bands, then turn back a quarter turn. Place the bottles either in a steamer or water bath and sterilise. (It can also be done in the oven though this method is less accurate and it is very easy to over-cook the fruit.)

For the water bath method

Place the bottles in a large vessel, cover with cold water, immersing completely if possible, or at least up to their necks. Heat gently on top of the cooker. Raise the temperature to 130F in 1 hour then to 180F in a further $\frac{1}{2}$ hour. Maintain the temperature at 180F — 8-10 minutes for gooseberries, cherries, pears and all stoned fruit. For peaches, apricots and plums which have the stone left in, allow 10-12 minutes.

Remove the bottles with tongs and tighten screw bands. When the jars are cool, remove the screw bands and carefully lift the jars by their lids to test whether a vacuum has been formed. If the lid comes off it is best to use up within a few days. Otherwise they will keep well in a cool dark place for at least a year.

Chapter Eight

CHEESE

Many's the long night I have dreamed of cheese — toasted mostly, and woke up again and here I were. . . . You might not happen to have a piece of cheese about you now?

Robert Louis Stevenson
Treasure Island, 1882

Poor Ben Gunn's first words to his rescuers, after being marooned for three years on Treasure Island, are echoed by Patrick Rance, cheese expert, owner of a famous cheese shop and author of The Great British Cheese Book (1982), when he says, 'If you offered me a desert island with just one kind of food, a farmhouse cheddar would be my unhesitating choice.'

This is indeed a rich area of gastronomy where passions run high and in which the Scots continue to play an important role. The main advantage in the past was that cheese preserved valuable protein during the summer months for use in the days when winter was winter and people had to survive on what they had 'put by'. It was portable, and much transfer of cheese went on particularly from Highlands to Lowlands in exchange for grain. Highlanders are said to have survived, at certain times of the year and during bad harvests, solely on cheese, fish and milk. The Highland cheeses were of the soft variety made mostly from skimmed milk, more usually from sheep than cows and made into what they called 'Crowdie', a light soft cheese with a sharp pleasing tang. This cheese was also known as 'hangman cheese' or 'hangie' since the curds were tied in a cheese-cloth and left to drain usually in the open air to dry for two or three days. To make a longer-keeping cheese they mixed the crowdie with butter and packed it into wooden barrels or stone crocks. This was called 'Crowdie Butter' and was kept throughout the winter.

There are people in the Highlands today who can describe with great enthusiasm the delights of 'Crowdie Butter' which they remember eating early this century, though it is no longer made. The nearest thing to it today is 'Caboc' from the old Scots word for cheese 'kebbuck' or 'kebec' meaning a whole cheese, which Susannah Stone and her husband revived at their farmhouse in Tain in Wester Ross. The Caboc which they make has a rich buttery curd and is made from double cream. Susannah Stone's family recipe for this 'Chieftain's cheese' has been handed down through many generations from Mariota de Ile, daughter of a 15th-century Macdonald of the Isles.

The Dairying areas of Caithness and Orkney have, in their time, produced considerable cheeses and there is still a thriving industry on Orkney producing both factory and farmhouse cheeses. Ayrshire and the South West of Scotland have always been the major cheese-producing areas where the rich grasslands combine with a moist climate to produce perfect conditions for dairy cattle and milk production. Because of these conditions, there has evolved over many centuries a special breed of cattle, known as 'Ayrshire', and prized throughout the world for the quality and quantity of milk it produces. Travelling through the Andes some years ago, we came across a herd of about a hundred Ayrshire cows grazing peacefully in the Sacred Valley of the Incas and discovered the reason why we had been enjoying such marvellous cheeses from the local markets.

Until the late 17th century in Scotland, cheese had been made mostly from the left-over skimmed milk from making butter, and mostly from sheep rather than cows. Barbara Gilmour and her Dunlop cows are given credit for changing all that. A farmer's daughter from Ayrshire, she had spent some time in Ireland fleeing persecution as a Covenanter, but returning to her native land in 1688, she settled in the 'Hill Farm' in the village of Dunlop with her farmer husband.

She started making the first sweet-milk, full cream, hard cheese with milk from her cows and in the space of sixty years the name of Dunlop Cheese and Ayrshire cattle had become nationally established as synonymous with the best cheese in Scotland. It virtually drove out all other varieties and at the end of the 18th century the milking of ewes for cheese came to an end. The 19th century saw many improvements and developments in making the Dunlop cheese, with advice and help coming from Cheddar-making areas of England. The changes in techniques produced a harder cheese than the original and so Scottish cheeses, like all others made in a similar way, took the name Cheddar to describe the technique which produced a different product from the original Dunlop.

According to Patrick Rance, the original Dunlop was still being made by three hundred farms in the South West in 1930. 'Each farm had a fully matured cheese open for cooking, and a softer one for eating. At breakfast, porridge was followed on alternate days by bacon and eggs or toasted cheese on a scone made of home-ground flour eaten in front of the fire.' Post-war has seen the decline of traditional farmhouse cheese and an increase in block Cheddar cheese made in creameries, which amounts to 70% of the cheese eaten in Scotland today. Plastic-wrapped 'modifications of a Dunlop type of cheese' (the official description) keep the name alive on the cheeses made in Arran and Islay. Other post-war developments in Scottish cheesemaking include farmhouse-made soft cheeses from Howgate in Midlothian; also the Barac Farmhouse Cheese made in Annan from ewes' milk and the Bonchester Cheese made from Jersey cows at Easteweems farm in Bonchester Bridge near Hawick. These are the ones being sold and marketed commercially, but there are other farms which are keeping the traditional cheese-making tradition alive. Odd cheeses will appear in specialist cheese shops where the owner has discovered a farmer who is making a few cheeses, usually from unpasteurised milk. Throughout Orkney you can buy traditional farm-house cheeses of varying flavours depending on the farm they've come from, when they are available in summer.

The advantages of traditional clothbound cylindrical cheese made from unpasteurised milk are of flavour and texture. Pasteurisation, while ensuring that the milk is clean and safe, also 'eliminates 99 per cent of the worthwhile organisms, including the bacteria and esters vital to the character of cheese' (Patrick Rance, Good Food Guide, 1985). The natural differences of locality and breed of cow are preserved in cheeses which are made from milk from one area only, a distinction which is often lost in the factory product when milk from numerous farms is mixed in 3000-gallon tankers. Moulding, pressing, coating and storing cheese also affects flavour, and clothbound traditional cheese has the advan-tage of being able to breathe, mature and ripen to a fuller flavour while the vacuum-sealed rindless blocks must be kept at a lower temperature, to prevent the cheese from 'blowing' the wrap, with a consequent loss of mature flavour. It may be that the consumer actually wants a milder cheese, and it has been suggested that only people who remember the mature 'bite' of a pre-war cheese still want to eat this product. Whether or not you prefer to eat a mature, well-flavoured hard cheese or a milder one, from a cooking point of view the mature cheese gives more character to the finished flavour. One of the major arguments for the rindless block cheese is that it means a reduction in waste since consum-ers are not willing to buy cheese with a rind and often expect to have it removed before it is weighed. There is still much to be said and written for and against, while those campaigning for 'Real Cheese' show every sign of continuing their crusade.

Milk Related Traditions

Besides the milk, buttermilk and whey, which was drunk by all classes, the Scots have a rich tradition of distinctive dishes made of milk. Travellers to Scotland noticed and commented on this fact, including the outrageously fat old gentleman who made rather a name for himself as an outspoken critic of the Scots and their food. 'A dinner in the West-ern Isles differs very little from a dinner in England,' says Dr Samuel Johnson, 'except that in the place of tarts there are always set different preparations of milk.' Journey to the Western Isles of Scotland (1775).

A very full explanation of a wide variety of these preparations with their traditional names is given in The Scots Kitchen by F. Marian McNeill (1929). The main ones she describes, and gives recipes for, are Corstorphine Cream or Ru'glen Cream which was a buttermilk and sweet milk curd mixed, sweetened and flavoured with nutmeg and cinnamon (see recipe on p. 252); Oon or Frothed Whey and Bland or Sparkling Whey from Shetland.

These traditions were based on a self-sufficient system of rural life where households had their own cows and were able easily to do things like milking the cow straight onto the buttermilk. It is true that many of these old traditions are obsolete but some will adapt and are worth preserving such as Hatted Kit (see p. 252), which has great similarities with the French Coeur à la Creme.

Guide to Scottish Cheeses

The Scottish Cheese Mark was introduced in August 1983 by the Company of Scottish Cheese Makers who administer the scheme. A round paper label with a blue circle in the centre and a blue wedge shape half in and half out of the circle and the words Scottish Cheese above, is applied to the wrapper of Scottish Cheddar and Dunlop cheeses of all sizes produced by all Registered Users. Its purpose is to monitor and control quality while at the same time providing information about the origin of the cheese at the point of sale.

The Company awards four grades — Choicest; First Grade; Graded; No Grade.

Choicest is the same quality as First Grade but must be capable of keeping for more than one year. First Grade is cheese with a clean flavour, firm body and close texture, with bright colour, no gas holes, free from mould and of a regular shape. Graded is a description given when there is a slight fault, possibly weak 'body' or over-acid, which means that the cheese will not mature well and should be eaten young. No Grade does not get a mark since it is unsuitable for counter sale and will be used for processing.

Starting at the beginning of the cheesemaking process there are:

1. Fresh Soft Cheeses

Made from milk which has been turned into curds and whey, either by using rennet to form the curd or the natural lactic acid in the milk. The curds are separated from the whey by hanging in muslin and draining. No pressing is involved.

Made with cream

CABOC (Highland Fine Cheese, Tain) Rich double cream cheese with a buttery texture is made in a 4 oz cylinder shape and rolled in toasted pinhead oatmeal. In prime condition it has a rich subtle flavour which is nicely contrasted by the mealiness of the oatmeal. For the cook it is just the right shape for slicing into $\frac{1}{4}$" rounds for use as a hard butter on all kinds of grilled and fried meat and fish. (4 oz roll)

GARLIC (Highland Fine, Tain) Full fat soft cheese with the chopped fresh leaves of the locally picked wild garlic herb, rolled in flaked oats, crumbled almonds and hazel nuts. (4 oz roll/2 lb cutting oval)
HIGHLAND SOFT CHEESE (Highland Fine, Tain) A mild flavoured, full fat soft cheese, suitable for cheesecakes. (6 lb tubs)
CREAM CHEESE IN OATMEAL (Howgate Cheeses, Penicuik) Made from cream, soured overnight without rennet, drained through a fine cotton bag, shaped and rolled in oatmeal.
Slightly lighter than Caboc but similar shape. (3½ oz roll)
May also be rolled in black pepper.

Made with low fat milk
CROWDIE

The great treat, though, was to have crowdie mixed with fresh cream and piled on an oatcake with fresh salted butter. Then you had a royal feast of flavours — acid, sweet and salt, and, better perhaps, a royal mixture of textures, soft, crisp and crunchy.

G. Wallace Lockhart
The Scot and his Oats. 1983

Traditional crowdie was a cottage cheese and originated as a staple food for the crofter. It was hand-skimmed on the croft when a little of the cream was left, making it, in modern jargon, a 'low fat' rather than a 'skimmed milk' cheese.

'The unusual thing about crowdie,' says Susannah Stone of Highland Fine Cheeses in Tain, 'is that it is semi-cooked. The fresh milk is soured naturally beside the stove and then "scrambled" over the heat and hung up to drip in a muslin cloth. This ancient cheese is unique to the Highlands and Islands of Scotland, and as far as we know was made nowhere else in Europe . . . it has special qualities. Firstly, because of the natural curding (12 hours) it has a lovely citric flavour. Rennet (forbidden by both Vegetarians and Orthodox Jews) was not traditionally used to speed the souring. We use no rennet on our large scale, lactic cultures, and stick rigidly to the old recipe and method. Secondly this semi-cooked cheese (believed to go back to Viking and possibly Pictish times) is very low in certain elements that are bad for kidney patients. Among them potassium and sodium.' Lactic or acid curd crowdie has a more refreshing sharper flavour than rennet-started crowdie.

Origin of the name
When the Scots mixed meal and water together in the 18th century they called this 'crowdie' and, because it was such a staple item of diet, the name for the dish became transferred to the meal itself. People talked

about Crowdie-time as the time to eat and because it took on this much broader meaning, it seems that all kinds of dishes had the word Crowdie added to them.

Crowdie-Moudie was a kind of steamed porridge made with milk; Cream-Crowdie or Cranachan was a special dish of harvest plenty when cream and oatmeal were mixed with fruits; Ale Crowdie was a mixture of ale oatmeal, treacle and whisky, also a harvest dish, while Crowdie Butter was curds with butter mixed through. Today the name is applied to the drained curd.

CROWDIE can be used in all recipes which use low or semi-fat soft cheeses (i.e. Quark, Philadelphia etc.): it is usually cheaper.

Basic crowdies

HIGHLAND CROWDIE (Highland Fine, Tain) A low-fat traditional crowdie with a moist texture and refreshing flavour. It is rennet free. ($5\frac{1}{2}$ oz tubs/6 lb tubs)

CLAYMORE CROWDIE (North of Scotland Milk Marketing Board Creamery, Kirkwall, Orkney) Low-fat, started with rennet. ($7\frac{1}{2}$ oz tubs)

HOWGATE CROWDIE (Howgate Cheeses, Penicuik) Low-fat, traditional crowdie made with unpasteurised milk. (5 oz cartons) Also sold in tubs mixed with other ingredients.

Crowdie variations

CROWDIE AND CREAM (Highland Fine, Tain) Two-thirds crowdie to one-third double cream. ($5\frac{1}{2}$ oz tubs/6 lb tub)

GRU DHU (Highland Fine, Tain) A crowdie and cream cheese mixture rolled in crushed peppercorns, giving it a unique flavour. (5 oz tubs/2 lb ball)

HRAMSA (Highland Fine, Tain) Crowdie mixed with chopped wild garlic lighter in flavour than continental garlic. 'Hramsa' is the Gaelic for wild garlic — the 'all healing herb'.

HOWGATE CROWDIE AND CREAM (5 oz tubs)

PEAT SMOKED SOFT CHEESE (Howgate Cheeses, Penicuik) A soft cheese, the curds are ladled into open ended moulds sitting on straw mats, giving characteristic marks, and turned once, gently smoked over peat. A fine delicate flavour. (5 oz packs)

GOAT CHEESE — Soft farmhouse goats' milk cheese is being made in small quantities mostly for local sale only. Worth keeping an eye open for in specialist cheese shops who track down supplies or may be able to give you further information. Howgate Cheeses sell it on the farm in summer time only.

2. Crusted Soft Cheese

Made with full cream milk, the curd is put into a mould and the whey drains out naturally — there is no pressing, and maturity is reached in about a month when a mould has formed. The mould spore is mostly sprayed on commercially now. The cheese is creamy and fairly mild in flavour — the texture buttery. There is a short period during which they are considered 'ripe', which is before they begin to start softening too much. This is a matter of taste; some like them quite runny. When they begin to smell of ammonia then it is not wise to eat.

BONCHESTER (Easter Weens, Bonchester Bridge, Hawick)
A brie-type of mature soft cheese which is made in much smaller rounds than the French brie. Jersey cows, unpasteurised, full milk. Richly flavoured.

LOTHIAN (Howgate Cheeses, Penicuik) A camembert-type of mature soft cheese.

PENTLAND (Howgate Cheeses, Penicuik) A brie-type mature soft cheese. (4 oz round or $2\frac{1}{2}$ lb)

3. Semi-Hard Cheeses

These are made with full milk but the curd is heated to a higher temperature and the separation of curd and whey is achieved by several processes including pressure and 'cheddaring', which describes how the curd is cut up. They are lightly pressed compared with hard cheeses so that more whey is left in, the texture is moister and crumblier, and the cheese will have a shorter life compared with the hard pressed variety.

4. Hard Cheeses

These are made in the same way as the Semi-Hard cheeses but the curds are subjected to much greater pressure so that the cheese is firmer-textured, takes longer to mature, keeps better and has a fuller flavour.

SCOTTISH DUNLOPS

Traditional farmhouse clothbound Dunlops are rare today since most are factory produced blocks or rounds with plastic coating — some is clothbound but usually for show purposes only. Dunlop is distinguished from Scottish Cheddar by the fact that it has a more mellow flavour and softer creamier texture, described by cheesemakers as a 'meatier' cheese.

ARRAN DUNLOP (Scottish Milk Marketing Board Creamery, Kilmory, Arran) Made in $2\frac{1}{4}$ lb small drums, plastic wrapped. Also in blocks. Some large clothbound rounds made. Pasteurised.

ISLAY DUNLOP (Isle of Islay Creamery) Small 1 lb/2 lb drums, plastic wrapped — also larger sizes.

Highland Herb — a flavoured cheese which is made with Islay
Dunlop, chives and Inniemore Scotch Mustard.
(5 lb rounds/$2\frac{1}{2}$ lb half rounds)
Highland Choice — a flavoured cheese which is made with Islay
Dunlop, Drambuie and flaked almonds.
(5 lb rounds/$2\frac{1}{2}$ lb half rounds)

SCOTTISH CHEDDARS

Traditionally these are more mature, fuller flavoured cheeses with a
firmer texture and longer keeping qualities. Mild Cheddar is matured for
about 4-5 months while Mature Cheddar is usually 9 months-1 year old
with some matured longer for a stronger flavour. About 70% of all the
cheese eaten in Scotland is of the Cheddar variety. It is mostly made in
blocks and wrapped in an impervious plastic material to exclude air;
only a small quantity are traditional round clothbound cheese. Flavour,
texture and 'body' of a cheese are dependant on the type of cow which
has produced the milk; its feeding; the bacterial culture which is added
to the milk to get the vital development of lactic acid started (known as
the 'starter'); the method of making and the length and conditions of
maturing. All these factors combine to produce different Cheddars from
different areas of Scotland.

Eating Cheese

Cheese is capital in the forenoons, or the afternoons either, when you've had nae ither denner, especially wi' fresh butter and bread; but nane but gluttonous epicures wad hae recourse to it after they hae been stuffing themsels, as we hae noo been doin for the last hour, wi' three coorses, forby hotch-potch and puddins.

Christopher North
Noctes Ambrosianae, 1822-1835

Less gluttonous modern epicures would disagree with James Hogg, the Ettrick shepherd, who made these remarks under the pseudonym of North, but it's all a question of the size and content of the dinner. Hogg and his friends, if accounts are anything to go by, consumed vast quantities of food at a sitting and yet the same shepherd on another evening is to be found ringing the bell for some toasted cheese. 'It's a gude while now sin' dinner,' he complains, 'and I'm getting roun' again into hunger.'

An important stand-by food just as much today as it was in the past, cheese has the huge advantage of being available at a moment's notice, allowing it the flexibility of fitting into any meal at any time of the day. Apart from the obvious advantage that it is cheaper than meat, it has the added attraction of providing endless variations of texture, flavour and aroma so that all palates can be satisfied. Specialist cheese shops are the best places to find the greatest range of cheeses and buying from them has some advantages. Firstly, it is possible to have cheese freshly cut from whole cheeses with the possibility of tasting before buying. Secondly the staff ought to be able to advise and discuss your likes and needs. While supermarkets may provide some excellent cheese, they seldom give this kind of service which is useful with such a huge and complicated subject. Small delicatessens providing a good cheese service are on the increase, and can only stimulate and encourage demand for good cheese which in turn is a boost to the industry.

Plainly served cheese, at about room temperature (it is best wrapped in cling film and stored in the vegetable compartment at the bottom of the fridge and needs about $\frac{1}{2}$-1 hour at room temperature before serving, unwrapping just before eating and re-wrapping just after), goes well with all the Scottish Oat and Barley breads and 'cakes', also scones. As described in the Ayrshire farmhouse earlier, it is excellent with a plain wholemeal scone. Texture contrasts, as with flavour ones, are good: the oatcake with crowdie or any other soft cheese; the scone with the hard Dunlop. Crusty bread goes well with both hard and soft cheeses. Finding a suitable fresh fruit to serve with cheese makes it into a well-balanced snack meal (see under Fruits p. 164).

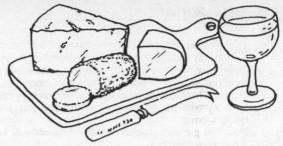

Despite the Ettrick shepherd's remarks, cheese, carefully chosen, can be used as a course in a three or four course dinner. The French, who eat three times as much cheese as we do,* are well practised in the art of the cheese course. They serve the cheese immediately after, or even with, the main course if it is being served with a wine which will be suitable for the cheese. White wines generally are not recommended with cheese.

TOASTED CHEESE

One of the nicest things about the onset of winter is sitting round a fire and eating toasted cheese. It is such a satisfyingly simple and easy meal with only two esssential elements, good bread and a ripe, well-matured hard cheese.

In the days before modern cookers, the cheese was placed on a plate in front of the fire and melted. The toast was made separately, buttered, and then the cheese poured over. Often, things were mixed into the cheese, and frequently the toast was soaked in wine or beer and the dish properly described as 'Toast and Cheese'. The Welsh can lay claim to making it a national dish. It appears that their description of it was entirely appropriate when they called it a 'rare bit' meaning something splendid. 'Rabbit' is a shortening of the original word and has nothing to do with the animal. This is the OED's definition — 'A dish consisting of cheese and a little butter melted and mixed together, to which are added ale, cayenne pepper, and salt, the whole being stirred until it is creamy, and then poured over buttered toast: also simply, slices of toasted cheese laid on toast.'

This is Hanna Glasse's decription of a 'Scots Rabbit' in her book The Art of Cookery made Plain and Easy, 1747.

'Toast a piece of bread very nicely on both sides, butter it, cut a slice of cheese about as big as the bread, toast it on both sides, and lay it on the bread.'

Her 'Welsh Rabbit' was similar but with mustard rubbed over the cheese while 'English Rabbit' had a glass of red wine poured over the toast before the cheese was put on top.

*Per head, per week: UK — 4 oz; French — 13 oz; Italians — 10 oz.

CHEESE AND EGGS

4 servings

This can be made by adding cheese to scrambled eggs, probably the commonest way of making it, but in this recipe it is the opposite procedure. The cheese is melted first with some milk then thickened with a little cornflour and finally cooked gently with some eggs till smooth and creamy. There is a higher proportion of cheese to eggs so the cheese flavour predominates and can be sharpened with some mustard just before serving.

8 oz/250 g grated Dunlop or Scottish Cheddar (2 c)
1 teaspoon cornflour
4 tablespoons milk
3 eggs, beaten
Salt and pepper
Mustard to taste

Dissolve the cornflour in the milk and put into a pan with the cheese. Heat very gently stirring all the time till the cheese melts. Now spoon some of the hot cheese mixture over the eggs and beat in, pour back into the pan and continue cooking, stir over a low heat till the mixture becomes runny and smooth. Taste for seasoning, pour over buttered toast and serve.

Note: In the Household Book of Lady Grisell Baillie (1692-1733) she frequently mentions 'Ramekins of Cheese' which referred to a kind of pie with a filling of cheese and eggs. The above mixture can be poured into ramekin dishes and eaten with fingers of hot buttered toast as a starter course to a meal. It can also be mixed with cooked Finnan Haddock (see p. 72) and used to fill a prepared 7″ (18 cm) pastry flan. It sets well and can be served cold.

Shaped Cheese

You will need a mould for this cheese and, apart from using a plastic flower pot with additional holes made with a red hot skewer, the alternative is to use the heart-shaped mould which is available in specialist kitchen shops and which is meant for a Coeur à la Creme. I have used both equally successfully. You may be lucky enough, on the other hand, to own an original antique 'curd mould' with a special shape and holes for draining the whey.

The traditional Scottish dish is a low fat unsweetened version which is a good contrast to ripe soft fruits or it may be served with oatcakes. The richer version is one I have enjoyed with Russians and Finns as part of their festive Easter food. Known as 'Kulich' they decorate the shape and eat it with slices of a rich yeasted cake (Pashka). I put it here as a variation of Hatted Kit though it correctly belongs with the Scandinavians in Chapter 9 (see p. 270).

HATTED KIT

PLAIN

'Take equal parts whole milk and butter milk and place them in a small keg in a warm spot. After two or three days a thick white paste or curd rises to the top. Remove this and strain. If too thick, thin with whole milk and sweeten to taste. Best eaten as a dessert with oatcakes when preferred. Can be flavoured with whisky. This can be repeated several times by adding milk and buttermilk to the keg. Hence the name. A warm weather dish.'

Anon

2 pt/11.5 dl sweet whole milk (5 c)
2 pt/11.5 dl cultured buttermilk (5 c)
While the recipe quoted above flavours with whisky, F. Marian
    MacNeill suggests nutmeg and cinnamon.
Bring sweet milk almost to the boil and pour over buttermilk. Pour into a colander lined with a muslin and leave for 2-3 hours till most of the whey has drained off. While it is still quite soft, pour into a muslin-lined mould with holes in it, cover and leave to drain. When it has stopped dripping, turn out and serve with cream and fruit or oatcakes and bread.

RICH

Beat together

7 oz/200 g unsalted butter (1¾ sticks)
7 oz/200 g caster or fine brown sugar (1 c)

Add

1 lb/500 g crowdie or cottage cheese (2 c)
2 egg yolks
4 oz/100 g raisins (¾ c)
1 tablespoon thick bitter marmalade
1 tablespoon blanched chopped almonds
Mix all together thoroughly and pour into lined mould, press down on top and lightly weight down overnight. Turn out and decorate with almonds and raisins. Eat as a spread for Plain Cookies or Hot Cross Buns or with a Rich Yeasted Cake (see p. 216).

CHEDDAR AND CROWDIE SALAD

4 servings

Four vegetables — cucumber, sweet red pepper, spring onion and tomato, blend with these cheeses to give interesting contrasts of colour, texture and flavour.
8 oz/250 g Scottish Cheddar
½ cucumber, chopped
1 sweet red pepper, chopped
1 spring onion, finely chopped
1 large tomato, chopped
1 lettuce
Black olives for garnish

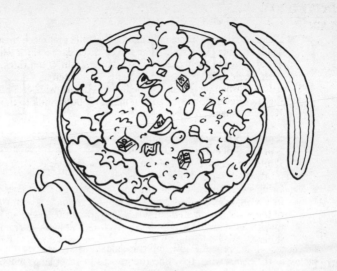

Dressing

Juice of 1 lemon
3 tablespoons mayonnaise
2 oz/50 g crowdie
$\frac{1}{2}$ teaspoon each — Arran mustard, tarragon, marjoram, basil, and
  horseradish
Salt and pepper

Assembling the salad

Mix the dressing ingredients well together and pour over cheese and
vegetables. Serve on a bed of fresh lettuce and garnish with black
olives.

CROWDIE CAKE

Combine in blender

4 cups crowdie or cottage cheese
4 medium eggs
1 cup buttermilk
$\frac{1}{2}$ cup sugar or honey
1 teaspoon pure vanilla extract
Juice and rind of 1 lemon
$\frac{1}{4}$ teaspoon salt
Pre-heat the oven to 375F/190C/Gas 5.
8″ (20 cm) flan tin with a removable base.
Pour into flan tin and bake for 45 minutes. Turn out and serve with
fresh fruit and whipped cream.

CHAPTER NINE

CULINARY INTERCHANGE

See the Manzil? A' the Pakki's are werring kilts oan Friday. They ur gonny be werring Pakki tartan and gie'in oot curried haggis.

Jack McLean
Glasgow Herald. 1985

The occasion was Burns' Night, and the Pakistanis are as versatile, it seems, as the Scots, when they find themselves in other lands among cultures which, by their sheer everyday presence, might cause an abandonment of national traditions. But it seems not. Like the haggis/curry compromise (not such a daft idea either), the Pakistani tartan is no stranger than the picture of a North American Chief of Scottish extraction (Waldo MacIntosh), resplendent in full Indian head-dress, kilt and sporran (Scottish Field, May 1985) — a symbol of how generations of Scots have integrated with their adopted nations around the world.

Maybe it's this ability to integrate which has made Scots particularly good at accepting and welcoming other cultures within Scotland. Without making Scotland any less Scottish, they add a rich and colourful dimension to the life of the country and not least in the realms of new foods and eating styles which they have introduced. The best ethnic restaurants which are particularly conspicuous in all the major towns, and some of the smaller ones as well (there is even a well integrated Asian community on the island of Lewis), are not only ambassadors for their distinctive cooking styles but also for the quality Scottish produce which they use daily. Chinese and Asian supermarkets, Italian and Greek delicatessens and lots of other shops selling ethnic foods have extended the dimensions of our gastronomic experiences. But none of them totally dominate, and Scots continue to consume large amounts of traditional fish and chips as well as favourites like every-day mince and tatties, whilst exploring the more exotic elements of Chicken Tandoori or Sweet and Sour Pork on occasions.

There are more Indo/Pak restaurants than of any other ethnic grouping, with Chinese coming second. While the men run the restaurants, wives tend to look after children at home and often have problems adapting, since they have no natural opportunity to socialise outwith their extended family and can often find themselves isolated by language. For these reasons, International Centres have been set up in the major cities where there are ethnic groups, to help them learn the language and integrate with the indigenous community.

Although they tend to cook and eat traditional foods at home, they are also interested in Scottish food, as I found during three years working in one of these centres in the heart of Glasgow, when we met weekly for an international cooking session. We ranged the globe, exchanging culinary traditions — watching the speed and skill of the Indian women making chapati; or the sheer artistry of the Japanese designing and presenting stunningly simple combinations which also tasted good; or learning how Moroccans actually make and eat Couscous in the desert. Without having to go more than half a mile down the road, I could travel the culinary globe.

This chapter is particularly dedicated to all those friends who shared so freely and generously their native culinary expertise. I hope some may still be making the odd piece of shortbread; I am grateful to have known the warmth and friendliness of their hospitality, and I wish them well with their curried haggis.

Italians

Birth of a new cuisine

Food historians give full credit to Italy as mother of the gastronomic revolution witnessed in the 16th century. It might never have moved out of Italy, had the fourteen-year-old Italian Caterina de Medici not married the French Dauphin (later Henry II) in 1533. A special armada of ships took the Medicis from Livorno to Marseilles, where the ceremony took place officiated by the Pope, and part of the huge retinue which accompanied them were Caterina's Tuscan cooks and 'gelatieri' (ice cream makers). They discovered that barbaric medieval food was still being served at the French court and they set about revolutionising the cuisine, seeking out the pure, unmistakable essence of each food, exalting it, and presenting it with all the means suggested by nature and their experience. It seems no different an aim than the one which present-day chefs would have us believe is a 'new' cuisine.

It was mainly because of new plants, fruits and vegetables (particularly olives) which spread widely after the Crusades and voyages of discovery that a new style came into being in this mild climate of North Italy. Also, Florence was the centre of a type of Italian cooking which owed its superiority to the simplicity of internal order and the beauty of its appearance. It was the product of a new sense of art and new produce from the land. The French learnt quickly. Heavy spicing was laid aside and the mortar and pestle no longer ground meat to an indistinguishable pulp.

Three centuries later, migrating Italians came to Britain, many to Scotland, and, while not exactly causing a revolution, certainly impressed many of their culinary traditions on our receptive palates. Some things, like ice cream, are now so well integrated that we hardly credit the Italians with bringing it to Scotland. Except, perhaps as you sit in an Italian café eating Italian Ice Cream, the like of which is still unsurpassed. While Italians have the reputation as the best ice cream makers, it seems they cannot lay claim to its invention. Ices were known in ancient times with records mentioning ice cellars in the time of Confucious. Alexander the Great is said to have enjoyed frozen mixtures of honey, milk and fruit juices while the Chinese mixed snow and fruit juice to make an iced sweet. Its connection with Italy developed as one of the many new and exciting ideas which Marco Polo brought back to Venice in 1292 from his journeys across Asia. In Peking he had enjoyed a delicacy made of frozen milk which was refined, developed and made popular by the Italian gelatieri.

Pasta and pizzas are probably the two other Italian things which we eat most of today and their popularity must be directly related to their ability to satisfy that basic need for fast-food every now and again.

PIZZA

makes 4

A genuine Italian Pizza has a thin layer of soft bread dough and a very slightly thinner layer of well-flavoured moist filling on top.
Pre-heat the oven to 450F/230C/Gas 8.

Making the dough

1 oz/25 g fresh yeast — $\frac{1}{2}$ oz/15 g dried yeast (2 pkg)
3 tablespoons warm water
Pinch of sugar
Mix all together and leave to stand in a warm place till the yeast begins to bubble
14 oz/500 g strong (high gluten) plain flour ($3\frac{1}{2}$ c)
8 fl oz/250 ml lukewarm water (1 c)
3 tablespoons olive oil
1 teaspoon salt
Stir flour and salt into a warmed bowl. Make a well in the centre and add yeast mixture, water and oil. Mix and knead into a ball for about 15 minutes till smooth and shiny. Leave to rise in a warm place till double in size.

Knock down dough and divide into 4. Knead each piece into a round ball and then flatten with your hands, turning the circle and pulling till it is about 7-8" (18-22 cm) across. Then roll and turn until it is about 10" (25 cm) across and $\frac{1}{8}$" ($\frac{1}{2}$ cm) thick. Crimp or flute the edge of the circle. Dust a baking tray with cornmeal and place pizza on top. Repeat procedure with other three pieces.

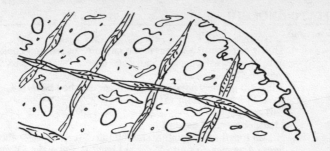

Making up the pizza

Pour about 6 tablespoons Tomato Sauce (see below) on each pie and spread it over with a pastry brush.

CHEESE PIZZA

Sprinkle with 6 tablespoons grated mozzarella, then 2 tablespoons grated parmesan. Dribble 2 tablespoons olive oil over and bake on lowest shelf. Reduce temperature to 400F/200C/Gas 6 after 5 minutes then cook for about 10 minutes till crust is lightly browned and filling bubbling hot.

ALTERNATIVE GARNISHES

Any sort of seafood, meat, vegetables, anchovies, sausage, pepperoni, prosciutto slivers, tiny meat balls, garlic slices, strips of green pepper, whole or sliced mushrooms, but always spreading with the tomato sauce first and finishing with parmesan and olive oil.

ITALIAN TOMATO SAUCE

Enough for 4-6 pizzas

Sauté in a large pan for ten minutes till the onion is cooked

3 tablespoons olive oil
1 large onion, finely chopped

Add

1 tablespoon crushed garlic
2 teaspoons fresh basil (1 dried)
2 teaspoons oregano (1 dried)
2 bay leaves
1 tablespoon sugar
3 tablespoons tomato purée
$\frac{1}{2}$ lb/250 g freshly chopped tomatoes (1 c)
1 × 1 lb 14 oz can chopped tomatoes

Simmer gently uncovered for about 1 hour till reduced to the consistency you require. Remove the bay leaves. Taste for seasoning — add salt, freshly ground black pepper and if necessary a little vinegar, though this may not be necessary if the tomatoes are sharp in flavour. This is a **Store Sauce** and will keep well covered in a cool place for at least a week.

POTATO GNOCCHI

4-6 servings

This is our Scottish potato scone mixture shaped and cooked differently. Served with Tomato Sauce and cheese it makes a useful cheap meal.

1 lb/500 g floury potatoes (cooked and mashed finely)
6 oz/175 g plain flour ($1\frac{1}{2}$ c)
Salt and pepper
$\frac{1}{4}$ teaspoon grated nutmeg

Mix all together thoroughly and roll into a long sausage about a finger diameter. Cut into 1" ($2\frac{1}{2}$ cm) lengths and make a dent in the middle of each so that it curls a little. Bring salted water to the boil and drop in a few at a time. Cook each batch about 3-5 minutes or until they rise to the surface. Scoop out with a perforated spoon and put into a buttered ovenproof dish. Keep hot till all are cooked. Dot with butter and sprinkle with parmesan cheese. Serve with tomato sauce or meat sauce. Sometimes they can be layered with thick tomato sauce and parmesan or mozzarella.

French

... For there is much, not only in the actual cookery but in the Domestic Economy of our ingenious neighbours, worthy of profound attention. In the hope that the foreign graces transplanted into this volume may considerably enhance its value to the practical cook, and in the belief that a culinary system superior to either the French or the English, may be drawn from the combined excellencies of both countries.

Med Dods
Cook and Housewives Manual, 1826

History

The French-Scottish connection began with the Normans in the reign of David I early in the 12th century; then William the Lion took a French wife in 1186. The first treaty between the two countries was not signed till 1295.

A little over three hundred years later (1603) the Scottish monarch James I went to London and the Scottish and English crowns were joined. To all intents this ended the close official ties with France though among some Scots, particularly Highlanders and Jacobites, links with France continued. With the fall of the French aristocracy in 1789 a new phenomenon occurred which affected Britain generally, rather than Scotland alone. Namely, the exodus of talented French chefs who were welcomed with open arms by the British aristocracy and upper classes. They firmly established, in British minds, that the French were masters in the kitchen and did so by establishing a highly sophisticated kitchen discipline which continues today in training colleges and hotels and restaurants.

Effects

Caterina de Medici found the French court pretty barbaric when she moved there in 1533 with her skilled Italian chefs and began the long spread of the Italian Renaissance gastronomic revolution. By that time the Auld Alliance only had another seventy years to run, during which time, of course, James V married the influential Mary of Lorraine (1538) and Mary Queen of Scots returned briefly to rule Scotland from 1561 to 1568.

Meanwhile, John Knox had started preaching a doctrine which regarded eating for nothing but pleasure as a sin, and despite Mary's desperate and ill-judged attempts to shut him up, the Scottish Reformation (1560-1690) gathered momentum. While it is clear from contemporary accounts that there were some fanatics who were intent on destroying wit, brightness, laughter and flavour with them, numerous accounts describe the warmth of Scottish hospitality. I believe that these few theological extremists were never more than partially effective in suppressing the natural features of humanity though they had some effect on the population. Certainly the 'sober-kail-and-brose' advocates did their best to reduce the Scottish diet to the barest necessities.

There were obvious divisions in the country, as the religious outlooks make clear. We were united, however, in the wide range of words which we had adopted from the French — many now obsolete, though some still surviving among indigenous Scots in common use to illustrate daily our separate history from England.

For example Ashet, meaning a large serving dish, comes from French, Assiette; Dresser, meaning a kitchen sideboard comes from French, Dressoir; Gean, meaning a wild cherry comes from French, Guigne; Gigot, meaning a leg of mutton comes from French, Gigot; Gout, meaning taste comes from French, Goût; Grosset, meaning gooseberry comes from French, Groseille; Hotch Potch, meaning vegetable soup comes from French, Hochepot; Howtowdie, meaning a young hen comes from French, Hetoudeau; Rizzarded, meaning dried in the sun comes from French, Resore; Sauty Bannock, meaning a pancake comes from French, Sauter.

The early Alliance had a considerable effect on the Scottish soup tradition by strengthening and refining it. Henry MacKenzie (1745-1831) tells us in his Anecdotes and Egotisms — 'The Old English cookery was only roast and boil, the roasts very raw; blood and butter were the savage accompaniments of their cookery. Ours in Scotland was much improved by our constant communication and alliance with France. From France we got several excellent soups, such as Hodge Podge, Friers Chicken, Hare Soup, Lambs Stove, Cocky Leeky and a soup maigre called Pankail . . . made with greens, butter, and a small quantity of oatmeal'.

The French 'dessert' was common in Scotland by the time Mary returned to Scotland in 1561. It was a more sophisticated form of service in which the tables were 'disserved' after the main meal and fruits and confections were then eaten in a separate room. England did not adopt the habit till half a century later.

Drink in Scotland was affected by its links with France and travellers frequently comment favourably on the excellent and abundant French Claret and Brandy which they enjoyed. Englishmen were surprised that the Scots did not put sugar into their wine, presumably because the French claret which was shipped to Edinburgh was less strong and finer flavoured than that sold in London. English wine connoisseurs regularly ordered wine from Leith. (For a full history, see Knee deep in Claret by Billy Kay and Cailean MacLean, 1983.)

Effects after the Union of the Crowns tend to become more British than purely Scottish such as the influence of Patrick Lamb, cook to Charles II, James II and William and Mary, who wrote in his Royal Cookery (1710) — 'Because many of the receipts are of French invention, we have been obliged to use several words and expressions of that language for want of proper terms in our own to express them.' His list includes; Bards of Bacon; Bisque; Braise; Court Bouillon; Entremets; Hors d'oeuvres; Lardons. All showing refinements which the French were busily working on.

The French Revolution (1789) meant that many refugees, among them chefs, came to Britain and established themselves and their customs among the aristocracy and upper classes of society so that by 1894, '5000 French cooks were distributed among the aristocratic houses, clubs, hotels and restaurants in Great Britain' (A. Suzanne — La Cuisine Anglaise, 1894). Inevitably they began to write in English and the British public began to follow their recipes. From the writings of Queen Victoria's own Royal Chef — Francatelli — onwards, the French influence in cookery instructions is considerable. Cookery writers with any pretensions knew and availed themselves of basic French terms so that, like the French themselves, when the Italians arrived to influence so radically their style of cooking, we in Britain in turn had the benefit of accumulated Italian and French refinements.

Louis Eustache Ude — chef at Crockfords, one of London's most famous clubs, explained the French way to the British and in 1814 published The French Cook. He held strongly to the French tradition which had by this time expanded and developed, making use of the new ranges and built-in ovens which gave more control over the heat, so that cooking was taken out of the fireplace, where it had been since the medieval period. French cooks developed the method of using the 'sautoire' for 'sautées'; they invented 'souffles', setting them to rise in the new ovens and they created a unique range of sauces which depended on the smooth blending of flour and butter and gentle simmering to develop flavour.

While the great French masters in the kitchen — Carème (1784-1835), Francatelli (1805-1876), Soyer (1809-1858), Escoffier (1846-1935) and others established in printed form detailed information on the now classic French cuisine, the British writers varied in their enthusiasm but most, like meg Dods (see p. 288), agreed that we should welcome this culinary influence and turn it to our best advantage. Alexis Soyer, perhaps the most influential, and certainly the most colourful French personality among chefs in Britain sums it up when he refers to the French word 'sauter' — '. . . having found no means of translating it to my satisfaction, I see no other plan but to adopt it amongst us, and give it letters of naturalisation, not for the beauty of the word but for its utility.'

Following Soyer's advice has meant that we have now naturalised words like — purée; braise; larding; au bleu; roux; soufflé; vol-au-vent; consommé; rissole; compôte; mayonnaise; meringue and others. Whether we should also naturalise French words which have a perfectly good English translation is open to debate. 'Menu' is a more concise form than 'Bill of Fare' though there may be occasions when it is more appropriate to use the latter. A 'gâteau' is a light creamy affair whereas a 'cake' has a more solid ring to it though I can't see why we should call broth, 'bouillon'; or fried bread, 'croûton', in our everyday language. In menu terminology it is a question of finding the appropriate word for the occasion, whether it be French or English. It is inevitable, given the fundamental nature of the French culinary influence, that naturalised French terms will crop up. The question at the moment is — do we adopt the ones for which there are good English translations? De Gaulle made it illegal to use English words in government documents, on street signs and in menus. His concern was that 'Franglais' — words like 'fish and chips', 'Irish stew', 'roast beef', 'football', 'pop music' and many others should not become naturalised and thus destroy the purity of the French language. While not necessarily going along with such extreme linguistic chauvinism, we should perhaps be more aware of the richness of the English and Scots language when talking of food.

As well as a culinary discipline, the French have given us the Restaurant. It originated in Paris in 1765 when Monsieur Boulanger started selling a variety of hot soups as quick restoratives or 'restaurants' in his shop. There was an outcry by cook-shop owners who took out a court action against him, since they thought that they had sole rights to sell cooked food. He won his case and gained much publicity in the process and 'restaurants' flourished. More than a hundred years passed before Britain saw the first one in London with the opening of Whiteley's Restaurant in 1873. Until then the coffee houses (later clubs), inns, taverns and cook shops had sufficed, serving at a common table, at a fixed price and time, a midday dinner or a supper at night. The restaurant changed all that.

It was the most influential and respected French chef Georges Auguste Escoffier (1846-1935) who shaped and formed the basis for our modern restaurant by creating the then revolutionary 'à la carte Menu' at the Carlton Hotel in 1899. He gathered round him a brigade of sixty cooks and concentrated on quickly made dishes which depended on a repertoire of basic sauces and garnishes rather than plain roasts and traditional accompaniments. Other well established restaurants in London followed — The Berkeley, The Ritz, Claridges, Oddenino's and the Café Royal — and all the menus were written totally in French.

A horizontal line has to be drawn at this point separating the wealthy classes who could indulge in this sophisticated and luxurious style of eating and those whose everyday fare continued more in the natural style of the country. 'Plain Roast and Boiled' was still basic fare for the mass of the population, though there is no doubt that there was a general 'filtering-down' to the extent that things like meringues became common fare for all.

Today, the long standing debate still rages about how much French influence we should encourage in our eating style. Should we continue to train chefs in Classical French cuisine? The fact is that the French set about establishing a highly successful kitchen discipline and the British did not. They developed and refined dishes in an original and imaginative way, their country encouraged them to do so, and they recognised the potential of regional and home-made dishes. They lifted out of oblivion dishes which they then made famous and established what was originally very basic fare as classic styles such as Bonne Femme — Housewife's Style; A la Bourgeoise — Simple Homely Style; A la Paysanne — Peasant Fashion; A l'Ancienne — Old Fashioned; A la Grandmère — Grandmother's Style.

The culinary influence from France has been greater than from any other country as the length of this piece illustrates, but it is not with the haute cuisine created by Escoffier at the Carlton Hotel at the turn of the century which I would like to end the story for the moment, but with the closing words from Jean and Pierre Troisgros in their Foreword to The Nouvelle Cuisine (1977). 'As it becomes simpler and lighter the chef's art is getting nearer to the home cook's art, and this is what we have set out to show in this book.'

GRATIN DAUPHINOIS

Potatoes baked in Cream
4-6 servings

In the Dauphine area on the Alpine border of France, cooks developed this gratin with its golden brown top and rich soft potato layers underneath.

Choose firm waxy potatoes which will hold their shape. The milk serves as the cooking liquid while the double cream poured on top browns in the oven to form the crust. Complications, such as cheese and eggs which are often added, compete with the natural cream and potato flavour and simple texture which, in this form, makes the best foil for all kinds of well-flavoured meat and fish dishes. Garlic is a matter of taste.

2 lb/1 kg large waxy potatoes
Salt and pepper
Grated nutmeg
2 oz/50 g butter ($\frac{1}{2}$ stick)
1 clove garlic (optional)
1 pt/600 ml milk ($2\frac{1}{2}$ c)
$\frac{1}{4}$ pt/150 ml double cream ($\frac{3}{4}$ c)

Preparing the dish

Peel potatoes and slice finely ($\frac{1}{8}''$ — 3 mm). Rub the inside of a gratin dish with the cut garlic clove. Leave to dry, then butter the dish thickly. Arrange the potato slices in rows overlapping and seasoning between each layer. The dish should be about two-thirds full. Pour in milk and put a layer of cream on top. Scatter the remaining butter in pieces on top.

Baking

Put the dish into a hot oven to begin with. Then after 15 minutes reduce to moderate and bake for another 45 minutes until the potatoes are soft and have absorbed all the milk and the cream has formed a golden crust on top. Serve.

TARTE TATIN

This is the classic French method of cooking an apple tart with the pastry on top rather than underneath, then turning just before serving. It has the definite advantage of keeping the pastry crisp but at the same time allowing a thick moist syrupy layer of apples for the filling without sogging-up the pastry. It is a Sologne dish called after Mademoiselle Tatin, the French cook who first delighted her customers by putting on her crust the wrong way.

Apple filling

2 oz/50 g unsalted butter ($\frac{1}{2}$ stick)
3 tablespoons caster sugar
2 lb/1 kg small eating apples

Melt the butter in a round pan 8″ (20 cm) which will go into the oven, sprinkle with sugar and heat over a very low heat till the mixture begins to caramelise slightly. Peel and core apples and arrange side by side close together. They may be halved if large. Cook over a low heat till the apples are just soft turning once; if halved the flat surface should be uppermost. Remove from the heat and then leave to cool.

Pastry

4 oz/100 g flour (1 c)
$2\frac{1}{2}$ oz/65 g butter ($\frac{1}{2}$ stick generous)
1 tablespoon caster sugar
1 egg yolk
Bake at 375F/190C/Gas 5.

Sift flour onto the board and rub in butter. Add sugar and make a well in the centre. Drop in the egg yolk and work in flour with your fingers till it is all incorporated and you have a smooth, firm paste — or blend together in the processor. Roll out to fit size of pan and lay over apples, turn in any surplus to make a double thickness round the edge. Bake 15-18 minutes till the pastry is cooked. Turn upside down onto a round dish.

Make a very light brown caramel in a small saucepan with 2 tablespoons sugar. Moisten with 2 teaspoons water and 2 teaspoons lemon juice.

Pour caramel, which should be soft and smooth, over the apples. Serve warm.

English

Today our Scots porridge and barley broth and scones and orange marmalade are as popular south of the Tweed as are ham and eggs, bath buns, and Yorkshire pudding in the north. But native dishes have a habit of deteriorating on alien soil, and, despite their similarity to a casual observer, the cuisines of the two countries remain, in many respects, curiously distinctive.

F. Marian McNeill
The Scots Kitchen, 1929

On my first visit to London, staying with some distant English relatives, they thought to make me feel at home with a plate of porridge for breakfast. It was made with fine ground oatmeal sweetened with sugar and cooked to a custard-like consistency, and I upset them badly by not recognising that it was supposed to be porridge. Ham is another area of difference. The Scots use the word 'ham' for what the English call 'bacon', which in Scotland is cut in very much thinner slices — and there are lots more.

When the Scottish and English crowns joined in 1603, the Scots, conscious of their separate history, and of the fact that they might lose identity, made an effort to preserve all things Scottish including their food traditions. Differences in indigenous raw materials meant other natural variations existed, making Scotland more of a fish/oat eating country rather than a meat/bread one. Also, centuries of feuding with one another had built up barriers of suspicion and mutual hostility which didn't encourage culinary interchange and it was not until Sir Walter Scott set about selling Scotland to the English that a better understanding developed. But it seems that, even so, Scots have borrowed least from their nearest neighbours.

Much Scottish produce was exported to English markets and the traditional Roast Beef of England was established on the strength of prime Scottish beef. Meat eating in England was synonymous with manliness in a way never established in Scotland because it was less readily available to the mass of the population. The fictitious John Bull was supposed to owe his vigour to meat while the Marlborough wars were said to have been won by the sturdy Englishmen fed on roast meats. Scots vigour, on the other hand, was attributed to a frugal oatmeal-based diet. When Carème (1784-1835) spent a brief period working in England, he was quick to realise the contrast between England and France. 'The cattle,' he says, 'are fat and of very good quality, as is the mutton veal and lamb; the roast beef is succulent much more so than ours in France. The English housewives are all experts at this roast beef, and this, and roast veal, mutton and lamb are the mainstay of the English table.'

Eating a pudding with meat is an English tradition which goes back to before the days of potatoes, when a boiled pudding was eaten with boiled meat (Boiled Pork and Pease Pudding) or a batter pudding cooked under the spit was eaten as a prelude to the roasted meat (Roast Beef and Yorkshire Pudding). Like the English version of porridge which I had found so strange, Yorkshire friends have difficulty in recognising some of the Yorkshire puddings which are served up in Scotland.

When George I of Hanover and Great Britain (1714-1727) came to the throne from Germany he brought with him a taste for sweet boiled puddings and earned himself the title 'Pudding George'. It is said that he was responsible for introducing the 'plumb pudding' as we know it today. While it was eaten with other meats its associations with Christmas and with Roast Beef are indicated in the Norfolk <u>Diary of a Country Parson</u> by James Woodforde when he writes that on the 25th December 1782 there was 'For the poor of the Parish, Surloin of Beef Rosted, Plenty of Plumb pudding, Mince pies for the first time today.'

ROAST ENGLISH SIRLOIN OF BEEF and Yorkshire Pudding

There are three types of rib roast. The sirloin end has the fillet on the inside of the bone — this is not an advantage since it will cook in a much shorter time than the meat on the outside of the bone so should really be removed and cooked separately. Next up from the sirloin is the Wing Rib, also known as an English Cut Sirloin. On the bone it looks like a giant cutlet and is easy to carve — this would be my choice for roasting. Further up, nearer the head, are the Fore Ribs which have an excellent flavour but they also have a thick 'lip' of meat and fat on the outer edge which tends to be slightly tougher than the rest of the meat and will take longer to cook.

Boned and rolled is perhaps easier to carve, but meat gains flavour from the bone; it protects the meat during the cooking and prevents it drying out and shrinking — it does not take any longer to cook either.

The English eat more meat on the bone than the Scots. Allow about 8 oz/250 g per person on the bone.

Preparing the meat

For a 4 lb/2 kg piece of meat to serve about 8-10, melt some butter and brush the meat, especially at the ends. Lightly brown 1 tablespoon flour in a pan and mix with 1 teaspoon freshly ground black pepper and 1 teaspoon powdered mustard. Rub this into the meat all over and leave at room temperature to absorb flavours before cooking. The fat surface may be salted lightly.

Roasting

Pre-heat the oven to 400F/200C/Gas 6.

Place the meat on a rack in a roasting tin or on a bed of roughly cut up vegetables or chopped bones. Roast, basting occasionally for 15 minutes per lb plus 15 minutes if you like the meat red and juicy in the middle: 20 minutes per lb plus 20 minutes if you prefer it medium to rare and 30 minutes per lb plus 30 minutes for well done.

Resting the meat

Remove from the oven, put on heated serving dish and keep in a warm place to allow the muscles to relax before carving. Remove vegetables or bones from the roasting tin and pour off excess fat — reserve dripping for making pudding.

Making the Pudding

Make up the batter in advance — at least an hour before cooking. Sift 6 oz/175 g strong plain flour into a bowl and add a pinch of salt. Make a well in the centre. Break in 2 eggs and $\frac{1}{2}$ pt/300 ml milk ($1\frac{1}{4}$ c). Beat till smooth then add another $\frac{1}{4}$ pt/150 ml milk ($\frac{3}{4}$ c) and beat till well mixed.

Pour 1 tablespoon of dripping from the roasting tin into each pudding tin and put into a very hot oven 450F/230C/Gas 8. Leave for five minutes till the fat is really hot, remove and then add the batter. Bake for 10-15 minutes till the puddings are puffed and golden.

Making the gravy

This can be made while the puddings are cooking. Add 2 cups of water to the roasting tin. Bring to the boil and scrape up all the residue in the tin, boil to reduce and concentrate flavours, season, strain and keep hot.

Serving

In Yorkshire I have always had the puddings first with gravy and the meat and vegetables after though it seems that this is not standard practice throughout the country. Serve with mustard (see p. 238) and horseradish sauce (grated horseradish mixed with cream).

SUSSEX POND PUDDING

A classic English sweet steamed pudding. It depends for its excellence on a number of features. The pudding is enclosed in a well-flavoured moist spongy suet pastry; inside this is a mixture of butter and sugar which melts and blends together during the long slow cooking whilst absorbing all the essential oils from the whole lemon in the centre; finally the softened lemon still intact with its centre sharp and tangy, adding instant contrast to the sweet buttery sauce. When cut open the sauce spills out to make the 'pond'.

For the pastry

12 oz/350 g self-raising flour (3 c)
1 level teaspoon baking powder
$\frac{1}{4}$ teaspoon salt
6 oz/175 g beef suet, finely chopped (1 c tightly packed)
Cold water
$3\frac{1}{2}$ pt greased pudding basin ($1\frac{3}{4}$ L)
Mix all the ingredients with water to make a soft dough, divide into $\frac{2}{3}$ and $\frac{1}{3}$ and roll out larger piece to fit pudding basin.

Filling

7 oz/200 g butter ($1\frac{3}{4}$ stick)
7 oz/200 g demerara sugar ($1\frac{1}{4}$ c)
1 large lemon, well washed and pricked all over with a fork
Put a layer of half the butter and sugar in the base, lay the lemon on top and cover with remaining butter and sugar. Put on pastry lid sealing well. Cover and steam for 3 hours. Turn out onto deep serving dish, an ashet is ideal but make sure there is enough room on the plate for the 'pond'. Cut up the lemon and serve a piece with each serving.

Irish

Amongst half a dozen families in the entry there was a broth exchange. Each family made a few extra quarts and exchanged them. Each can was emptied, washed, refilled and returned.

'Did ye ever think, Jamie, how like folks are to th' broth they make?'

'No,' he said, 'but there's no raisin why people should sting jist because they've got nothin' but nettles in their broth!'

The potatoes were emptied out of their pot on the bare table, my father encircling it with his arms to prevent them from rolling off. A little pile of salt was placed beside each person, and each had a big bowl full of broth. The different kinds had lost their identity in the common pot.

Alexander Irvine
My Lady of the Chimney Corner, 1966

When St Columba sailed the Irish sea and settled in Iona he was only the first of many to make this crossing from one Celtic country to another.

With much interchange in subsequent centuries the Irish find themselves today as much at home in Scotland as the Scots are in Ireland. Cultural similarities apart, they both share similar food traditions which have led to broadly similar eating patterns. Cooking food in a large iron pot over a slow burning peat fire and baking with a girdle rather than an oven are only two cooking methods common to both countries. Both are also oat-growing and fish-eating and in addition have reared cattle more for selling than eating in the past.

The parallels are many; the main difference is in the fact that the Irish were more enthusiastic about potatoes than the Scots. Original and frequent use of potatoes in their diet was the result; they made bread with potatoes (Boxty); they made cakes with potatoes (Fadge, similar to Scots Potato Scones; also Potato Cakes which are more like a Scone, as well as Pratie Oaten which was a Potato Scone with oatmeal); and they developed interesting potato and vegetable dishes like Colcannon and Champ, which are also to be found in the Scottish repertoire. They combined their most common meat with potatoes and onions to make Irish Stew, which has had many variations throughout the Western world but originally depended on a combination of only three basic flavours, potatoes, onions and mutton, with some herbs as available. The Irish peasantry gave up growing everything else for potatoes with tragic results when the crop failed in 1845/46 and caused the deaths of so many during the Potato Famine.

IRISH STEW

6-8 servings

The dish originated in the Irish cabin. In it utensils were scarce — a frying pan, a griddle, a kettle and a potato pot sometimes constituting the entire cooking apparatus. When a pig or sheep was killed at the 'big house' the griskin, spare-ribs, or scrag-end of the neck of mutton were shared with the peasants. Having limited vessels and more limited experience, the potatoes were peeled when meat was used, otherwise they were boiled in their 'jackets'; and meat, potatoes and onions were put in the pot, covered with water and all boiled together. So Irish Stew was made, and without much change has remained as a popular dish to this day.

Florence Irwin
<u>The Cookin' Woman</u>, 1949

It should have a thick creamy consistency similar to Scottish Stovies.

3 lb/1½ kg neck of lamb chops
3 lb/1½ kg mealy potatoes, peeled
1 lb/500 g onions, sliced
Salt and pepper
Parsley and thyme

Put the meat into a heavy based pan. Cover with water and bring to the boil briefly, skim. Slice about a third of the potatoes very thinly; these will disintegrate and thicken the stew. Leave the rest in larger pieces. Add the thinly sliced potatoes, onion, salt, pepper and herbs to the meat and stir well. Place the larger potatoes on top, cover and simmer gently till the meat is tender. Taste for seasoning and finish with more chopped parsley.

Often served in Ireland with **Pickled Red Cabbage:** Shred a large cabbage finely, spread out on a large tray and lightly cover with salt. Leave for 2-3 days, turning daily. Drain the cabbage and pack into jars then cover with spiced vinegar (see p. 239). Put a cayenne pod and a few peppercorns into the jars, cover and seal. Ready for use in a fortnight.

Variation

Use a leftover joint, removing all meat from the bones. Cover the bones with water and simmer for about 2 hours to make a stock. Strain. Prepare the potatoes and onions as above and add to the stock, cook till tender then add the cooked meat thinly sliced and heat through.

COLCANNON

6-8 servings

I find it useful to make Colcannon into a main meal dish by adding crowdie (cottage cheese) and some sour cream. It is versatile and lends itself to many variations.

Sautéing the onions and cabbage

3 medium onions, finely chopped
4 tablespoons butter
2 tablespoons oil
½ teaspoon salt
1 lb/500 g shredded cabbage (4 c)

Heat the butter and oil together in a large pan and add the onions. Cook till soft and yellow. Add the cabbage and sauté the cabbage till just tender.

Preparing the other vegetables
> 4 medium potatoes
> 2 medium carrots
> Half a small turnip
> 12 oz/375 g crowdie (cottage cheese) (1½ c)
> 4 fl oz/125 ml sour cream (½ c)
> Cook and mash the potatoes, turnip and carrots. Season and while
> still warm add crowdie and sour cream.

Finishing the dish
> Mix together the two lots of vegetables. Add ½ teaspoon ground
> caraway (optional) and 2 tablespoons cider vinegar. Taste for
> seasoning. Spread in a 2½ pt (1¼ kg) gratin dish and cover with
> 2 tablespoons grated cheddar cheese. Brown under the grill or finish
> in the oven. (400F/200C/Gas 6).

Scandinavians

The Scandinavians are widely known as brilliant designers, and
much of what they have designed, crafted and sent out into the
world for the past three decades has been for the beautification
of the table — porcelain, silverware, crystal, linen. It is not so
widely known that they are excellent cooks as well. It should
stand to reason, however, that a people who could care so
much about the way a table looks would also care vitally about
food, and the Scandinavians do.

Dale Brown
The Cooking of Scandinavia, 1969

While the Irish naturally had more contact with the West of Scotland,
then the East was more influenced by Scandinavia. They shared a strong
fishing tradition which encouraged much interchange and as recently
as 1469 the Islands of Orkney and Shetland were still part of the Norwe-
gian crown's lands. They were pledged for 58,000 florins which was to be
the unpaid dowry of their Princess Margaret when she married James III
in 1470. From 1472 they were annexed to the Scottish crown though
the Norwegians constantly tried to get them back and only gave up in
1749.

There was also strong Norse influence on the outer Islands of the
Hebrides which can be still seen in the Norse place names like Ness
('nes' — Norse for headland) on Lewis.

Norse culture in Shetland remains strong and the islanders continue to celebrate the end of Yule by burning a viking ship at the Up-Helly-A' ceremony. Interchange of food traditions with Scandinavia are many. The Shetlanders' extensive use of livers, heads and roes in the past, when they were a by-product of salting large white fish, is one similarity. They also shared with Scandinavians a liking for fermented fish and while they no longer go in for things like Sookit Piltacks (Saith left in the open to ferment for 10 days) or Klossed Heads (Fish heads pressed between stones and left to ferment) they do still salt and eat herring. Salted mutton (Reested mutton) can be bought in butcher's shops in Lerwick (I am not aware that it is available in any other part of Scotland) and Shetlanders use it to make an excellent broth.

Other evidence of Scandinavian influence is the extensive use of cabbage and the use of onions with herring which is not common in the rest of Scotland. At the Yule breakfast they drink Whipkull (see p. 160) which is another tradition which they share with Norway. This is a light frothy mixture of eggs and sugar beaten over heat and called Eggedosis in Norway. The Scandinavian tradition of salting and pickling herring and using it as a central part of the cold table (Smorgasbord), with many variations, has kept alive old herring cures. Today modern manufacturers in Scandinavia have exploited these interesting cures and are now buying Scottish herring and mackerel, processing the fish and selling it back.

Here are some Scandinavian recipes which Scots could easily make instead.

SALT HERRING WITH LEEKS

4 servings

This Finnish combination has a strong personality of contrasting flavours. It should be eaten with plainly boiled or baked potatoes.

8 salt herring, boned and skinned
3 medium leeks white and pale green only, cleaned and finely sliced
2 hardboiled eggs
2 oz/50 g unsalted butter, melted and very hot ($\frac{1}{2}$ stick)
4 large baked potatoes

To assemble

Arrange the herring in a row up the centre of an ashet. Put the hardboiled eggs on one side and the leeks on the other. Pour the very hot melted butter over everything and serve immediately with baked or boiled potatoes.

MARINATED FRIED HERRING

The method is in two parts, first the frying then the marinading. In theory it is the same idea as sousing but frying the fish first gives it a firmer texture and fuller flavour.

Coat 8 herring fillets in seasoned flour. Fry in butter till golden brown on both sides. Leave to cool.

Bring to the boil and cool

$\frac{1}{2}$ pt/300 ml cider vinegar (1$\frac{1}{4}$ c)
$\frac{1}{2}$ pt/300 ml water (1$\frac{1}{2}$ c)
6 tablespoons granulated sugar
1 bay leaf
6 peppercorns
1 medium onion, finely sliced

When both are cold pour marinade over the fish and leave overnight before using. Serve cold with brown bread and butter. The dish will keep in a cold place for about a week.

GRAVLAX

Salmon marinated in Dill
8-10 servings

3 lb/1$\frac{1}{2}$ kg fresh salmon, middle cut
1 large bunch fresh dill, may be chopped or left whole

Mix together

2 oz/50 g caster sugar
1 teaspoon crushed white peppercorns (optional)
$\frac{1}{4}$ cup coarse salt

Begin by filleting the fish. Place half the fish, skin side down, in a deep dish or casserole. Wash the dill and chop or leave whole and place on the fish (use all the stalks). Sprinkle salt/sugar mixture over and cover with the other half of the fish, skin side up. Cover the fish with foil and place a board or plate on top. Weight down and place in the refrigerator for 2-3 days. Turn every 12 hours, basting it with the liquid marinade and separating the halves to baste the salmon inside.

To serve

Remove from the marinade, scrape away the dill and seasonings. Slice the salmon as thinly as possible on the diagonal (usually a little thicker than smoked salmon) and serve with mustard sauce (see p. 238). Traditionally served in Sweden as part of a Smorgasbord. May be eaten as a main course or as a starter with rye bread or crispbread and chilled schnapps.

Pakistanis/Indians

Chana-jora-garam!
Brother, I have come from a long, long distance
To bring you this unimaginably tasty
Chana-jora-garam.
I use the most excellent and secret masala —
You can know, because all kinds of famous people
Eat my chana-jora-garam.*

Indian street seller's song

For a country with at least a hundred different spices known in its cooking it is not surprising that it was these spices which first stimulated British interest in India. Queen Elizabeth I began the association by founding the East India Company in 1600, but it was not until 1784 that Pitt's 'India Bill' formally shared the ruling of the country between this now powerful company and the British Government. In the intervening years the British had beaten off attempts by the Portuguese, Dutch and French to take over India; and had taken control of Bombay, Madras and Calcutta. But the decisive battle was won against the French by Clive at Plassey in 1757.

While there has been much use of spices in traditional British cooking throughout the centuries as a result of this contact, it seems that the British version of an Indian Curry, as is so often the case on foreign soil, bore little resemblance to the real thing. The native dish deteriorated in the hands of the British and it was not until the people of the Indian subcontinent gained their Independence in 1947 and started coming to Britain to settle that we really learned what authentic Indian food was all about. Restaurants throughout Britain now provide a wide range of dishes exploiting all the subtleties of this varied cuisine with many 'Indo/Pak' restauranteurs taking advantage of the interchange with their native country by going themselves to buy the best supplies of herbs and spices from markets in India and Pakistan.

The Scots' enthusiasm for good Indian food is conspicuous by the number of Indo/Pak restaurants evident in the major cities while on the counters of food shops of all kinds you can indulge in subtleties of Pakoras, Samosas and Halva.

*A spicy savoury snack.

PAKORA

These deep fried vegetables are traditionally eaten as snack food, though they may also be part of an Indian meal. Indians never eat them, as they are often eaten in restaurants by Westerners, as the start to the meal — 'indescribables'. In India they are sold at street corners or in bazaars for the people to nibble during the day. The same applies to Samosas, which are triangular meat-filled deep fried pastries. Every Indian or Pakistani woman I have known has made a different version of Pakora — the combination of vegetables and spices is a matter of taste and availability; the gram flour and the method of deep frying seem the only constant factors.

1 lb/500 g besan (gram) flour* (4 c)
½ lb/250 g onions
½ lb/250 g potatoes
1 lb/500 g fresh spinach or cabbage
1 tablespoon salt
1 tablespoon chilli powder — or to taste
1-2 tablespoons tomato paste

Halve the onions and slice lengthways into paper-thin slices. Peel and slice the potatoes into very thin slices. Chop the cabbage or spinach finely. Put all the ingredients into a bowl and mix well. Fry in spoonfuls in deep fat. Drain and serve hot or warm.

Serve with Tomato Chutney

Blend together in liquidiser or processor: 2 green chillies; 1 onion; 2 cloves garlic; 2 tomatoes; sprig of mint; 1 teaspoon Mango powder (soak for 1 hour); ½ teaspoon salt.

GULAB JAMAN

makes 40-45

A rich milky dough is made first, then pieces rolled into small balls and deep fried. The final stage is soaking the browned balls in a cardamom and rose-water flavoured syrup which puffs them up while at the same time imparting its delicate flavours.

Must be speared with forks to eat; these are typical soft sticky Eastern sweets.

For the syrup

12 oz/350 g granulated sugar (1¾ c)
2 pts/11.5 dl water (5 c)
1 teaspoon rose-water
12 cardamom seeds

Put the water and sugar into a pan and bring to the boil, dissolving the sugar. Simmer for about ten minutes. Remove from the heat and leave to cool then add rose-water and cardamom seeds.

*Besan (gram) flour is made from grinding dried chick peas — it is widely available in specialist food shops.

For the milk balls

    7 oz/200 g baby milk powder (1¾ c)*
    3 oz/75 g semolina (½ c)
    2½ oz/65 g self-raising flour (½ c gen)
    2 tablespoons ghee (melted butter)
    Milk to mix
    Put the milk powder, semolina and flour into a bowl and add the
    melted butter. Mix with milk to a soft putty-like dough — it should
    not be too stiff or they will be heavy; on the other hand, if too soft
    they will be difficult to handle. Roll into balls about the size of a
    large marble and deep fry in oil. When well browned, drain and add
    to prepared syrup. Leave for at least 4 hours before serving to allow
    them to puff up and absorb the flavours.

MRS ANWAR'S CHICKEN

    The subtleties of cooking chicken in yogurt were revealed to me by Mrs
    Anwar when we made this dish together. The delicate spicing and the
    gradual evaporation of the yogurt during cooking leaves the chicken
    moist inside but with a crisp nicely-flavoured skin. The crucial point is at
    the end of the cooking when the outer skin is crisping. Too long in the
    oven will dry out the meat, too short a time and the skin will still be
    soggy.
    1 × 3½-4 lb/1¾-2 kg chicken, jointed (see p. 187)

Curry powder

    Grind in blender till powdered:
    2 oz/50 g coriander seeds
    2 oz/50 g cumin seeds
    4-6 small dried chillies
    2 oz/50 g turmeric
    5 cardamom pods
    ½ oz/15 g cinnamon
    ¼ oz/7 g each of cloves; nutmeg; mace
    2 oz/50 g fenugreek

Flavouring

    1 teaspoon curry powder or to taste
    10 fl oz/300 ml natural yogurt (1¼ c)
    2 green chillies, finely chopped
    1″ (2½ cm) piece of ginger root, peeled and grated
    ½ teaspoon powdered cumin
    1 grated onion
    1 pinch turmeric
    Salt

Marinading in yogurt

    Mix all the flavouring ingredients together in the yogurt and add the

*This is a useful substitute which Indian women use instead of reducing the milk to a thick con-
sistency which is the authentic Indian method. Ordinary milk powders will not do since their fat
content is too low.

chicken. Leave overnight and turn chicken once or twice.

Roasting the chicken

Pre-heat the oven to 375F/190C/Gas 5.

Cut up 2 oz/50 g butter ($\frac{1}{2}$ stick) into small pieces and place over chicken which should be skin side up. Roast in the oven for about an hour or until the skin is brown and crisp and nearly all the yogurt has evaporated.

Serve with Chapati

Put into a bowl $\frac{1}{2}$ lb/250 g wholemeal flour (2 c) and rub in $2\frac{1}{2}$ tablespoons ghee or melted butter. Make a well in the centre and add 3 tablespoons lukewarm water. Continue adding water 3 tablespoons at a time till the dough comes together into a firm compact ball. Knead the dough till it becomes smooth and elastic. Leave to rest for 30 minutes. Shape into small balls about the size of a small egg and roll out to a 5" (12 cm) round. Cook on a heated, but ungreased girdle or large frying pan till lightly brown on both sides. Serve warm.

Chinese

... One can compare Chinese cooking with Chinese painting and calligraphy, where the aim is to achieve a very high degree of delicacy and refinement within a traditional and sometimes stylized framework, but at the same time never lose sight of the need for character, quality and meaning which should be the foundation of every artistic expression.

Kenneth Lo
The Chinese Cookery Encyclopedia, 1974

Like many other Chinese, Kenneth Lo came to Britain before the Second World War to study. When China joined the Allies, her diplomatic missions abroad were enlarged and expatriate Chinese were employed (during the war he worked at the Chinese Consulate in Liverpool and was later Vice-Consul in Manchester). Many other new Chinese representatives arrived with their families and their cooks. When the war was over they stayed on and then the Revolution in China left them stranded. In 1951 Mao's regime was officially recognised by the British Government, which left the staff of the Nationalist Chinese Embassies out of a job. The cooks opened restaurants. Many more Chinese, fleeing the Revolution, went to Hong Kong and there discovered that they could go to Britain to satisfy the increasing demand for Chinese food rather like French chefs had done in the aftermath of the French Revolution.

Though the first Chinese restaurant in Britain was the Cathay in Piccadilly Circus — opened in 1908, it was not till after the Second World War that demand for Chinese food really developed. American and Commonwealth troops had a liking for Eastern food and when the Far Eastern ports were occupied by the Japanese, large numbers of Chinese sailors used British ports, and restaurants of a more humble variety than 'The Cathay' were to be found in dockland areas. During the war British forces serving in the East enjoyed the oriental food and they also created a demand when the war was over.

Restaurant interpretation of this sophisticated and varied cuisine has not always given Westerners the correct impression of true Chinese dishes. Native Chinese will shop around carefully before deciding on the authenticity and quality of an establishment. But despite this, the Chinese influence on us has been considerable. While noodles and rice are now commonplace, the Chinese treatment of vegetables is a rich area of exploration for Western cooks. It was in the kitchens of Buddhist temples and monasteries that vegetarian cookery was most highly developed. They catered for large communities and the most frequent and popular method of cooking was stir-frying.

'Chow' or stir-frying is only one of forty different methods of cooking used by the Chinese and listed by Kenneth Lo. Only a small amount of oil is used and the usual practice is to stir-fry the stronger vegetables first (garlic, ginger, onions) so that the oil becomes impregnated with their flavour. The heat should be very high; the materials to be cooked cut into strips, or small pieces. The blending of flavours and textures is a skill learnt only by practice. Watching a good Chinese cook throwing together foods of widely different substance and texture to create a whole with so many different facets in the space of a few minutes is a stunning theatrical performance.

CHINESE STIR-FRIED VEGETABLES

Cut vegetables on the thin side and in bite-sized pieces. Any combination can be used but allow about 2½ cups per person.

Separate vegetables into four groups
1. ONION, GARLIC, ROOT GINGER
2. HARDER, LONGER-COOKING TYPES — turnips, carrots, celery, broccoli stems, cauliflower stems
3. SOFTER, QUICKER-COOKING TYPES — courgettes, sweet peppers, tomatoes, broccoli heads, cauliflower heads
4. LAST MINUTE ADDITIONS — herbs, spinach, watercress, lettuce, chopped spring onions, sesame seeds

Cooking

Heat 2-3 tablespoons oil in a large sauté pan or wok for about 4 portions. Begin over a high heat by cooking the onions, garlic and ginger — this flavours the oil. Then add group 2 and toss till almost tender. Then add group 3 and finish cooking quickly with last minute additions. Keep tossing the vegetables all the time, season with salt and pepper if necessary. Serve immediately.

Jews

The real crystallisation of Jewish cuisine took place in the 16th century, when the Jews were confined to ghettos by edict. It may seem surprising that interest in food should blossom in a ghetto, especially one devoted to religious worship; but people focused on their home life as an antidote to the misery and degradation outside. Hospitality became a means of survival and the celebration of religious festivals . . . made it possible to remain indifferent to the world outside the gates. Banquets were held on top of the bakehouse which was the hub of bustling activity where housewives exchanged hints, stuffed necks and cabbage leaves, rolled meat balls and dumplings, fried potato pancakes and grated horseradish while they waited for their goose and chicken drippings to melt down and their pickled beef to boil.

Claudia Roden
The Good Food Guide, 1985

Although there is a large Jewish population in Scotland their food traditions have not had anything like the impact of the Chinese or Indians simply because they have not had an influence through restaurants. Traditional Jewish food is not conducive to general restaurant eating since so much is intimately related to religious ritual. There are some kosher restaurants in and around London which cater for the local Jewish population. Some East European Jews, however, brought with them superb baking skills and set up bakers' shops some of which have grown into well-established quality bakers.

Plaited white bread is known by Jews as Challah (pronounced halla) and is eaten on the Sabbath, but it has also found its way into many bakers' shops whether of Jewish origin or not. The bread takes its name from the Jewish 'act of Challah' in which the woman takes a small piece of the dough and puts it in the oven to burn as an offering, thereby re-enacting her origin at the Creation when she sprang from man's rib. The Hebrew law of Challah requires that the quantity of flour to be kneaded into dough be no less than the weight of 43 and $\frac{1}{5}$ eggs; or $2\frac{1}{2}$ quarts; or $3\frac{1}{2}$

pounds. The portion to be separated as the Challah offering is to be no less than the size of an olive.

CHALLAH

A handsome plaited white loaf, glazed and decorated with poppy seeds, it rises in the middle and tapers at the ends. Jews plait it with four strips (not difficult) to make an interesting weave though it is equally attractive in the usual three-plait.

$1\frac{1}{4}$ lb/625 g strong white flour (5 c)
2 tablespoons sugar
$1\frac{1}{2}$ teaspoons salt
1 oz/50 g fresh yeast, 2 teaspoons dried (2 pkg)
2 oz/50 g butter/margarine at room temperature
$\frac{1}{2}$ pt/300 ml warm water ($1\frac{1}{4}$ c scant)
3 eggs + 1 white
Glaze — 1 yolk from egg white above with 1 teaspoon water
$\frac{1}{2}$ teaspoon poppy seeds
Pre-heat the oven to 400F/200C /Gas 6.
Greased baking tin

Making up the dough

Reconstitute the dried yeast by mixing in a little of the measured water. Leave till it froths. Mix the fresh yeast with a little sugar till a smooth paste.

Put into a mixing bowl a little less than half of the flour, sugar, salt, yeast and butter. Gradually add the water, do not add all at once since it may not all be needed, and beat by hand or with an electric beater for two minutes. Then add the eggs and beat for another two minutes. Add remaining flour gradually till the dough is fairly firm. Turn out onto the board and knead till it is smooth

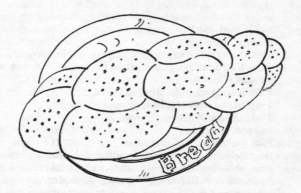

and elastic. Grease a clean bowl with oil. Put in the dough and turn it in the bowl to coat the top surface. This will prevent it drying out. Cover with a piece of cling-film and leave in a warm place till doubled in size.

Shaping the dough

Knock down the dough and knead out the bubbles. Divide in four. Roll out each piece into a rope about 12″ (30 cm) long, thicker in the centre and tapering at the ends. **To make a four plait loaf** place the four pieces in the form of a cross, joining the four tapered ends together at the centre of the cross. Lift the ends of the two opposite ropes and twist them over the other pair to reverse their positions but still preserve the cross shape. Then lift and reverse the other pair. Repeat lifting and reversing one pair at a time to weave the four ropes into a compact plait rising in the middle. Tuck loose ends under the loaf and leave in a warm place to rise for 30 minutes. Brush with glaze sprinkle with poppy seeds and bake for about 30-40 minutes till golden brown and crusty.

JEWISH FRIED FISH

Cold fried fish may not have the most appealing ring to it but Orthodox Jews cook it on Friday and eat it on their Sabbath (Saturday) since they are not allowed to cook on that day. There was a popular and flourishing trade in 'Cold Fried Fish' in the streets of London in the 19th century when itinerant sellers provided the public with a satisfying food which must be the forerunner of that sold in the Fish and Chip shop. Jews coat the fish with Matzo meal which can be bought in specialist food shops and some supermarkets. It is made from unleavened Matzo biscuits and comes in two grades, fine and medium. They also reverse the usual order of preparing fish for frying by dipping first in the meal then in egg which means that the fish actually has a nicely browned egg surface rather like French Toast which greatly improves its appearance and eating qualities when cold.

Medium grade is used for frying fish — it is also a useful coating for all other fried food as an alternative to breadcrumbs and without any artificial colourings, etc.

4 fillets haddock, sole, whiting etc
1 egg beaten with 1 teaspoon water
3 tablespoons Matzo meal, medium
Salt and pepper
Pan of oil about 2″ (5 cm) deep
Heat the oil and cover the fish with matzo meal. Dip immediately into the beaten egg. Allow to drain and put into the hot oil. Cook for 5 minutes or until cooked — this will depend on the thickness of the fish. Drain on kitchen paper. Leave to cool and serve cold with salads. Will keep for up to two days but is really best eaten the day it is cooked.

GEFILLTE FISH BALLS

Another version of Jewish cold fried fish, also using matzo meal. They are especially good served for snacks or at parties — good mouthful-food, which can easily be eaten with a fork or fingers. For children, a popular variation on the ubiquitous 'fish finger'.

1 lb/500 g white fish (haddock, cod, whiting, hake, bream, carp, pike or any mixture) minced
1 grated onion
1 beaten egg
Salt and pepper
Sugar to taste
5-6 tablespoons matzo meal, medium
Oil for deep frying

Mix the fish, onion, egg and seasoning. Add 1 tablespoon of matzo meal to make a fairly firm consistency. Add more if you think it is too wet. Shape into small balls and roll in the remaining meal. Leave in a cool place to set for about an hour (not essential) and then fry till a golden brown turning frequently. Drain on kitchen paper and eat cold.

Americans

Today American cookery is at a crossroads somewhere between technology and tradition.

James Beard
American Cookery. 1980

The exodus of Scots to America over the years has developed strong cultural links and led to much culinary borrowing to and fro. This informal interchange has been given new dimensions in the years since the Second World War with firstly the influence of thousands of American service men stationed in Scotland during the war; then with the development of American fast-food restaurants and take-away chains; and now with an influx of Americans to the North East of Scotland as a result of the oil based industry.

The GIs enthralled their Scottish hosts during the war with such goodies as heavy rich fruit cakes, brownies, cookies and sugar candies which had been sent from home in food parcels and which the Americans gave freely to the Scots in return for their hospitality. They were welcomed by the sweet-loving Scots, deprived as they were during wartime of such luxuries, and although not always directly imitated, their style enriched already existing traditions in this field.

Of more lasting significance was the American liking for fast foods. This first hit Britain after the war in the form of restaurant chains operating a franchising system where the native population ran the operation but had to conform to the brand image by producing standardised food in a form laid down by the parent company, and the British were introduced to the hazards of mass-produced hamburgers, hot dogs, fried chicken, pizzas and ice cream, *et al.*

All of this food is a blessing to busy cooks. The theory is fine; the results sometimes lack quality and good basic raw materials, which does no service to their American originals.

SOUTHERN CRISP FRIED CHICKEN with Cream Gravy

4-6 servings

The colour should be an even golden brown, the crust crisp but tender and the meat moist and well-flavoured. It is just as good eaten cold for a picnic with salads. Americans eat it with plain boiled rice; sometimes they flavour the cream gravy with lemon juice and add a little chopped parsley which makes an excellent combination. The gravy is always served in a separate sauce boat and never poured over. They also serve it with a Sweet Potato Pudding and with Hot Biscuits. Their biscuits are thinner than our scones but not as crisp as our biscuits, which the Americans call cookies. They eat their biscuits as a bread. Another variation is the Maryland one which may include sweetcorn, bacon and banana in some form or another. I find the best way to do this is to make the sweet corn into golden brown fritters and wrap the bacon round the banana and grill it, which is a good fast-food for children on its own.

3 lb/1½ kg roasting chicken, jointed (see p. 187)

For coating

4 tablespoons wholemeal flour
1 teaspoon salt
½ teaspoon ground pepper

For frying

½ pt/300 ml vegetable oil (1¼ c)
Heat the oil or lard in a 10-12″ (25-30 cm) frying pan. Put the flour for coating, salt and pepper (some recipes add a teaspoon of cinnamon) into a polythene bag, mix well and then add the chicken pieces two or three at a time and toss in the bag till they are well coated. Remove and repeat with remaining chicken and shake off excess flour. Heat the fat till it is moderately hot — it should be about 2-2½″ (5 cm) deep, and add the chicken legs and thighs first since they will take longer. After about five minutes add the rest and brown evenly on both sides. Maintain heat at a moderate temperature, allowing the crust to brown slowly; there should be no smoking fat or spluttering — the frying process should take about three-quarters of an hour. Pile on serving dish and keep warm.

For the sauce

> Use the left-over flour from coating, about 2 tablespoons
> 4 tablespoons chicken or other suitable stock
> $\frac{1}{4}$ pt/150 ml single cream ($\frac{3}{4}$ cup)
> Salt and pepper
> $\frac{1}{2}$ teaspoon fresh thyme
> 1 tablespoon lemon juice
> Pour off all but about two tablespoons of fat in the frying pan and
> add flour. Stir for a few minutes then add the chicken stock and
> cream. Simmer gently to reduce till the correct consistency. Add
> thyme, taste for seasoning and serve with the chicken.

Corn Fritters

> Put 6 oz/150 g sweetcorn kernels ($\frac{1}{2}$ c) into a bowl and add
> 4 oz/125 g self-raising flour (1 c); 1 egg; salt and pepper; and
> $\frac{1}{4}$ pt/150 ml milk ($\frac{3}{4}$ c) to make a dropping consistency. Drop in
> spoonfuls into the hot oil and cook both sides till golden brown.

Banana and Bacon Rolls

> Roll some streaky bacon round a peeled banana and grill till crisp,
> turning once or twice.

AMERICAN BROWNIES

> Though they have no raising agent, these rise surprisingly well in the
> oven. When cooled, the centres are moist and pregnant with chocolate.
> Americans often cover them with icing and nuts though I find this
> unnecessary. This version has no authentic American pedigree but is
> merely my own attempt to recreate the best Brownies I have tasted in
> America.
> 12 oz/350 g butter or margarine (3 c)
> 12 oz/350 g soft brown sugar ($2\frac{1}{2}$ c)
> 4 eggs (large)
> 4 oz/125 g plain or wholemeal flour (1 c)
> 3 oz/75 g cocoa powder (1 c)
> $1\frac{1}{2}$ teaspoons vanilla
> Pre-heat the oven to 350F/180C/Gas 4.
> 7 × 11″ (17-27 cm) Swiss roll tin, greased
> or 2 × 9″ (22 cm) round sandwich cake tins
> Cream the butter and sugar together till light and creamy, beat in
> the eggs gradually. Add the vanilla. Mix in and then sift in the flour
> and cocoa powder. Mix in well but do not beat. It should have a
> fairly thick consistency. Spread into the tin and bake for
> $\frac{3}{4}$-1 hour or until risen and firm on top. Remove from the oven. Leave
> to cool for about five minutes then cut into squares and take out,
> cool on rack. Can be iced with chocolate icing and decorated with
> nuts. May be served warm with vanilla ice cream for pudding.

PANCAKES AND STRAWBERRIES with Maple syrup

4 servings

This is the kind of thing which Americans eat for breakfast but there seems no reason why we should not utilise Scottish pancakes which are after all more akin to the American variety than any other, and serve this as a sweet or even as the main course for lunch with bacon. The pancakes are made with yogurt and orange juice which gives them a lovely sharp flavour. Maple syrup and strawberries make a perfect combination.

To make the pancakes

$\frac{1}{4}$ pt/150 ml orange juice ($\frac{3}{4}$ c)
$\frac{1}{4}$ pt/150 ml plain yogurt ($\frac{3}{4}$ c)
1 large egg
2 tablespoons softened butter
4 oz/125 g plain flour (1 c)
1 teaspoon baking powder
$\frac{1}{4}$ teaspoon salt

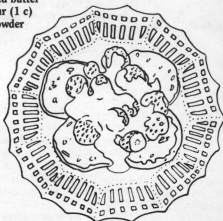

Pre-heat the girdle till fairly hot.
Mix the orange juice, yogurt, egg and butter together and then sift in the flour, salt and baking powder. Mix the batter lightly till well combined but do not beat. It should be a soft dropping consistency; add more orange juice if necessary. Drop in spoonfuls (3" − 7 cm) on the girdle and turn after a few minutes when they start bubbling. Cook till evenly brown and then place on heated serving dish. Brush or spread with butter and keep hot.

To finish the dish

4 oz/125 g strawberries (1 c)
$\frac{1}{4}$ pt/150 ml sour cream or natural yogurt ($\frac{3}{4}$ c generous)
4 fl oz/125 ml maple syrup ($\frac{1}{2}$ c)

Arrange about five pancakes in a cluster on the plate and top with a spoonful of sour cream/yogurt. Slice strawberries if too large or leave whole and arrange on top of yogurt. Serve with lightly warmed maple syrup.

SCOTTISH REGIONAL RECIPES

The picture of Scottish food would not be complete without mention of the fact that the country has wide geographical differences which, along with some other cultural, social and political factors, have created different dishes in different areas. The following is an indication of the regions and the dishes which especially belong within them.

Edinburgh and the Lothians — Midlothian Oatcakes; Petticoat Tails; Edinburgh Gingerbread; Edinburgh Tart; Edinburgh Rock; Tantallon Cakes; Cock-a-Leekie Soup; Tweed Kettle; Stoved Howtowdie; Holyrood Pudding; Barley Pudding; Newhaven Cream; Musselburgh Pie.

Angus and Fife — Forfar Bridies; Lowland Game Pie; Dundee Marmalade; Dundee Cake; Montrose Cakes; Angus Fruit Cake; Angus Toffee; Arbroath Smokies; Angus Fish Soup; Largo Potato Soup; Kingdom of Fife Pie; Fife Broth; Kilmeny Kail; Fife Bannocks; Aberdeen Angus Beef.

Glasgow and Clydeside — Glasgow Broth; Glasgow Tripe; Glasgow Toffee; Helensburgh Toffee; Glasgow Punch; Het Pint; Apple Frushie.

Ayrshire — Cheese; Ayrshire Meat Roll; Cod with Mustard Sauce; Ayrshire Shortbread; Sweet Haggis.

The Border Counties — Friar's Chicken; Selkirk Bannock; Yetholm Bannock; Teviotdale or Benalty Pie; Rumbledethumps; Soup n' Stovies; Original Border Tart; Eyemouth Tart; Border Sweeties; Eyemouth Fish Pie.

Dumfries and Galloway — Roast Upland Lamb; Drumlanrig Pudding; Ecclefechan Butter Tart; Solway Scallops; Galloway Beef.

The North East — Finnan Haddock; Ham and Haddock; Fisherman's Stew; Findon Fish Pudding; Aberdeen Whiting; Aberdeen Sausage; Aberdeen Angus Steak; Sea Pie; Burnt Cream; Neep Bree; Kailkenny; Skirlie; Morayshire Apples; Aberdeen Preserved Apples; Mrs MacNab's Scones; Balmoral Shortbread; Pitcaithly Bannock; Portnockie Shortbread; Aberdeen Crulla; Butteries or Buttery Rowies; Fochabers Gingerbread; Aberdeenshire Rich Fruit Cake.

The Highlands and Inner Hebrides — Fried West Coast Herring; Islay Scallops; Limpet Stovies; Croppen Head; Sutherland Venison; Pocha Buidhe; Roast Red Grouse; Roast Pheasant; Highland Game Soup;

Nettle Kail; Chicken Stovies; Pan White Pudding; Tatties and Crowdie; Stapag Uachair (Crowdie Cream); Fuarag; Cranachan; Atholl Brose; Gromack; Highland Oatcakes; Highland Cakes.

The Outer Hebrides — Hebridean Shellfish; Whelks in Sauce; Whelk Soup; Lobster Hebridean; Fried Cockles; Carageen Mould; Fried Skate; Port of Ness Cod; Lewis way of frying Brown Trout; Boiled Fish Roe; Roe Cakes; Kale Soup; Lewis Kailkenny; Sweet Maragan; Greiseagan; Barley Bannocks; Bonnach Imeach.

Orkney and Shetland — Orkney Pork and Kale; Clapshot; Orcadian Oatmeal Soup; Tatties and Cream; Fatty Cutties; Sour Skons; Orkney Pancakes; Orkney Broonies; Shetland Fish Soup; Flats; Fried Herring and Onions; Sassermaet and Brönies; Roast Leg of Shetland Lamb; Boiled Mutton; Boiled Pork; Lentil Brö; Gooseberry Sauce; Potatoes with Milk; Bride's Bonn or Bridal Cake; Brunnies; Brunnies of Rye; Whipkull; Beremeal Bannocks.

PROFILES

Early Scottish Cookery Writers

Mrs McLintock
Mrs McLintock's Receipts for Cookery, Glasgow 1736

Thought to be the first collection of Scottish recipes, it is a rare little book (only two copies are known to exist, both in Glasgow University Library) and Mrs McLintock has clearly been influenced by the need for preservation of food since more than half the book is taken up with recipes for pickling, potting, preserving and making wines. This perhaps explains why there are few Scottish national dishes. No Haggis, Barley Broth or Black Bun, though there is a recipe for Shortbread. She has one or two excellent soups, a Lobster Soup which is finished with oysters and mussels and a basic soup recipe which starts with, '3 great whole onions stuck with cloves, a bunch of sweet herbs,' and lots of beef and veal bones. It is finished with toasted bread floating in the soup and a cooked marrow bone in the centre of the plate.

Mrs Johnston
Mrs Johnstons Receipts for all sort of pastry, creams, puddings, etc., Edinburgh 1740

A small collection of recipes for plain basic fare thought to be either copied from Mrs McLintock or written by her under another name. Of the 117 pages in the book the first 92 are the same as in Mrs McLintock's 1736 edition.

Elizabeth Cleland
The Practice of Cookery, pastry, pickling, preserving, containing . . . a full list of supper dishes . . . directions for choosing provisions: with two plates, showing the method of placing dishes upon a table etc., Edinburgh 1759

Mrs Cleland also had a cookery school in Edinburgh and her book has the feeling of an elementary manual of instruction — there is much emphasis on methods of preservation. A whole chapter is dedicated

'To pot and make hams' but Scottish national dishes are also well represented.

Susanna MacIver
Cookery and Pastry, Edinburgh 1773

She began by selling cakes, jams, chutneys and pickles from her shop, but later opened a cookery school where she taught a sophisticated range of dishes to the well-to-do of Edinburgh. In 1773 her pupils encouraged her to publish her recipes. The collection is well mixed with French influence. Unlike many contemporary English books which are at pains to denounce the French as spoiling good English fare, possibly because of the long Scottish assocation with the French, she, like most Scots, seems to have had a more relaxed attitude to their incursions.

She includes a fair representation of Scottish dishes, like Scotch Haggies, Parton Pies, Rich Bun, Shortbread, Diet Loaf, Chip Marmalade, To Make Tablets and To Make Barley Sugar. It seems, though, that she was not a broth-lover since no recipe appears for the universal Scotch Broth which was considered so much of a national institution both at home and abroad that it is included in The London Art of Cookery by John Farley (1785).

Mrs Fraser
The Practice of Cookery and Pastry, Edinburgh 1791

She helped to run Mrs McIver's cookery school, took over after her death and then published her own recipes. This is a more sophisticated and comprehensive collection than Mrs McIver's. Her aim was to 'reconcile simplicity with elegance, and variety with economy'. She has organised the book in a more logical structure, dividing it up into three parts — I Cookery; II Pastry; and III Confectionery, which includes all the preservation methods. Plain simple fare predominates with all the basic Scottish dishes and little French or foreign influence besides the odd 'ragoo' and 'fricassy'. Curiously she also, like Mrs McIver, has no recipe for Scotch Broth among her nineteen soup recipes of which only three could be termed traditionally Scottish. In place of Cock-a-Leekie she has a poor version of Leek Soup with prunes but no chicken.

Mistress Margaret (Meg) Dods of the Cleikum Inn, St Ronan's
The Cook and Housewife's Manual, Edinburgh 1826

Meg Dods was a fictitious character whom Sir Walter Scott created in his novel St Ronan's Well but is said to have modelled on Miss Marian Ritchie, the landlady of his local inn, the Cross Keys in Peebles. Meg was a capricious and eccentric old landlady with a detestable bad humour. Potential guests were turned away if she disliked the 'cut of their jib', and the ones who stayed had to be prepared for her blunt couthy ways.

Her saving grace, and the reason why gourmets flocked to her inn, was that she was a superb cook.

The real author of the cookery book was Mrs Isobel Christian Johnston, wife of an Edinburgh publisher and friend of Scott. He is said to have written the Introduction on 'The St Ronan's Culinary Club'. Mrs Johnston is the first Scottish cookery writer of the century to make an accurate assessment of the changes taking place, cutting her cloth accordingly, while at the same time carrying out the task with expert professionalism. Public horizons were widening far beyond the basics of Plain Roast and Boiled, although these were still important. Curiosity and the desire to learn were cultivating the made dishes of beef, mutton, veal and venison, etc. In the second chapter the whole system of French Cuisine is thoroughly explored while the next deals with national dishes — Scottish, Irish, Welsh, German, Spanish and Oriental. She is one of the first cookery writers to isolate these subjects, recognising the public interest in them. Both before, and after her, the tendency has been to create a hotch-potch of foreign and national dishes with no clear distinction.

She was careful also not to adopt these dishes purely for their novelty, but claims that she has set out to embody 'all in Foreign culinary science that is considered really useful'. She was a very practical lady.

Mrs Dalgairns
The Practice of Cookery, Edinburgh 1829

First published only three years after Meg Dods, and competing with her for popularity, this is a large cookery book with 1434 recipes. It seems, however, that the public did not take to Mrs Dalgairns with the same enthusiasm they felt for Meg Dods. Certainly Mrs Dalgairns does not have an entertaining Foreword written by Sir Walter Scott but her book is just as large and comprehensive. Despite this, there is a feeling of muddle about the structure of the book. There are all the basic Scottish national dishes but French, English, Irish and other foreign dishes occur randomly throughout the book. Apart from the lack of form she has a vague style of writing so that when you read the recipes you are constantly frustrated by lack of quantities and instruction. None of these criticisms apply to Meg Dods, which explains why her book was reprinted frequently throughout the century and Mrs Dalgairns' was not.

Lady Clark of Tillypronie
The Cookery Book of Lady Clark of Tillypronie, Arranged and Edited by Catherine F. Frere, London 1909

Lady Clark was an obsessional collector of recipes. When she died her husband asked Catherine Frere to edit her manuscript collection. She took on the task of sorting out 'the gatherings of many years' which consisted of sixteen books of various sizes, containing nearly three thousand pages of manuscript, some of the pages written on every available margin, plus recipes written on loose sheets pinned in; or on backs of envelopes; or on backs of paid bills; or any available piece of paper.

The collection begins in 1841 when emigrés from the French Revolution stayed with Lady Clark's family. Her culinary curiosity was aroused by them and consolidated when she travelled with her family to Italy and France. When she married in 1851, her husband was in the Diplomatic Service and they lived in both Paris and Turin. Her collection has a strong hidden implication that if you give fifty different chefs the same recipe they will all produce a different dish. She spent so much time gathering recipes from so many different people that there are many variations of the same recipe, reflecting always the personality of the individual. It makes interesting reading; especially since her roots were in the North East of Scotland and it was to this part that she returned frequently, absorbing also the culinary traditions of her home.

F. Marian McNeill
The Scots Kitchen, Its Traditions and Lore Blackie, 1929
(new edition Mayflower Books — Granada Publishing, 1974)

Because she thought that our old national dishes were in danger of sinking into oblivion through modern standardisation of food she set about preserving everything hallowed by age.

She ranged the country from North to South from palaces to island sheilings in her search for the authentic food of the people. Being by profession a historian, she also sketched the development of Scottish food throughout the centuries and set about showing how 'the pagent of Scottish History is shadowed in the kitchen'. She highlights the distinctive traditions and customs not out of 'antiquarian zeal' but from a 'healthy national sentiment' and our debt to her is infinite.

William Heptinstall
Gourmet Recipes From a Highland Hotel Faber and Faber, 1967

Fortingall menus were beautifully balanced and offered an astonishing mixture of haute cuisine and bourgeois dishes from all over Europe. At lunchtime there was a limited choice but at dinner the guests were obliged to take what was offered or do without. It was only in this way that 'Hep' as he was known, was able to offer such good food at such moderate prices, for no effort or ingredients ever need be wasted.

Gregory Houston Bowden
British Gastronomy, 1975

In the 1920s when railway hotels were the only outposts of serious gastronomy in Scotland, an enterprising Yorkshire-born chef, with a formidable international reputation, bought Fortingall Hotel — eight miles from the nearest railway station and on a quiet back road in Perthshire.

During the thirty-five years of Heptinstall's reign at Fortingall he not only created an outstanding hotel off the beaten track, but stimulated, encouraged and trained many young chefs who continue to keep his cooking philosophy alive in hotels and restaurants in Scotland and further afield. He was particularly well known for his Cold Table, only offered once a week, preceding Sunday lunch. On an average Sunday, forty dishes could appear on the table, half of which probably had to be prepared before breakfast. He felt that the start to a meal was vitally important — 'Just as a good or bad start may win or lose the race,' he said, 'so may hors-d'oeuvres make or mar a meal. Unless they are dainty, little, and tasty, they will dull the keen edge of your appetite.'

In Gourmet Recipes he exploits the natural produce of Scotland with originality and flair but mindful always of the practicalities — his infectious enthusiasm shines through.

People who kept Records in Household Books; or wrote Journals of Travel; or Letters; or kept Diaries

Lady Grisell Baillie
The Household Book of Lady Grisell Baillie 1692-1733
Edited by Robert Scott-Moncrieff, 1911

Besides much information on household expenditure, Lady Grisell also kept a special book in which she recorded 'Bills of Fare'. Not all of the hundred and seventy in the book are meals in her own family home, but she recalls meals with friends and in other countries. The list of dishes give an indication of the types of foods which were popular at this level of society. She has carefully preserved the exact layout of the dishes on the table, so that the book shows clearly the style of eating in the days when they arranged everything on the table at once.

Edward Burt
Letters from a Gentleman in the North of Scotland 1726

Edward Burt was an English engineer who served with General Wade building roads in the Highlands from 1724-28. His letters are unique since he was travelling in the area before the very roads he was helping to build brought 'travellers' to the Highlands. His record of the manners and conditions of the people is vivid and detailed, interspersed with much humour — a good read.* He lived for some time in or near Inverness and made a number of journeys along the Great Glen and into some of the adjacent country.

---

*'I was invited to sup at a Tavern. The cook was too filthy an Object to be described: only another English Gentleman whispered me and said, he believed, if the fellow was to be thrown against the Wall, he would stick to it.'

Ochtertyre House Book of Accomps 1737-1739
Edited by James Colville, Edinburgh 1907

While Grisell Baillie's bills of fare give an indication of the dinner party fare of sophisticated Edinburgh society, then the Ochtertyre House Book gives the picture of the standard of daily living in an average baronial establishment just before the 'Forty Five. It is a detailed catalogue of daily meals, purchases and home-grown or home-produced food. You can follow the rhythm of the seasons in the foods they ate and see the way they utilised all the odds and ends in a most economical way when beasts were killed.

Thomas Pennant
Tour in Scotland, 1771 (Describes a journey made in 1769)

According to Pennant his book was such a success that Scotland was, as a result, 'inondée with Southern visitors'. He was one of the most eminent naturalists of the 18th century and as a traveller showed a lively curiosity about people and customs as well as the natural things of the country. His comments on the things he saw growing, and which the people were eating, are an important record of the Scots diet. His 1769 Tour in Scotland went into five editions between 1771 and 1790. He made another tour round the West Coast and the Islands in 1772 but this was less popular with the public since these areas were much less accessible.

Christopher North (Professor John Wilson)
Noctes Ambrosianae 1822-1835

Ambrosian nights in an Edinburgh tavern were brought to life by Wilson, a professor of philosophy, in a series of imaginary colloquies which entertained the readers of Blackwood's Magazine for more than a decade. They were so popular that Blackwood's allowed other writers besides Wilson to write the dialogues when, for one reason or another, he couldn't contribute. But none of them could match his style and the published collection in four volumes is confined only to Wilson's work.

His principle characters, Christopher North (Wilson himself), Timothy Tickler (Robert Sym) and James Hogg, The Ettrick Shepherd, only bear the slightest resemblance to the original people. They formed the prototypes, and Wilson's imagination expanded and developed them. Besides talking a great deal, they also ate.

Most of the vivid and detailed descriptions of what and how they would have eaten in early 19th century Edinburgh ring true. There is just the occasional doubt that Wilson's imagination has elaborated over much. His description of the 'Deluge of Haggis' likening it to a flood when the haggis was first burst open, while highly entertaining, goes way beyond the bounds of reality by the time he is finished.

His comments, though, on attitudes to food indicate current taste and style and occasional pieces on things like how they ought to eat these new things called 'pineapples'* are both revealing and amusing.

Samuel Johnson and James Boswell
Johnson's Journey to the Western Islands of Scotland, 1775
Boswell's Journal of a Tour to the Hebrides with Samuel Johnson, 1785

The 64-year-old English lexicographer and the 33-year-old Scot spent four months together on a tour which took them round a large part of Scotland and into many different types of Scottish homes. They went from Edinburgh northwards to Aberdeen, then along the Morayshire coast to Inverness. This was the easy part. In Inverness they bade 'farewell to the luxury of travelling' and continued on horseback across to Glenelg, over to Skye, down to Coll, across to Mull and back to the mainland at Oban. From there they travelled south to Glasgow and then into Ayrshire before going back to Edinburgh.

Boswell's journal is more detailed and, according to literary experts, also a better travel book than Johnson's. Johnson seems to allow his prejudices about the Scots and their customs to influence his opinions, and his likes and dislikes, while interesting and relevant, perhaps don't always reflect the true nature of things. He was, after all, a brilliant critic and he naturally came, not like the Wordsworths in 1803, to see and feel, but to pass his own judgment. He was a colourful character, highly amusing, witty and notoriously rude, which was occasionally matched by his Scottish hosts. When he was eating Hotch Potch at his Edinburgh landlady's she is reputed to have asked him, 'And how do you like the Hotch Potch, sir.' 'Good enough for hogs,' replied Johnson. 'Shall I help you to a little more of it, then?' retorted the landlady.

Besides all kinds of opinions on all kinds of topics the two men both noted how the people lived. They described the conditions, the traditions and the diet of the people and have provided a revealing and valuable account of life in different parts of Scotland and at different levels of society in the late 18th century.

---

*'Shep. And what ca' ye thae, like great big fir cones wi' outlandish-looking palm-tree leaves arching frae them wi' an elegance o' their ain . . . What ca' ye them?
North. Pineapples.
Shep. I've aften heard tell o' them — but never clapped een on them afore. And these are pines! Oh! but the scant is sweet, sweet — and wild as sweet. . . . I'll join you noo in a pair o' pines.
[NORTH gives the SHEPHERD a pine-apple]
Hoo are they eaten?
Tickler. With pepper, mustard, and vinegar, like oysters, James.
Shepherd. I'm thinking you maun be leein.
Tickler. Some people prefer catsup.
Shepherd. Haud your blethers. Catchup's gran kitchen (relish) for a' kinds o' flesh, fish and fule, but for frutes the rule is 'sugar or naething,' — and if this pine keep the taste o' promise to the palat, made by the scent he sends through the nose, nae extrawneous sweetness will he need, self sufficient in his ain sappiness, rich as the colour o' pinks, in which it is sae savourily enshrined. — I never pree'd ony taste half sae delicious as that in a' ma born days! Ribstanes, pippins, jargonels, peaches, nectrins, currans and strawberries, grapes and grozets, a' in ane!'

Select Bibliography — Cookery Books

Beard, James Delights and Prejudices, 1964. James Beard's American Cookery Little, Brown and Company, 1972
British Deer Society (Scotland) Venison Recipes
Boyd, Lizzie (Ed.) British Cookery Croom Helm, 1976
Brown, Catherine Scottish Regional Recipes Molendinar, 1981/Penguin 1983
The Glasgow Cookery Book: Queens College Glasgow John Smith, Revised Edition, 1962
Clayton, Bernard The Complete Book of Breads Simon and Schuster, 1973
Clifton, Claire Edible Flowers Bodley Head, 1983
Craig, Elizabeth The Scottish Cookery Book Deutsch, 1956
David, Elizabeth English Bread and Yeast Cookery Allen Lane, 1977
Davidson, Alan North Atlantic Seafood Macmillan, 1979
Drysdale, Julia The Game Cookery Book Collins, 1975
Escoffier, Auguste Ma Cuisine 1st published Flammarion, 1934, Paul Hamlyn, 1965
Fitzgibbon, Theodora A Taste of Scotland Dent, 1970
Fletcher, Nichola Venison, The Monarch of the Table Nichola Fletcher, 1983
Fulton, Willie The Hebridean Kitchen Buidheannfoillseachaidh nan Eilean an Iar, 1978
Grigson, Jane Good Things M. Joseph, 1971. Fish Cookery Penguin, 1975. Jane Grigson's Vegetable Book M. Joseph, 1978. Jane Grigson's Fruit Book M. Joseph, 1982
Harben, Philip Cooking Penguin, 1960
Heptinstall, William Gourmet Recipes from a Highland Hotel Faber, 1967
Katzen, Mollie The Mosewood Cookbook Ten Speed Press, California, 1977. The Enchanted Broccoli Forest Ten Speed Press, California, 1982
King, A. and Dunnet, F. The Home Book of Scottish Cookery Faber, 1967
Mabey, Richard Food For Free, A guide to the edible wild plants of Britain Collins, 1972. Mabey, David and Rose The Penguin Book of Jams, Pickles and Chutneys Penguin 1975
Menhinick, Gladys Grampian Cookbook Aberdeen University Press, 1984.
Murray, Janet Wartime Cookery Book Fraser, 1944. Janet Murray's Cookery Book London, 1950. Traditional Recipes from Scotland BBC, 1964. With a Fine Feeling for Food Impulse, 1972.
Nelson, Janet M. (Ed.) A Mull Companion Mull 1977
Nice, Jill Home-Made Preserves Collins, 1982
Olney, Richard Simple French Food Penguin, 1983
Phillips, Roger Wild Food Pan, 1983

Reid, Nancy (Ed.) Highland Housewives' Cook Book Highland Printers, 1971

Scottish Women's Rural Institutes Traditional Scottish Recipes Cookery Book 6th Edition, 1946

Simmons, Jenni A Shetland Cook Book Thuleprint, 1978

Stout, Margaret B. The Shetland Cookery Book Manson, 1968 — First published in 1925 as Cookery for Northern Wives

Taste of Scotland Ltd. and Catherine Brown Chef's Manual 4th edition, 1985

Troisgros, Jean and Pierre The Nouvelle Cuisine Edited and Adapted by Caroline Conran, Macmillan, 1980

Whyte, Hamish Lady Castehill's Receipt Book, A selection of 18th Century Scottish Fare Molendinar, 1976

Wolfe, Eileen Recipes from the Orkney Islands Gordon Wright, 1978

Select Bibliography — General

Anderson, W. The Poor of Edinburgh and their homes Menzies, 1867

Brown, P. Hume (Ed.) Early Travellers in Scotland Edinburgh, 1891

Burt, Edward Letters from the North of Scotland 5th ed. London, 1822

Campbell, John An Exact and Authentic Account of the Greatest White-Herring Fishery in Scotland, carried on yearly in the Island of Zetland Edinburgh, 1750

Chambers, Robert Walks in Edinburgh Edinburgh, 1825. Traditions of Edinburgh 2nd ed. Edinburgh, 1868. Domestic Annals of Scotland Edinburgh, 1859

Chapman, R.W. (Ed.) Johnson's Journey to the Western Islands of Scotland and Boswell's Journal of a Tour to the Hebrides with Samuel Johnson Oxford University Press, 1961

Cheke, Val The Story of Cheese Making in Britain Routledge, 1959

Colville, James (Ed.) The Ochtertyre House Book — 1737-1739 Scottish History Society, Edinburgh, 1907

Cutting, Charles L. Fish Saving (Leonard Hill, 1955)

Edmonston, Elizabeth Sketches and Tales of Shetland Edinburgh, 1856

Faujas de Saint-Fond, B. Travels in England, Scotland and the Hebrides etc. London, 1799

Fenton, Alexander Scottish Country Life Donald, 1976.

Foulis, Sir John Foulis of Ravelston's Account Book, 1671-1707 Scottish History Society, 1894

Fyfe, J.G. Scottish Diaries and Memoirs, Volume I (1550-1746), Volume II (1746-1843), Maclean, 1928

Grant, Elizabeth Memoirs of a Highland Lady London, 1898

Hodgson, W.C. The Herring and its Fishery Routledge, 1957

Jamieson, John Etymological Dictionary of the Scottish Language new ed. 1879-82

Jamieson, J.H. The Edinburgh Street Traders and their Cries, in Book of the Old Edinburgh Club, Volume II, Constable, 1909

Kitchen, A.H. The Scotsman's Food Livingston, 1949

Lochhead, Marion The Scots Household in the 18th Century Moray Press, 1948

Lockhart, G.W. The Scot and His Oats Luath Press, 1983

MacCarthy, Daphne (Ed.) Prodfact 1985, a Comprehensive Guide to British Agricultural and Horticultural Produce British Farm Produce Council, 1985

MacClure, Victor Scotland's Inner Man Routledge, 1935. Good Appetite, My Companion Odhams Press, 1955

Martin, Martin A description of the Western Islands of Scotland, etc. 1703 Stirling, 1934

Mitchison, Rosalind Life in Scotland Batsford, 1978

Newton, Lily A Handbook of British Seaweeds British Museum, Natural History, 1931). Seaweed Utilisation (Sampson and Low, 1951)

Page, E.B. and Kingsford P.W. The Master Chefs Arnold, 1971

Plant, Marjorie The Domestic Life of Scotland in the 18th Century Edinburgh University Press, 1952

Pococke, Richard Tours in Scotland, 1747, 1750, 1760 Scottish History Society, 1887

Ramsay, Dean Reminiscences of Scottish Life and Character, 1st published 1857, Robert Grant, 1947

Robertson, Una A. Let's Dine at Hopetoun Published in aid of the Hopetoun House Preservation Trust, 1981

Salaman, Redcliffe N. The History and Social Influence of the Potato Cambridge University Press, 1970

Samuel, A.M. The Herring: Its effect on the History of Britain Murray, 1918

Sibbald, Sir R. What the Poor might eat; Provision for the Poor in time of Dearth and Scarcity Edinburgh, 1707

Sinclair, Sir John (Ed.) The Statistical Account of Scotland Edinburgh, 1791-99. General View of the Agriculture of the Northern Counties and Islands of Scotland Edinburgh, 1795

Southey, Robert Journal of a Tour in Scotland in 1819 The Mercat Press, 1972

Steven, Maisie The Good Scots Diet Aberdeen University Press, 1985

Stuart, Marie W. Old Edinburgh Taverns Hale, 1952

Sutherland, Douglas The Salmon Book Collins, 1982

Tannahill, Reay Food in History Stein and Day, 1973

Thornton R. and Sieczka J.B. Potato Atlas International Potato Centre, Lima, 1978

Torry Research Station Fish Handling and Processing

Victoria, Queen Leaves From a Journal of Our Life in the Highlands, 1846-1861

Wilson, C. Anne Food and Drink in Britain Constable, 1973

Youngson, A.J. Beyond the Highland Line, Three Journals of Travel in 18th Century Scotland Collins, 1974

RECIPE
& FOOD INFORMATION INDEX

Page numbers in **bold type** indicate a recipe

GENERAL INDEX